Public Law in Germany

A Historical Introduction from the 16th to the 21st Century

MICHAEL STOLLEIS

Translated by

THOMAS DUNLAP

OXFORD
UNIVERSITY PRESS

OXFORD
UNIVERSITY PRESS

Great Clarendon Street, Oxford, OX2 6DP,
United Kingdom

Oxford University Press is a department of the University of Oxford.
It furthers the University's objective of excellence in research, scholarship,
and education by publishing worldwide. Oxford is a registered trade mark of
Oxford University Press in the UK and in certain other countries

First Edition published in 2017

Published in the United States of America by Oxford University Press
198 Madison Avenue, New York, NY 10016, United States of America

British Library Cataloguing in Publication Data
Data available

Library of Congress Control Number: 2017938215

ISBN 978-0-19-879896-5

This translation of the book published as Michael Stolleis,
Öffentliches Recht in Deutschland. Eine Einführung in seine Geschichte, is
published
under licence from Verlag C.H.Beck oHG, München

PUBLIC LAW IN GERMANY

Preface

I wrote this introduction to the history of public law in Germany to provide a concise and simplified summary of my longer work *Geschichte des öffentlichen Rechts in Deutschland*.[1] It offers students at the beginning of their studies access to a sphere of legal thinking that is so clearly shaped by politics and history.

"Public law" (*ius publicum*, imperial constitutional law, state and administrative law, international law) is a historically variable formula that is accompanied by an equally variable scholarly literature. The early modern state that arose everywhere out of the medieval polities in Europe also prompted the creation of a "public-law" discipline that was unique to it. In Germany it stretches from the early seventeenth century to contemporary Europeanization, internationalization, and globalization. The question that arises today concerns not only the self-understanding of public law, but fundamentally the future of the state as well. Will the future forms of public authority that might replace it display the same qualities of democratic legitimacy, rule of law, and social balance?

To understand and shape future developments, one must understand the history that has given rise to the present. And by "history" I mean not only the factual and normative changes, but also the way these have been grasped linguistically and intellectually. While history, history of law, and the history of jurisprudence can be grasped as distinct fields, they are not truly separable from one another. We are always dealing with the interaction between conceptual understanding and historical change, with thinking at times rushing ahead of events, at times following them with commentary and interpretation.

Again, I have to thank Thomas Dunlap for his excellent translation. He has been my overseas companion for a great number of years and is quite familiar with my writings as well as with German public law in general.

All mistakes are my own. Suggestions and criticism should be given directly to me: stolleis@rg.mpg.de.

Michael Stolleis
Frankfurt

[1] *History of Public Law in Germany*, vol. 1 (Munich, 1988), 2nd edn. (Munich, 2012), vol. 2 (Munich, 1992), vol. 3 (Munich, 1999), vol. 4 (Munich, 2012).

Contents

1

Introduction

Subject, Methodology

1. LAW AS A HISTORICAL SUBJECT

The historical view of the law is that of an observer; it is directed at the law from the outside. Its motivation is the curiosity of the historian who seeks to discover how older law functioned, how it ordered social relationships, what "rules" applied, and how violations were punished.

This view presupposes that law is experienced and understood as changeable in the first place, and that it is possible to inquire of documents of the past what ideas of the law their authors held and how they communicated about it. Such questions become possible only when societies conceive of themselves as historical, when they reflect upon how their existence and their legal systems move along the temporal trajectory from the past into the future. None of this is self-evident and inevitable, since many human cultures have lived and live with models of cyclical return and periodic renewal. The notion that they are part of a movement toward the "end of the world" or a "Last Judgment" was and is alien to them. Cultures that are marked by the idea of return tend to think "unhistorically," in terms either of cycles or of graduated perfection. The role of the individual and his or her rights is also different. It cannot be separated from the contexts of family and kinship. In such a worldview, the individual is not—as presupposed by modern Western thinking—a singular entity endowed with subjective rights to whom material and immaterial goods are allocated. It is only by transcending the traditional Eurocentric perspective that one can ascertain the deeper reasons for tensions between cultures.

At the same time, if one wants to understand one's own legal system, it is necessary to engage with general European history and the European mindset. Since the Christianization of Europe, that mindset has seen the historical process as the linear progression toward a distant goal, whether that was a salvation history with the hope for final redemption, or a secularized, progressive history of an internal liberation from coercions, beset by occasional "setbacks," or simply a process with an open horizon and uncertain outcome: at various times the goal has been seen differently. A definitive pattern for interpreting the concepts of history advocated in Europe does not exist, but they all have one thing in common: they see themselves bound into a geographical realm of "Europe" and into a temporal continuum reaching from late antiquity to the present.[1]

Within this Europe, the beginning of the "modern era" can be dated in different ways. There is much to suggest that one should date it quite early, in order to recognize long-term processes and shifts in the social foundations.[2] "Early" here refers to the twelfth and thirteenth centuries. During that period one can observe the emergence of a law-based world church and of communication, politics, and the law based increasingly on writing; the growth of urban landscapes; increasing population density; significant technical innovations (such as clocks, windmills, and watermills); and improvements in shipbuilding and architecture. At the same time, theology and philosophy grew apart.[3] When it comes to legal history, the modern period begins traditionally with the rediscovery of the Digests in northern Italy, the "codification" or "compilation" of Roman law enacted in East Rome (Byzantium) in 533. A single preserved manuscript of this collection of legal extracts compiled in late antiquity became the basis for the work of "jurists" from the middle of the twelfth century, first in Bologna, then in Padua and Pavia, and later throughout Europe. By

[1] Michael Stolleis, "Europa," in *Handwörterbuch zur Deutschen Rechtsgeschichte* (hereafter *HRG*), 2nd edn., vol. 1 (Berlin, 2004), pp. 1439–41. A superb global overview has been written by Jürgen Osterhammel, *The Transformation of the World: A Global History of the Nineteenth Century*, translated by Patrick Camiller (Princeton, 2014).

[2] This is meant in the sense of the *longue durée* of the French historian Fernand Braudel (1902–85). See his first major work, *La Méditerranée et le monde méditerranéen à l'époque de Philippe II* (Paris, 1949), English translation: *The Mediterranean and the Mediterranean World in the Age of Philip II*, 2 vols., translated by Siân Reynolds (London, 1972–3).

[3] Kurt Flasch, *Das philosophische Denken im Mittelalter: Von Augustin zu Machiavelli*, 2nd edn. (Stuttgart, 2000).

teaching and explaining the Roman texts, they were also commenting on them, adapting them to practical needs, and in the process creating the Roman–Italian law of the Middle Ages.

Equally important was the contemporaneous assembly of the scattered regulations of church law (the product of a thousand years) into a compendium (1140) which soon took on an official character. Its creator was the monk Gratian, who was also teaching in Bologna.[4] Henceforth there were two kinds of "learned law": secular Roman–Italian law and the law of the universal Roman church.

Secular Roman law, largely based on the Digests, developed via Italy, France, the Netherlands, and Germany into the "common" (shared) law of southern and Western Europe, while it made few or no inroads into England, Northern Europe, and Eastern Europe. Southeastern Europe, to the extent that it was ruled by Byzantium in the Middle Ages, lived until the fifteenth century under the uninterrupted tradition of "Roman" law, in the special form in which it had taken shape there within the context of orthodox religious life. Eventually, the aggregate of the various texts was called the Corpus Iuris Civilis, and out of it developed the general rules of civil law. It was only in the eighteenth and nineteenth centuries that it was replaced throughout Europe by national law codes. And in Germany, which was not able to embark upon a national codification until 1870, the common law was in force until it was replaced by the Civil Law Code (Bürgerliches Gesetzbuch, BGB) on January 1, 1900.

The church's "canon" law—so named after the *canones* (rules)—was cultivated and expanded upon at the universities in the late Middle Ages, and it was given its official form in the second half of the sixteenth century. As the Corpus Iuris Canonici, it was in force within the Roman Catholic Church until 1917. Following the reformations of the sixteenth century (Luther, Zwingli, Calvin), the reformed churches did create their own legal codes, but they continued to regard the traditional church law as valid in a subsidiary form, to the extent that it did not contradict the Evangelical confession.[5]

From the sixteenth century on, following the slow emergence of a sense of national identity, there was also a growing interest in domestic

[4] Peter Landau, "Gratian (von Bologna)," *Theologische Realenzyklopädie* 14 (1985), 124–30; Anders Winroth, *The Making of Gratian's Decretum* (Cambridge, 2000); Christoph Link, *Kirchliche Rechtsgeschichte*, 3rd edn. (Munich, 2017), §6.

[5] Link (Note 4), §§10 ff.

law. The humanist jurists of the sixteenth and seventeenth centuries, mostly Calvinists or Lutherans, began with editions of early tribal laws (*leges barbarorum*) from the time of the Germanic migrations. But they also took a special interest in the medieval struggle between the emperor and the Pope in their efforts to come up with arguments in the confessional conflicts.[6] Village and city laws also began to attract the attention of learned jurists, partly for practical reasons (to prevail in court), partly out of patriotic and scholarly curiosity.

In other words: the discipline of legal history as practiced in Germany today has three main fields: the first is occupied by ancient Roman law and the "common law" derived from it. It deals mostly with topics of modern civil law; that is, personal law, law of obligations, property law, and law of succession. The second field contains the native legal system prior to and alongside the Roman or common law: it deals with the "Germanic" law that is very difficult to ascertain in the sources; early medieval tribal laws; medieval and early modern law, with its urban and rural law codes and court books; and, finally, the development of "German" law, composed of many particular special rights. The third field is made up of church law, which was initially universal for "Latin" Europe, but then evolved along more or less separate tracks after the reformations of the sixteenth century.

2. *IUS PUBLICUM*—PUBLIC LAW

Less attention was paid in legal history to the emergence and functioning of public law. Ancient Roman "state law" had vanished with the fall of the empire during the Germanic migrations. It lived on in East Rome (Byzantium), where it flowed into a characteristic symbiosis with orthodox church law. This line of tradition ended in 1453 when Byzantium fell to the Ottoman Turks.[7]

What was newly constituted in terms of state law (if that is what one can call it) in the western Middle Ages consisted of customary

[6] Michael Stolleis, "Gelehrte und politische Editoren mittelalterlicher Texte um 1600," in Jacques Krynen and Michael Stolleis, eds., *Science politique et droit public dans les facultés de droit européennes (XIIIe–XVIIIe siècle)* (Frankfurt, 2008), pp. 613 ff.

[7] Richard Potz and Eva Synek (in collaboration with Spyros Troianos), *Orthodoxes Kirchenrecht: Eine Einführung* (Freistadt, 2007).

law, a few central political documents, and a few maxims developed by medieval jurists,[8] out of which the *leges fundamentales* (basic laws) emerged in France and Germany. The German "basic laws"—the Golden Bull of 1356, the Eternal Peace of the Land and Code of the Imperial Chamber Court of 1495, the Electoral Capitulations from 1519 to 1654, the Augsburg Religious Peace of 1555, the Peace of Westphalia of 1648, the Recent Imperial Recess of 1654, and so on—will be discussed further on. Taken together they formed a normative conglomerate that was soon called the "imperial constitution." This constitution, which in the eyes of eighteenth-century observers was turning increasingly into a "Gothic ruin," was formally preserved until the period of the Napoleonic Wars. The last imperial law in 1803 was the Reichsdeputationshauptschluß (Final Recess), which led to the disappearance of many spiritual and many small secular territories. In 1806, under pressure from Napoleon, the states of the Confederation of the Rhine seceded from the empire, and a few days later, on August 6, 1806, Emperor Franz II abdicated the throne.

This matter of the imperial constitution was initially the subject of "imperial history" (*Reichshistorie*), which began in the seventeenth century to explain the constitution of the Holy Roman Empire of the German Nation as the product of a historical process. It soon developed into a discipline of its own, which was cultivated at first mainly in Halle, but then intensively in Göttingen.[9] When the empire fell and the political energies were focused on the constitutional movements in the individual states, the discipline changed its name and was now called *Staatengeschichte* (history of states). In the wake of the constitutional movement of the nineteenth century, it was called "constitutional history" (*Verfassungsgeschichte*) from the middle of the century on.[10] It was in charge of "external" legal history and was overseen either by "German" legal historians or by constitutional jurists. The course of study prescribed by the National Socialist state

[8] The basic work is that of Ernst H. Kantorowicz, *The King's Two Bodies: A Study in Medieval Political Theology* (Princeton, 1957), 2nd edn. in German (Munich, 1990). On the current state of the discussion, see Gerhard Dilcher and Diego Quaglioni, eds., *Die Anfänge des öffentlichen Rechts*, vol. 1, *Gesetzgebung im Zeitalter Friedrich Barbarossas und das Gelehrte Recht* (Bologna, 2007), vol. 2, *Von Friedrich Barbarossa zu Friedrich II.* (Bologna, 2008), vol. 3, *Auf dem Wege zur Etablierung des öffentlichen Rechts zwischen Mittelalter und Moderne* (Bologna, 2011).

[9] Notker Hammerstein, *Jus und Historie* (Göttingen, 1972).

[10] Georg Waitz, *Deutsche Verfassungsgeschichte*, 7 vols. (1844–78), new edn. vols. 1–4 (1865–85).

in 1935 then created the parallel disciplines of "the history of private law of the modern period" and "the constitutional history of the modern period."

At this time, the constitutional history of the modern period seems to be disappearing again from the curricula, even though it has numerous general works, textbooks, and outlines.[11] Material in legal history is offered in general introductory courses for beginning students, and in greater depth in follow-up seminars, depending on the capacities or specialties of the faculties. What has all but disappeared is the history of church law. The "history of ancient law," which once constituted the foundation for all of private law as "Roman law," exists in part still as a learned niche discipline, and in part it still thinks of itself as the ideal preparatory course for civil law, especially if it leads right up to the present via the history of the discipline and dogmatics of private law of the modern period. "German legal history," which reaches from the faint traces of Germanic origins, via the *leges barbarorum*, the tribal law of late antiquity, to the Middle Ages and the modern period and right up to the present, breaks apart into individual fields of research, one of which deals with the "imperial constitution" from the Middle Ages to 1806, and as "constitutional history" also beyond that. On the whole it must be said, though, that today all "basic subjects" lack a fixed place in the educational track and that the curricula contain too much positive law material. This is creating a difficult situation for legal history, legal philosophy, legal theory, and legal sociology, and at the margin also comparative law, though in the wake of Europeanization and globalization the latter is gaining in intrinsic importance and outside appreciation. The more recent diagnoses of the current state of legal history are in agreement in this respect.[12] That is why the proposals adopted by the Perspectives of Legal Science scientific council on November 9, 2012, recommend a vigorous strengthening of the basic subjects, in part with a view to

[11] For overview, see Dietmar Willoweit, *Deutsche Verfassungsgeschichte: Vom Frankenreich bis zur Wiedervereinigung Deutschlands*, 7th edn. (Munich, 2013), §3.

[12] Filippo Ranieri, "Romanistik/Rechtsgeschichte," in Manfred Landfester, ed., *Der Neue Pauly*, vol. 15/2 (Darmstadt, 2002), cols. 960–70 (with bibliography); Dieter Simon, "Rechtsgeschichte," in Axel Görlitz, ed., *Handlexikon zur Rechtswissenschaft*, vol. 2 (Munich, 1972), pp. 314–18; Michael Stolleis, "Rechtsgeschichte, Verfassungsgeschichte," in Hans-Jürgen Goertz, ed., *Geschichte: Ein Grundkurs* (Reinbek, 1998), pp. 340–61 (with bibliography); Franz Wieacker, "Methode der Rechtsgeschichte," in *HRG*, vol. 3 (Berlin, 1984), cols. 518–26 (followed by M. Stolleis in the 2nd edn., 2016, cols. 1475–83); Franz Wieacker, *Ausgewählte*

international communication, in part out of a concern to preserve the scholarly character of university training. Whether the universities and the state judicial administration responsible for the training of lawyers will follow up with actions remains uncertain. Of course, the representatives of the basic subjects are called upon to organize themselves better and to present their knowledge in a form that can be taught and tested in examinations.

3. HISTORY OF A DISCIPLINE

This introduction takes on a narrower, previously neglected, sector in the field of legal history, namely the history of the discipline of public law from the early modern period to the present. This neglect is explained by the fact that the central interest of constitutional history was, naturally enough, directed at the "constitution(s)." Constitutional history describes "those rules and structures that shape the community and thus the political system,"[13] which means that it is using an open concept of constitution, one that is also useful for the premodern era. In the process, the efforts of contemporary jurists (including women, starting in the twentieth century) disappeared within the environment, as it were. Although they are not disregarded, with a view toward the constitution as a whole, they constitute only the accompanying intellectual element. In the same way, within the framework of the more feebly developed history of administration and administrative law, the theorists of administration are heard only as voices on the margin. Only in exceptional cases, as for example in the major work by Hans Maier, are they recognized as a historically formative force.[14]

The primary concern here is therefore to recognize and unlock the thinking, talking, and writing about these very rules and structures of constitutions and administrations over the course of more

Schriften, vol. 1, *Methodik der Rechtsgeschichte*, ed. by Dieter Simon (Frankfurt, 1983); Link (Note 4).

[13] Willoweit (Note 11), § 1, II.I.

[14] Hans Maier, *Die ältere deutsche Staats- und Verwaltungslehre* (Neuwied and Berlin, 1966), 2nd edn. (Munich, 1980), paperback edn. (Munich, 1986); also Hans Maier, *Gesammelte Schriften*, vol. 4 (Munich, 2009).

recent history. This is a literary history of the scholarly compilation and the doctrinal permeation and systematization of public law from about the year 1600 to the present. Until the end of the Old Empire in 1806, that history—in part intellectual, in part related to praxis—took place in Germany largely at the universities. They were the centers of training and of intellectual life. The written output is university literature: lecture course outlines, textbooks, commentaries, collections of cases, and a vast number of dissertations and disputations, the latter an invaluable source today for reconstructing the intellectual profile of a period, of a university or a school of learning, and of the fashionable topics and innovations, but also of the migratory movements of students throughout Europe.[15] The dominance of the universities and of the world of scholars that becomes evident is specific to Germany, while in countries like France or England the capital-based salons, clubs, or academies held the intellectual leadership roles.

This kind of history presupposes the development of power relationships, of wars and peace treaties, of the de facto existing structures, of institutions and human actors. In other words: a broadly conceived constitutional history forms the basis and the background of political and legal thinking. After all, doing and thinking are historically intertwined to the point of being indistinguishable, and they shall remain thus also in the present study. Still, the primary focus will be on the history of the "science" of public law, even if in the period from the sixteenth to the eighteenth centuries the talk was not of science in the modern sense, but mostly of jurisprudence (*iuris prudentia*).

Anyone who establishes a connection with others beyond theoretical writings, who helps to shape the public discourse and becomes one of its elements, is at the same time also an actor. Theorists often think "ahead" and guide the debate to a point where it can be turned into political action. Just as often they analyze in an illuminating way what has happened, casting what is not understood into "concepts," and in this way once again creating starting points for new thinking. Human thinking is time-dependent, but it always displays also a will of its own and a relative autonomy. It neither moves only at lofty heights, nor can it be reduced to an appendix of the "facts." In that

[15] The Max Planck Institute for European Legal History (Frankfurt a. M.) has a collection of nearly 100,000 organized and catalogued dissertations of this kind. See www.rg.mpg.de.

sense, an effort has been made in recent times to find a meaningful way of writing an *histoire sociale des idées*, an "intellectual history" or "histories of mentalities" that oscillates between political history, social history, and the conventional "history of ideas." We will treat not just the "master thinkers" in a kind of summit tour, but also the sometimes much more influential minor and mid-level authors, their lifeworlds, their dependencies, and their political environments. All told, this much is true: the "state" is not only the concrete substrate of public services, buildings and things, budgets, and legal rules, but also what all of us think and do. The state "is" as we imagine it to be, and how we act within these notions. To that extent, a study of the thinking about the state is the study of the state itself. What our ancestors thought about it and how they shaped it is something we must understand at least in outline in order to decide what it is that we ourselves want to do in the state and with the state. If we decide that we want to have as little as possible to do with the state and refuse to become engaged on its behalf, we must answer the questions of who is to protect us against violence; who is to be responsible for the services necessary for living and for the conveniences we take for granted; who will maintain transportation and communication systems; who will finance universities, libraries, museums, and much else. Since every generation sets other emphases in this regard, moving ahead into the future is—whether we like it or not—also an engagement with the past.

4. METHODOLOGICAL RECOMMENDATION AND AUXILIARY TOOLS

One's approach to the historical material in libraries and archives should be as unbiased as possible. Notwithstanding the fact that we are all entangled in the net of the present, thinking and acting within it, that we can therefore never free ourselves fundamentally from biases, the following methodological rules are recommended: one's own customary ways of thinking and conceptualization should not be uncritically assumed, but should be critically examined and used to understand the historical "Other." The historical material is the "Other," even if its language may still sound comprehensible to us today. There is no objection to the use of modern terms, provided one is aware of the danger of anachronisms and deploys modern terminology in a thoughtful way. In fact, because of its alienating effect, it can be quite helpful. However, the primary goal is to study the usages of the words in the past to decipher what those words "meant" back then. One should beware of discerning in the course of history all too readily a rising curve of progress or a declining curve of decay. The commanding height of one's own convictions is perhaps nothing more than a molehill. Above all, one must not block out everything that cannot be superficially related to contemporary constitutional and administrative law. This kind of separation of historical material into "dead" and "alive" not only degrades history into being the prehistory of the present, but also cuts off important possibilities of understanding. What did not prevail in the mainstream or even failed can be of the utmost interest.

The following account seeks to sketch the basic lines and is therefore concerned with conciseness. For biographical information about the authors, the reader is referred to the standard resources.[16] References to the literature are also only sparsely provided. What made that decision easier is that my detailed treatment of the entire complex is now complete and can be used to pursue a more in-depth study.[17] A similar approach was taken by Manfred Friedrich's newer *Geschichte der deutschen Staatsrechtswissenschaft* (History of the German Science of State Law).[18] Recent years have also seen the publication of Andreas Kley's *Geschichte des öffentlichen Rechts der*

[16] They can be accessed through Michael Stolleis, ed., *Staatsdenker in der Frühen Neuzeit*, 3rd edn. (Munich, 1995); Michael Stolleis, ed., *Juristen: Ein biographisches Lexikon*, 2nd edn. (Munich, 2001); Gerd Kleinheyer and Jan Schröder, eds., *Deutsche und Europäische Juristen aus neun Jahrhunderten*, 5th edn. (Heidelberg, 2008).

[17] Michael Stolleis, *Geschichte des öffentlichen Rechts in Deutschland*, vol. 1, 1600–1800 (Munich, 1988), vol. 2, 1800–1914 (Munich, 1992), vol. 3, 1914–45 (Munich, 1999, also in a paperback study edn.), vol. 4, 1945–90 (Munich, 2012). The following translations of these volumes have been published to date: vol. 1 (French, Italian), vol. 2 (English, Chinese, Italian, French), vol. 3 (English, Chinese). The volumes were accompanied by Michael Stolleis, *Staat und Staatsräson in der frühen Neuzeit: Studien zur Geschichte des öffentlichen Rechts* (Frankfurt am Main, 1990) (Italian: *Stato e ragion di stato nella prima età moderna* (Bologna, 1998)); Michael Stolleis, *Konstitution und Intervention: Studien zur Geschichte des öffentlichen Rechts im 19. Jahrhundert* (Frankfurt am Main, 2001); Michael Stolleis, *Recht im Unrecht: Studien zur Rechtsgeschichte des Nationalsozialismus* (Frankfurt am Main, 1994), 2nd edn. (Frankfurt am Main, 2006) (English: *Law under the Swastika* (Chicago, 1998); French edn. (Lyon, 2016).

[18] Manfred Friedrich, *Geschichte der deutschen Staatsrechtswissenschaft* (Berlin, 1997).

Schweiz (History of Public Law in Switzerland).[19] The newer literature on constitutional history can be accessed best through Dietmar Willoweit's textbook.[20] Abundant material on administrative history, including early modern *Policey* and modern administrative law, can be found in the five-volume work *Deutsche Verwaltungsgeschichte* (German Administrative History).[21]

[19] Andreas Kley, *Geschichte des öffentlichen Rechts der Schweiz* (Zurich and St. Gallen, 2011).

[20] Willoweit (Note 11); Dietmar Willoweit, *Reich und Staat: Eine kleine deutsche Verfassungsgeschichte* (Munich, 2013).

[21] Kurt G. A. Jeserich, Hans Pohl, and Georg-Christoph von Unruh, eds., *Deutsche Verwaltungsgeschichte*, vols. 1–5 (Stuttgart, 1983–7), and index volume.

2

The Emancipation from Roman Law and the Change in the Sources of Constitutional Law

1. THE STARTING POINT: ROMAN LAW

Roman law as practiced and applied to the medieval world of Italy since the thirteenth century had spread, in teaching and praxis, from Bologna to the universities of Western and Central Europe. Learned jurists were increasingly consulted on all legal questions, and were given important posts as advisers and experts, negotiators or diplomats, and gradually also as judges. They were familiar with the famous division of legal studies into public and private law. Public law, in the words of the late Roman jurist Ulpian (died 223 CE), concerned the "Roman state" (*ad statum rei Romanae spectat*), private law the utility for each individual (*ad utilitatem singulorum*).[1] The subjects of public interest included, alongside the state cult, religious and priestly law, public offices, and also all obligatory norms of private law (e.g., marriage law, adoptions, wills, the regulations of time limits, procedural law, and more). However, public law and private law formed an imagined unity of "the law." This unity encompassed not only secular and religious law, but also the particular laws in the city and the countryside, as well as special rights specific to certain groups. A categorical division into "private" and "public" law was unknown in theory and practice. The more specialized rule took precedence over the more general one. Where special rules were absent, the "common law" or the "imperial law" were consulted: initially in

[1] Dig. I.I.2; Inst. I.I.4.

a subsidiary capacity, but the more trained jurists took control, the more the balance shifted in favor of common law. If experts in the fifteenth and sixteenth centuries were called upon on questions concerning the imperial elections, proxy representation of the emperor, the imperial diets, or controversial sovereign rights or dues, they gathered the necessary elements wherever they found them—from Roman–Italian law including feudal law, but also from the *Sachsenspiegel* and the basic electoral law of the empire, the "Golden Bull" of 1356, and from the "imperial customs" derived from customary law. Arguments derived from the Old and New Testaments also readily found their place here.

To be sure, since the high Middle Ages there had existed a differentiation between, on the one hand, the public–political, sovereign, and in this sense "public" sphere, whose legal rules were included in the *ius publicum*,[2] and, on the other, the private sphere of life in which the legal rules applicable to everyone had to be observed—however, the boundaries were barely discernible. Land and authority were passed down in accordance with family and inheritance law, but often also according to purchase or lien law. When dealing with serious crimes, criminal law belonged to the public sphere; when it came to lesser offenses, it belonged to the private sphere, where one sought compensation through "fines." Only slowly did early modern authorities put forth a claim for a "public right to punishment" and distinguished between private actions and "official legal proceedings."[3] But the classifications were in a sense the polar opposites of today. In the thinking of that time—which barely separated private and public, or at least did so differently—cursing and swearing, invocations of the devil, magic and witchcraft, adultery and other sins, were problems of public order, because they brought God's wrath upon the community and thus endangered it. It took just as long before the notion of

[2] See Gerhard Dilcher and Diego Quaglioni, eds., *Die Anfänge des öffentlichen Rechts*, vol. 1, *Gesetzgebung im Zeitalter Friedrich Barbarossas und das Gelehrte Recht* (Bologna, 2007), vol. 2, *Von Friedrich Barbarossa zu Friedrich II.* (Bologna, 2008), vol. 3, *Auf dem Wege zur Etablierung des öffentlichen Rechts zwischen Mittelalter und Moderne* (Bologna, 2011).

[3] On this development, see the results of a research project published by Klaus Lüderssen, Klaus Schreiner, Rolf Sprandel, and Dietmar Willoweit, *Konflikt, Verbrechen und Sanktion in der Gesellschaft Alteuropas*, 10 vols. (Cologne, Weimar, and Vienna, 1999–2006); and a series of monographs written in conjunction on the topic of pre-state criminal law.

"indivisibility" established itself on the central question whether land was in the family ownership of a dynasty; that is, could be bequeathed, divided, sold, and mortgaged. Accordingly, indivisibility was a crucial precondition for the "state formation" of the early modern period. In this way, the territory was removed from the private sphere and took on supra-individual contours. In line with this development, the image of the ruler changed gradually to that of the "highest servant of the state," and although he considered himself the head of his dynasty and endowed with the grace of God, he now saw himself obligated to the abstract entity of the "state."

2. NEW CONDITIONS

The medieval legal order, which was overarched by secular "imperial law" and by church law but was chiefly oriented toward village law, territorial law, city law, feudal law, special professional law, the law pertaining to social estates, and countless privileges and special privileges, invariably ran into difficulties—with its mix of legal customs and written law, learned and unlearned law—when living conditions and mentalities changed dramatically at the end of the fifteenth century and during the sixteenth. Striking innovations multiplied. New armies of mercenaries replaced the old knightly armies, knighthood declined materially and socially, the increasingly prosperous burgher class rose, the large long-distance trading houses inserted themselves into politics and mutated into a moneyed aristocracy, the Reformation caused considerable instability within the structure of the empire and raised entirely new constitutional questions, for example, about the theoretical possibility of a Protestant emperor. Since the German cities were weakened by a financial crisis in the second half of the sixteenth century and the large merchant houses had lost the eastern Mediterranean to the Turks, the political weights shifted.[4] The nobility, too, was no longer a closed caste. The unity of the church had been broken once and for all with the Council of Trent

[4] Karl S. Bader and Gerhard Dilcher, *Deutsche Rechtsgeschichte: Land und Stadt: Bürger und Bauer im Alten Europa* (Berlin and Heidelberg, 1999), pp. 688 ff. (Dilcher).

(1545–63). Thereafter it was no longer possible to bring together Roman Catholicism, Lutheranism, and Calvinism into a single ecclesiastical entity. The Eastern Orthodox Churches, too, had long since become independent. What the ecclesiastical powers lost in secular influence in this way accrued to the territorial prince. The latter no longer defined himself as a judge, but primarily as a lawgiver. As a "sovereign" he sought to round out his territory and endow it with boundaries within which his law and his fiat were effective.

The law and fiat of the territorial ruler gradually replaced the previous legal order. The rule now was that the newer law superseded the older one. With that, the entire legal structure was upended, since previously the older law was considered more venerable ("good old law"). The lawgiver was now the authoritative, central figure. Particular rights were displaced, and privileges were taken away, though a wealth of new privileges was also handed out by virtue of the new law. The new lawgiver could now—at least in theory—abrogate also Roman law, which had lost its nimbus as "imperial law," and replace it with new statute law.

In the wake of these efforts to move lawgiving and the office of the ruler into the center (efforts inspired by late antiquity), the idea also arose in the early sixteenth century of propping up the wavering authority of Roman law by declaring that it was valid not only by virtue of authority, quality, or custom, but also because the whole of it had been made legally binding by Emperor Lothar III of Supplinburg (1075–1137). This "Lotharian legend" was refuted once and for all as early as 1643,[5] but the fact that it could emerge in the first place reveals a good deal about the persuasive power that the word "lawgiving" now unfolded.

This fundamental process of the relativization of Roman law by the new, lawgiving "state power" was also supported by the fact that Roman law—traditionally seen as intrinsically coherent, indeed inviolable—had suffered cracks at the hands of humanist philology and a new historicizing perspective. With their keener look at the texts, the great humanist lawyers of the sixteenth century (Andreas Alciatus, Guillaume Budé, Jacques Cujas, Hugo Donellus) destroyed the notion of the inner unity of the law that should be preserved or

[5] Hermann Conring, *Der Ursprung des Deutschen Rechts* (Frankfurt, 1994) (translation of *De Origine Iuris Germanici Commentarius Historicus* (Helmstedt, 1643)).

rather established by a harmonizing interpretation. Now one saw various "textual strata," differentiated the individual classic authors, discovered inconsistencies and blatant contradictions. Roman law was no longer the sacralized unitary law of the West, but a historically transmitted mass of texts that also showed defects and led to countless conflicts over interpretation.

When the rising absolutism now established itself as a lawgiver in order to reorganize the legal system, it was in principle free to use Roman law as its material, and there was much to suggest that this treasury of subtle rule making, differentiation, and life experience should not be wasted. And so, as early as the sixteenth century, the idea arose that one could use Roman law as the foundation for a comprehensive codification of the law, supplement it with the tried-and-tested territorial law, and impart to all of it a rational form in keeping with the new spirit of mathematics and the natural sciences. Of course, a direct transfer of Roman state law to the conditions of the sixteenth century was out of the question. The components of Roman law that were usable in this regard were limited. What supported the claim of a centralized power were the late classical titles, symbols, and legal formulas employed by the imperial publications since the twelfth century: for example, that the prince's will has the force of law (*quod principi placuit legis habet vigorem*); that the prince is above the law (*princeps legibus solutus*), yet is bound to unchangeable natural law and divine law; that the ruler should be seen as lord of the world (*dominus mundi*), as father of the land (*pater omnium*); that he can not only make laws, but also change, interpret, and abrogate them. All of this was now gratefully picked up again.

In addition, the stock of Roman law was used according to all the rules of the art of interpretation. When the prince, as the "father of his land," commanded the power of the father (*patria potestas*), one could apply the rules of inheritance law to the princely testaments and declare that land and people were heritable; but one could also deduce that the patrimony should be kept together as much as possible. The notion about the power of the father turned people into *Landeskinder* (literally "children of the land") and subjects. The extent of the land was determined in accordance with the Roman definition of the word *territorium*. The income was derived from the princely family's own possessions and from the feudal right that was considered part of Roman law (*regalia*). To protect the economically threatened nobility, one developed out of the Roman law concerning entailed estates a special law of noble family estates that were inalienable and could not be burdened with debt.[6]

Roman law, interpreted with flexibility, thus still offered numerous points of connection for the changed constitutional situation, but it no longer fit together into a system that would have been usable for the constitutional reality of the sixteenth and seventeenth centuries. Even in Germany, which advanced the claim of the emperorship to continue the Roman emperorship, it became clear that the ancient emperorship was no longer comparable to the contemporary one. The constitutional state of affairs had altered completely. Moreover, one of the most important elements of Roman *ius publicum*, namely sacral law, had turned into church law. In the Reformation it had fragmented, turned into special law, and was no longer suitable as a strong bracket of the imperial constitution. All previous rules about church property, about the bishop's official powers, about marriage law and divorce, about property and inheritance law of the residents of monasteries, and about many other matters had to be newly regulated.

3. THE NEW CONSTITUTIONAL LAW

The "anti-Roman sentiment" at work in the Reformation additionally supported the tendency to justify the emperor and the empire on the basis of their native roots, and to replace the papal version of the transfer of the late Roman Empire by the Pope to Charlemagne in 800 CE with its own secularized construct. The fact that this empire was nevertheless referred to as "Holy" and "Roman" until its end did impart a certain splendor to it. In the age of dynastic great-power politics, however, it meant virtually nothing anymore, especially in the period after the end of the Thirty Years War (1648) and the end of the empire itself (1806).

The focal point of Roman law thus continued to lie in the law of obligations, in specialized contract law, in lien and mortgage law, and in law of inheritance. It was chiefly important for training the legal method of argumentation, intellectually standardizing the increasingly important "legal profession," and providing it with tools to

[6] Philipp Knipschild, *Von Stammgütern: Tractatus de fideicommissis familiarum nobilium* (Ulm, 1654).

justify judicial decisions or expert opinions rationally and based on texts.[7] That is also true for criminal law, which had been formed out of native traditions and had by now been overlaid with Roman canonical procedural law. Only remnants of the old Roman criminal law still existed, and they too vanished once the Reich had been able to create its own penal code in 1532. This Constitutio Criminalis Carolina (CCC) was now considered imperial law, until it was replaced in the eighteenth and nineteenth centuries by other law codes, the last instance being the Imperial Criminal Law Code of 1871.

All told, the altered constitutional situation since the Worms Diet and its reform laws of 1495, the Reformation of the church that reverberated into all spheres of life, the confessional rupture and the religious wars gave rise to completely new conditions for "those rules and structures that shape the community and thus the political system."[8] The Holy Roman Empire of the German Nation, as it had been called since the late Middle Ages, could no longer be governed with Roman–Italian law. The legitimation of Roman law had become brittle. The modern state announced itself as a lawmaking state, with the claim, namely, that it was casting aside previously valid law.

[7] Michael Stolleis, "Juristenstand," in *HRG*, 2nd edn. (Berlin, 2011), pp. 1440–3.

[8] Dietmar Willoweit, *Deutsche Verfassungsgeschichte: Vom Frankenreich bis zur Wiedervereinigung Deutschlands*, 7th edn. (Munich, 2013), p. 2.

3

Elements of the Emerging Public Law

1. "POLITICS"

Like Roman law, the "theory of politics" (*politica*) was another legacy from antiquity. The text used at the universities throughout the Middle Ages was Aristotle's *Politics*, dating from the fourth century BCE. Translated into Latin by Wilhelm von Moerbecke around 1260, it formed the basis thereafter for questions about the emergence of the state and the place of citizens within it, about the state forms of monarchy, aristocracy, and polity, along with their degenerate forms of tyranny, oligarchy, and democracy. This text was also used to discuss the virtues of the monarch, "just rule," constitutional change, the curing of "ailments of the state," and the education of citizens.

But in the training of jurists in the late Middle Ages, this "constitutional theory" played only a minor role. It was taught in faculties of arts (later faculties of philosophy), where it formed, alongside ethics (the individual) and economics (the household), the third stage of human social association (the state). There is reason to doubt whether jurists participated in this preparatory study in larger numbers. They had more than enough on their hands with Roman law and canon law.

After the Reformation had interrupted teaching on the basis of the "pagan" Aristotle for a decade, a new flowering of neo-Aristotelianism began at the Protestant universities in 1530–1 with the authority of Philipp Melanchthon. It extended to about the second third of the seventeenth century. This period saw the publication of numerous works on "politics" that reflected quite different intellectual traditions, confessions, and political conditions, but which time and again allowed the original Aristotelian image to shine through. They were penned by Lutherans (Henning Arnisaeus, Georg Schönborner,

Hermann Conring), Catholics (Francisco de Suárez, Pedro de Ribadeneira, Gregorius Tolosanus, Adam Contzen), and members of reformed confessions (Lambertus Danaeus, Johannes Althusius, Bartholomaeus Keckermann). Especially Lutheran universities saw a flood of disputations, dissertations, handbooks, systemizations, and specialized tractates on politics, "simultaneous with the establishment of the Jus publicum."[1]

These works on politics were tied to religion to varying degrees. Some sought a supra-confessional vantage point, as for example the 1589 book by the brilliant Dutch philologist Justus Lipsius, which was largely a compilation of quotes from Tacitus. It was sensationally successful, not only because of its stylistic elegance, but also because Lipsius preached the confessionally unified, well-ordered, strong state, and because he moderated the scandalous theses of the Florentine politician Niccolò Machiavelli (1469–1527) and communicated them as a skillful intermediary. The key questions were whether politics and religion belonged to separate spheres, and whether the acting statesman was permitted to use deception and force. Machiavelli had advocated the autonomy of politics against the claims of the church, and under certain circumstances he had no qualms about granting the politician the right to employ deceit and force. Within Machiavelli's circle, and probably still during his lifetime, the formula of the "reason of state" (*ragione di stato*) appeared in Florence and Venice. Ever since, acting in accordance with the reason of state has meant soberly calculating one's own strengths and those of others in the political struggle (*ragione* = "calculation"), and pursuing the goals of the polity with no more than tactical consideration given to religion and morality. These theses, extraordinarily bold for his time, led not only to the church banning Machiavelli's writings, but also to the demonization of immoral politics as "Machiavellian."

Anyone who wanted to examine Machiavelli's questions—as to the permissibility of deceit or ruses of war, for example—without mentioning his name could do so using the writings of the ancient author Publius C. Tacitus (*c.*58–120 CE). Following his rediscovery in the fifteenth century, Tacitus was especially popular in Germany because

[1] Horst Dreitzel, *Protestantischer Aristotelismus und Absoluter Staat: Die "Politica" des Henning Arnisaeus (ca. 1575–1636)* (Wiesbaden, 1970), pp. 412 f. See also Christoph Strohm, *Calvinismus und Recht: Weltanschaulich-konfessionelle Aspekte im Werk reformierter Juristen in der frühen Neuzeit* (Tübingen, 2008).

he had painted an image of the virtuous ancient Germans in his work *Germania*. More important for Europe, however, were his *Annals* and *Histories*. Commentaries on these writings gave rise to a debate about practical ethics and politics, a debate that was called "Tacitism" and which split, in turn, into two main currents, one republican and one absolutist.[2]

2. NATIONAL SOURCES OF LAW

However, for the jurists who had to counsel and advise their city authorities, territorial lords, or the emperor in Vienna at the end of the sixteenth century, the paltry components of Roman law that dealt with the law of the state and references to the new commentaries on Aristotle or to Cicero's *De re publica* were no longer adequate. The Bible, too, was an aid far too subject to interpretation, as were the medieval writings on the state rediscovered by the humanists, who typically favored those that opposed the papal claim to power.

To craft arguments that were legally promising, one had to turn to the imperial constitution itself. The Lutheran Reformation and the Peasants' War of 1525, the religious wars and the imperial crisis in the final third of the sixteenth century—all of this called urgently for an interpretation of the norms that were essential to the empire and its "constitution." But which norms were essential? For contemporaries they were the "basic laws of the empire" I mentioned at the outset.

The highest-ranking law of this kind was unquestionably the Golden Bull of 1356, which stipulated above all the procedure for electing the emperor. It gave the initial number of seven electors and fixed the electoral processes.[3] A set of important imperial laws was added in 1495, chiefly the curbing of feuds (i.e., permitted private wars) through the declaration of a "Permanent Territorial Peace" (*Ewiger Landfriede*), and the establishment of the Imperial Chamber Court (*Reichskammergericht*), which was soon followed by the Imperial

[2] Jürgen von Stackelberg, *Tacitus in der Romania* (Tübingen, 1960); Else-Lilly Etter, *Tacitus in der Geistesgeschichte des 16. und 17. Jahrhunderts* (Basel, 1966); Kenneth C. Schellhase, *Tacitus in Renaissance Political Thought* (Chicago, 1976).

[3] In 2013, the extant copies of the Golden Bull were declared a World Cultural Heritage.

Aulic Council (*Reichshofrat*) in Vienna. Beginning with the election of Emperor Charles V, an electoral capitulation was issued at every imperial election; that is, a document containing the agreements made between the candidate and the imperial estates.[4] In 1555, the Peace of Augsburg guaranteed a framework for imperial constitutional law within which Catholics and Lutherans could coexist side by side.[5] In 1648 these "basic laws" were joined by the Peace of Westphalia, a central document for the religious parties, for the internal order of the empire, and for the system of international law. All of these documents were now also considered fundamental or basic law. The same quality was accorded to the more important laws passed by the imperial diet (*Reichstag*), the so-called imperial recesses (*Reichsabschiede*) that were printed immediately following each imperial diet.[6] Of those laws, the Imperial Police Ordinance (Reichspoliceyordnung, 1530) and the Imperial Penal Code (Constitutio Criminalis Carolina, 1532) were considered especially important.

If one puts all of this together, around the middle of the sixteenth century, the material was at hand for the jurists working on the imperial constitution for the Holy Roman Empire of the German Nation, the *Ius Publicum Sacri Imperii Romano-Germanici*.[7] De facto, this empire—with its approximately 1,000 political subunits of emerging states, individual lordships, ecclesiastical territories, free Hanseatic cities, imperial cities, imperial villages, imperial abbeys, and so on[8]—thus had a constitution. It was an elected emperorship (though in practice this was an office passed down within the House of Habsburg), as well as a body of electors, a college of princes, an assembly of the estates called the imperial diet, two supreme courts (the Imperial Chamber Court, the Imperial Aulic Council), extensive regional groupings (the *Reichskreise*, "Imperial Circles"), and an imperial army (the *Reichsaufgebot*) that was levied as needed. What

[4] "Capitulation" (*Kapitulieren*) in this sense means recognizing a text arranged by chapters (*Kapitel*) as binding.

[5] Martin Heckel, *Deutschland im konfessionellen Zeitalter* (Göttingen, 1983).

[6] At the conclusion of an imperial diet, it was "recessed," or it adopted (German *verabschieden*) its resolutions.

[7] Barbara Stollberg-Rilinger, *Das Heilige Römische Reich Deutscher Nation: Vom Ende des Mittelalters bis 1806* (Munich, 2006).

[8] Gerhard Köbler, *Historisches Lexikon der deutschen Länder: Die deutschen Territorien vom Mittelalter bis zur Gegenwart* (Munich, 1988), 7th expanded edn. (Munich, 2007).

the empire was unable to create was an effective imperial administration, a productive tax system, and a comprehensive judicial administration with enforcement authority. Moreover, no central residence comparable to Paris, London, or Madrid emerged. Vienna, located at the periphery of the empire, was always more the capital of the Habsburg realm than of the "German" empire.

This complex political entity was now about to be given a legal structure. The impulse for this came largely from the dangerous political stalemate between the emperor and the empire and between the confessional camps. A series of conflicts that arose in the 1570s, in spite of the Peace of Augsburg, alarmed the Protestant side. It was interested above all in clarifying the questions of the imperial constitution, and it had promoted the training of jurists at its twenty-two universities, while the twenty-eight Catholic universities, all of which (with the exception of Salzburg) were run by Jesuits, neglected legal training for a long time. It was therefore overwhelmingly Protestant authors who now busied themselves with the *Ius publicum (sacri) Imperii Romano-Germanici*, created lecture courses on the subject, organized disputations, and arranged for dissertations to be written. This body of material soon gave rise to the first compilations and textbooks. The leaders in this effort were the Lutheran universities in Altdorf, Jena, Strasbourg, and Giessen, as well as reformed centers like Marburg, Heidelberg, and Basel. An expanded circle included also Tübingen, Frankfurt an der Oder, Helmstedt, Herborn, and Gdansk. A consensus soon emerged that one was dealing with a new and important discipline that had previously been neglected. Roman law became obsolete, for it contained nothing useful about the currently valid imperial law, the religious constitution, or the law of war and alliances; no specialized knowledge about the administration; and nothing about imperial diets, *Deputationstage* (meetings of the electors and princes), *Reichskreistage* (assemblies of the imperial circles), the treasury, or the army. The treatises on politics, too, were not concrete enough.

The new discipline flourished between 1600 and 1620. It soon became customary to fill at least one professorship at small universities with a representative of the *ius publicum*. The reluctance to address the *arcana* of the state and the administration in public teaching was soon overcome—too obvious was the advantage of finally having experts available in this area. The *Ritterakademien* (academies for knights) that were reserved for the nobility and served as a school for future officials, military officers, and diplomats also incorporated public law into their curricula without delay.[9]

The rapid acceptance of the new discipline can be explained: for one thing, on the Protestant side one felt the political pressure emanating from the constitutional quarrels on the eve of the Thirty Years War. That side, too, was philologically prepared through European late humanism and was familiar with the native texts. These new "publicists" (*Publizisten*), as they were soon called, were methodologically trained in Roman law, which furnished them with the rational style, the specialized language, and the specific mode of argumentation. The Catholic side was no less familiar with the native texts, but it invested hardly any scientific energies in interpreting them. Instead, it largely continued to cling to the previous position that Roman law, as "imperial law," formed the real source of legitimacy and the reservoir of argumentation.

Here is an example: when the Protestant city of Donauwörth, because of an insignificant incident, was seized by Duke Maximilian of Bavaria with the emperor's approval, the Bavarian Council argued in 1610 that according to the law of the Roman principate, the Imperial Aulic Council in Vienna was in charge of such a *Reichsexekution* (imperial enforcement action). The Protestant side responded in 1611 that it now seemed "sufficiently clear that a considerable difference existed between the old Latin and today's German emperors, and that therefore the form of this entire German constitution (*ipsa totius reipublicae Germanicae forma*) must be taken, not from the Latin laws, or from Bartolo and Baldo, as the *relator* ... very foolishly construed, but rather from the traditions of the empire and from the old constitutions stemming from them, from the Golden Bull, imperial and royal capitulations, imperial recesses and constitutions."[10] This statement now became the general conviction.

[9] Klaus Bleek, *Adelserziehung auf deutschen Ritterakademien* (Frankfurt am Main, 1977); Norbert Conrads, *Ritterakademien der frühen Neuzeit: Bildung als Standesprivileg im 16. und 17. Jahrhundert* (Göttingen, 1982).

[10] Sebastian Faber and Ludwig Müller, *Beständige Informatio facti & Juris wie es mit den am Keiserlichen Hof wider des H. Römischen Reichs Statt Donawerth außgangenen Processen/und darauff vorgenommenen Execution/aigentlich und im Grund der Warheit beschaffen seye* (n.p., 1611).

4

Reichspublizistik, Natural Law, International Law, *Gute Policey*

1. *REICHSPUBLIZISTIK*

The period between 1600 and the end of the Old Empire in 1806 saw the development of *Reichspublizistik*. This label refers to scholarly engagement with the above-mentioned legal sources on the imperial constitution and their transmission to the next generation of jurists. Since all universities were state universities and were subject to a territorial ruler or a free imperial city (Strasbourg, Nuremberg), it was only natural that the expertise that was developing here would be put to political use. University professors of public law were not only active on the side as judges when they worked on cases as part of the usual "consignment of files" by the courts to the law faculties. They were also the perfect experts in all disputes touching on territorial sovereignty or *Reichsunmittelbarkeit* (the status of being directly subject to the emperor). In the process, they had to defend the interests of their employer. Thus "objectivity" (a deceptive illusion to begin with) could simply not be expected, and neither could a kind of modern academic freedom, which was propagated only in the late eighteenth century and implemented to some extent in the nineteenth.[1]

The development of a new discipline typically begins with collections of material, with initial probing disputations, which existed at the time both as a form of exercise and as closing events, and with more

[1] On this, see Ingolf Pernice, "Kommentierung des Art. 5 Abs. 3 GG," in Horst Dreier, ed., *Grundgesetz Kommentar*, 2nd edn., vol. 1 (Tübingen, 2004), pp. 715 ff.

or less systematically structured "dissertations." The latter were often written by the professors themselves and handed to a candidate to be publicly defended. University printers then published thematically arranged anthologies of such dissertations, and it was only a small step from these to regular textbooks. That step was taken in Herborn under Johannes Althusius, in Jena under Dominicus Arumaeus, in Giessen under Gottfried Antonius, and in Marburg under Hermann Vultejus. Thematic focal points were the questions of who held public authority (*iurisdictio, maiestas*, sovereignty), what legal constraints the ruler was subject to, whether he could impose taxes on the estates of the land without their consent, and whether the Imperial Chamber Court or the Imperial Aulic Council had jurisdiction over who was in possession of specific *regalia* (privilege of minting coins, customs, natural resources, hunting and fishing, market protection, protection of the Jews, and so on). Equally important were all disputes about the rights of possession of the confessions; that is, the landholding of churches and monasteries, incomes, and church treasuries. At the level of the empire, the issue revolved around the demarcation of the spheres of the emperor and of the imperial estates; that is to say, the locus of "sovereignty," which Jean Bodin in his epochal work *Les six livres de la République* (1576) had defined as "puissance absolue & perpétuelle d'une République" ("absolute and perpetual power of the Republic").

This was the theoretical formula of absolutism. It was not applicable in the empire, for the power of the emperor was not total, nor was the authority of the imperial estates *absolute*. Bodin had described the form of government in Germany as an aristocracy, which sparked much disagreement. The problem was really quite intractable, and so one resorted to the option of separating the legal title (*maiestas*) from its actual execution (*imperium*). A distinction was likewise drawn between the sovereignty of the community (*maiestas realis*) and that of the ruler (*maiestas personalis*). This form of government could not be subsumed under Aristotle's classic theory of state forms; it was therefore declared to be "mixed," similar to that of ancient Rome, which had also contained monarchic, aristocratic, and democratic elements and for that very reason was believed to have been especially stable.[2]

[2] Wilfried Nippel, *Mischverfassungstheorie und Verfassungsrealität in Antike und früher Neuzeit* (Stuttgart, 1980).

The literature devoted to these questions grew at an astonishing rate in the seventeenth and eighteenth centuries. It contributed significantly to the admired and feared "baroque mountain of books." The first great summation appeared in 1619, the *Tractatus de Regimine Seculari et Ecclesiastico* from the pen of Dietrich Reinkingk (1590–1664), a professor at Giessen, who championed a piously Lutheran, pro-emperor, and monarchic point of view.[3] More strongly inclined toward the cause of the imperial estates was the nine-volume work of Johannes Limnaeus (1592–1663), a lucidly structured handbook overflowing with material (1629–34).[4] He solved the sovereignty issue by assigning to the empire (more precisely the imperial estates) the real sovereign power, and to the emperor the personal sovereign power, which was tied, though, to a higher law. This was the theoretically balancing meaning of the formula "emperor and empire."

When the "Great War" erupted in 1618 and laid the land waste in several stages, university activities were interrupted only locally and temporarily. Disputations and dissertations on public law continued to appear, along with short works and pamphlets of every kind, depending on the course of the war. The (false or true) reason of state was discussed over and over. A particularly harshly anti-Habsburgian work was the famous tractate *On the Reason of State of Our Romano-German Empire* (*Dissertatio de ratione status in Imperio nostro Romano-Germanico*), written in 1640 or 1647 by Bogislaus Philipp von Chemnitz, who called himself Hippolithus à Lapide.[5] It was an attempt to push Habsburg aside and shift the power of the empire to the imperial diet—an interesting parallel to the Glorious Revolution in England, which ended the effort of the Crown to establish absolutism and eventually led to a balance between king and Parliament ("king in Parliament").

The long-desired peace agreement of Münster and Osnabrück in 1648 changed the imperial constitution, created a new religious law, and was the starting point for a new international legal order of Europe. The "empire," a now weaker entity between the powers of France, Sweden, and Habsburg, did survive. But the individual

[3] Christoph Link, "Dietrich Reinkingk," in Michael Stolleis, ed., *Staatsdenker in der Frühen Neuzeit*, 3rd edn. (Munich, 1995), pp. 78–99.

[4] Rudolf Hoke, "Johannes Limnaeus," in Stolleis (Note 3), pp. 100–17.

[5] Chemnitz = Slavic *Stein* = Latin *lapis*. See Rudolf Hoke, "Hippolithus a Lapide," in Stolleis (Note 3), pp. 118–28.

imperial estates were granted the *ius territorii et superioritatis*, which differed from full sovereignty only by the verbal consideration accorded to the emperor and the empire. In a further fundamental law, the sovereign rights of the emperor were tied to the consent of the Imperial Diet (*jüngster Reichsabschied* ("recent recess"), 1654). On the religious question, the parties agreed to go back to the "normal year" 1624, the reformed Calvinists were included in the peace as the third confession deserving protection, and procedural guarantees were to ensure that religious questions could no longer breach the imperial constitution. Unresolved questions were postponed to the future and remained such until the end (1806). The Imperial Chamber Court resumed its work and was moved to Wetzlar following the destruction of Speyer in 1689. The Imperial Diet established itself as a "Perpetual Diet" in Regensburg, as a permanent congress of delegates, institutionally consolidated but, at the same time, with limited capacity to take political action.

Thereafter, the imperial constitution, also called the "imperial system" by contemporaries, was considered cumbersome and old-fashioned, while all around Europe—with the exception of Italy and Poland—powerful nation states were arising, chiefly the France of Louis XIV as the model absolutist state. In the empire itself, the rising Brandenburg-Prussia and the Habsburg multi-ethnic state were the main powers, between which Germany moved as a conglomerate of medium-sized and small states. Finally, the Peace of Münster and Osnabrück established a system of international law in that it was concluded with the involvement of European guarantor powers and henceforth served to secure the continental balance of power (the "Westphalian order").

Reichspublizistik responded to this partly new, partly consolidated constitutional situation after 1648 with a wealth of publications, even if the universities were crippled by the war. The smaller Protestant universities (Altdorf, Wittenberg, Rinteln, Herborn, Helmstedt, Duisburg, Königsberg) continued to languish, while Jena, Marburg, Giessen, Strasbourg, and Tübingen quickly started up again. Heidelberg suffered from several confessional changes, and it was subsequently not only destroyed twice (1689, 1693), but as a Jesuit university after 1700 it also lost touch again with public law. Kiel University, founded in 1665, was affected by the Northern War, and Greifswald belonged to the Swedish state after 1637, even if it retained its German-language university.[6] On the whole one could observe a shift in intellectual life. To be sure, Hermann Conring (1606–81) taught in Helmstedt as professor of medicine and politics, and the young Samuel von Pufendorf (1632–94) taught briefly in Heidelberg, but Europe's leading natural scientists and humanistic scholars—the likes of Francis Bacon, Baruch Spinoza, René Descartes, Blaise Pascal, or Gottfried Wilhelm Leibniz—worked outside the universities. The learned societies, new academies, salons, and reading societies attracted more and more talent. Discussions there were more open and without formalities, experiments were demonstrated, and books were exchanged. The latest knowledge circulated through an extraordinarily dense network of letters. The universities, by contrast, paid attention to the transmission of chairs within scholarly dynasties, to a schematization of the curriculum and publishing, to the guild spirit and closure against the outside. The universities in Catholic territories (Ingolstadt, Trier, Würzburg, Mainz, Cologne, Salzburg) were under ecclesiastical supervision, placed little value on jurisprudence, and until the middle of the eighteenth century opened themselves only hesitantly to the spirit of the Enlightenment. Public law was taught at them only selectively, at most, while a nearly complete—if qualitatively diverse—offering of lectures on the imperial constitution existed around the year 1700 at the Lutheran and Reformed universities as well as at the knightly academies.

2. NATURAL LAW AND INTERNATIONAL LAW

Alongside the constitutional law of the empire, the *ius publicum* in the narrower sense, two other disciplines that can be included in public law in the broader sense established themselves over the course of the seventeenth century: natural law and European international law. Though not identical, the two disciplines were closely interconnected.

To the degree that absolutism asserted itself in terms of power politics and reorganized the internal structure of the respective territories, it became necessary to find a new legal system of communication

[6] Kjell Å. Modéer, *Gerichtsbarkeiten der schwedischen Krone im deutschen Reichsterritorium* (Stockholm, 1975), pp. 423 ff., 458 ff.

also for external relations. The notion of a world ruled by the emperor as the *dominus mundi* had lapsed already in the fourteenth and fifteenth centuries. Feudal law, too, which had long fulfilled a pacifying function similar to international law, lost its original military meaning. By now the dogma of sovereignty ruled, which was deployed as an instrument to ward off all outside or external influences. To be sure, the demarcation of rights of rulership and zones of influence is not a phenomenon specific to the modern era. But only the sovereignty of the European states that was becoming aware of itself internally and externally made it possible and necessary to formalize relations and lift them to a new stage of interstate law (*ius gentium*). "The idea of international law," Immanuel Kant wrote in 1795, "presupposes the separate existence of many independent but neighboring states."[7] Only this "separate existence" made it possible to demarcate territories by treaty, to treat them as legal entities and above all as contracting parties. The relevant state ceremonial followed this development.[8]

Initially, one could observe among the humanistically educated authors in the sixteenth century a striking rise in works on military affairs, weaponry, tactics, and fortifications. The commentaries on the classical authors Vegetius, Frontinus, and Aelianus (which had begun in the Middle Ages) intensified and also had practical repercussions in the "military reform of the House of Orange," which led to much-noted military innovations inspired by classical models. A wealth of military tractates spread across Europe (Machiavelli, Pierino Belli, Balthazar de Ayala, Alberico Gentili, Justus Lipsius, Heinrich von Rantzau, Lazarus von Schwendi, Bernardino de Mendoça, Johann Jacobi von Wallhausen, Elias Reusner, and others). Alongside technical questions, they were concerned above all with the justification of war (*ius ad bellum*) and with the permissibility of inherently illegal means when waging war (*ius in bello*). Was it permissible in case of war, and possibly in time of peace, to lie and deceive for reasons of state? What could be done with prisoners of war, what with conquered lands and the subjects living there and

[7] Immanuel Kant, *Perpetual Peace: A Philosophical Sketch*, 1795, First Supplement, 2: www.constitution.org/kant/perpeace.htm.

[8] Miloš Vec, *Zeremonialwissenschaft im Fürstenstaat: Studien zur juristischen und politischen Theorie absolutistischer Herrschaftsrepräsentation* (Frankfurt am Main, 1998).

with their possessions? The tractates on war thus transmuted into tractates on the international law of war, and they dealt also with reprisals, right of escort, law of plunder and law of prize, and the treatment of prisoners of war and of pirates.

At the same time, numerous treatises were written on alliance law, the law of envoys and delegations, on diplomatic traffic and its symbolic forms, in which the complicated hierarchies of the European theater of states were embodied. The primary concern, though, regarded treaties: when states, represented by their monarchs, entered into treaties, the question of their binding force immediately arose. Does the treaty apply "forever," does it also bind the next ruler, can it be abrogated unilaterally if the political situation changes and is it therefore subject to the proviso that the "situation" remain unchanged (*clausula rebus sic stantibus*)? Or does the implacable rule hold that treaties must be adhered to verbatim regardless of changing circumstances (*pacta sunt servanda*)?

In the sixteenth century, all of these questions were discussed in Spain and Portugal against the backdrop of the wide-ranging discoveries and conquests in Central and South America, especially in the "school of Salamanca" of Francisco de Vitoria (1483/93–1546), Domingo de Soto (1494–1560), Fernando Vasquez (1512–69), and Francisco de Suárez (1548–1617). They were motivated by the very controversial justification of war, its limitations, the legal status of indigenous peoples, and the freedom of the seas, both theologically and in terms of the law of nations.

The emergence of European international law, which cannot be described here,[9] took place primarily in the western geographical arc extending from Salamanca over the Spanish Netherlands through the Protestant Netherlands to England. It culminated in a treatise that was a work of both legal philosophy and international law: *De Iure Belli ac Pacis libri tres in quibus Ius Naturae et Gentium*, written by the Dutch polymath Hugo Grotius (1583–1645) and published in Paris in 1625.[10]

[9] Arthur Nussbaum, *Geschichte des Völkerrechts* (Munich and Berlin, 1960); Wilhelm G. Grewe, *The Epochs of International Law*, translated and revised by Michael Byers (Berlin and New York, 2000); Karl-Heinz Ziegler, *Völkerrechtsgeschichte*, 2nd edn. (Munich, 2007).

[10] Hasso Hofmann, "Hugo Grotius," in Stolleis (Note 3), pp. 52–77; Robert Feenstra, "Grotius," in Stolleis, *Juristen*, pp. 265–8.

Its subtitle promised that it would also discuss the most important points of the *ius publicum*. It was an epochal work, one that would also shape the teaching of natural law and international law at the German universities in the seventeenth and eighteenth centuries. After a certain delay on account of the war, an extensive Grotius literature began there, and professors were lecturing on natural law and international law "according to Grotius"—with the result that separate bibliographies were necessary at the end of the seventeenth century to get a grip on the wealth of material.[11]

3. NATURAL LAW (*IUS NATURAE ET GENTIUM*)

In the same way, and—as we have seen—closely interconnected with international law, natural law flourished beginning in the sixteenth century. As a theoretical-philosophical subject within legal education, it offered a general theory of law that presented the human being argumentatively as an individual and endowed with rights and obligations (toward himself, toward others, toward God) within the family, society, and the community. To the extent that natural law also examined questions of the constitution of the rights and obligations of governments, it overlapped here and there with the *ius gentium*. This can be seen especially in Grotius.

The reasons behind the rapid growth of natural law in the seventeenth and eighteenth centuries resemble those I have indicated in the case of international law. But especially the penchant of natural law for stringent systematization needs to be separately examined. "Natural law" rested on reflections that reached back all the way to the oldest texts in the history of philosophy. They then migrated from Greece into the introductory titles of the late classical Digests and Institutes, and from there into the theological interpretation of the Ten Commandments and the Church Fathers by medieval theology, in which the trinity of revealed law, natural law, and human positive law emerged. Likewise, Aristotle's *Politics* offered a starting point for natural law, for example, on the question of slavery, the regulation of marriage, or the proper conduct of citizens. The European world

[11] Ernst Reibstein, "Deutsche Grotius-Kommentatoren bis zu Christian Wolff," *ZaöRV* 15 (1953–4), 76–102.

thus possessed a rich stock of natural-law arguments in the fifteenth and sixteenth centuries.[12] However, there was neither a "system" in the more exacting sense, nor a developed discipline of "natural law" within legal education.

The upheavals of the sixteenth century fundamentally altered the known world in Europe. The religious schism gave rise to divergent views on questions of natural law. For example, Lutherans rejected a right to resistance grounded in natural law, Zwinglians took guidance from the Golden Rule and the Sermon on the Mount, while Calvinists imputed that creation tended toward rationality and accordingly devised a rational *Politica Christiana.* Because the Netherlands had ties to Spain, it also witnessed a broad reception of the moral–theological natural law of the school of Salamanca. This made available the argumentative material that was now used for legal questions concerning the New World, but also for the elementary problem of freedom of religion, for the catalogue of human obligations, and for the general question about the power of natural law to prevail against unjust or deficient positive law.

Even if the elements I have mentioned were available, they did not yet amount to a developed system of natural law with the kind of claim to stringency that came to prevail with the "scientific revolution" of the seventeenth century. What was needed following the discovery of America and the circumnavigation of Africa was a natural law for the "whole" world, including the so-called primitive peoples, the "savages." The Copernican revolution expelled this world from the center of the universe and placed it into an orbit around the Sun.[13] Its Earth was demoted to a round planet, but at the same time humans could now take full possession of it.[14] This suggested the idea that natural law could be a universal legal entity.

At the same time, the rising absolutism needed a tool to overcome the social conditions of the late Middle Ages and transform them into a uniform model of rulership with centralized guidance.

[12] Merio Scattola, *Das Naturrecht vor dem Naturrecht: Zur Geschichte des "ius naturae" im 16. Jahrhundert* (Tübingen, 1999).

[13] Hans Blumenberg, *Die Genesis der kopernikanischen Welt* (Frankfurt am Main , 1975), three-volume paperback edn. (Frankfurt, 1981).

[14] Wolfgang Reinhard, *Geschichte der europäischen Expansion*, 4 vols. (Stuttgart, 1983, 1985, 1988, 1990); Jörg Fisch, *Die europäische Expansion und das Völkerrecht: Die Auseinandersetzungen um den Status der überseeischen Gebiete vom 15. Jahrhundert bis zur Gegenwart* (Stuttgart, 1984).

Natural law offered such a tool by promising a rational and geometric order that leveled out all differences based on social estates. Contemporaries began to devise supreme principles for such an order, principles from which logical deductions could be drawn step by step. The procedure that was used in the process was inspired by the new natural sciences, which were rushing from one discovery to the next around the year 1600. What Copernicus, Brahe, Kepler, Galileo, and Bacon were discovering were "laws of nature." Nothing seemed more self-evident than to apply their procedures also to "natural law." The "book of nature" that was studied with reverence for God's omnipotence lay side by side with the book of natural law, whose rules God had inscribed upon the human heart. For the first time there were also attempts to free oneself from the "God premise." René Descartes's *Discours de la méthode pour bien conduire sa raison, et chercher la vérité dans les sciences* (1637) clearly expresses that the new, methodologically developed science, which was to take the place of the obsolete scholastic method, was not only supposed to lead to scientifically secure results, but also aimed at the rational justification of normative propositions of morality and the law. And Thomas Hobbes affirmed that for the theory of the state, one needed the mathematical method "free from controversies and dispute."[15]

In line with this thinking, the image of the "state as machine" now also appeared. The state should be constructed like a clockwork that functioned with precision according to "natural law."[16] In other words, the certainty of natural laws appeared as a quality that one was hoping to transfer to the social world. Not only had God, as the clockmaker, organized the entire world according to his law, possibly in such a fixed manner that he could no longer deviate from his own natural law (the problem of miracles),[17] the sovereign, too, as God on earth, should have the power, as lawgiver, to organize the social world according to his will, but should likewise be bound by his own laws. If this machine is animated by a single force, that of

[15] Thomas Hobbes, *The Elements of Law, Natural and Politic*, ed. by J. C. A. Gaskin (Oxford 1994; first published 1640), Epistola dedicatoria.

[16] Barbara Stollberg-Rilinger, *Der Staat als Maschine: Zur politischen Metaphorik des absoluten Fürstenstaats* (Berlin, 1986).

[17] Lorraine Daston, *Wunder, Beweise und Tatsachen: Zur Geschichte der Rationalität*, 2nd edn. (Frankfurt am Main, 2003).

the sovereign, one would also have the ideal reinforcement for the unifying absolutism that governed consistently from top to bottom.

If this kind of standardization and decluttering according to mathematical maxims were possible, it would be a victory over history and could mean the solution to all problems of human community. For if one could ascertain the natural laws of the social world, there would be only a single truth. To be sure, this kind of mathematical optimism confronted the beliefs in original sin, the negative anthropology of "evil," and the realization of humankind's occasional weakness. But Gottfried Wilhelm Leibniz's fantasy of a mathematized law, and the great textbooks of natural law by Samuel Pufendorf, Christian Thomasius, and especially Christian Wolff,[18] tended to be borne by the optimism that clarity could be created, at least in principle. This all unfolded at a time before Immanuel Kant, with his critical writings, jolted and constrained the certainty regarding the possibilities of human understanding.[19]

The literary boom of natural law at German universities began in the second half of the seventeenth century and peaked in the eighteenth century. The reasons behind this boom are found in the shift of the political powers. At first, there was a close alliance between absolutism and its theoretical equivalent, the derivation of normative propositions from a supreme principle. Just as the ruler at the top of the pyramid of the polity sought to implement his orders downwards, the geometrically ordered natural law was to govern the polity, down to the smallest social unit of marriage. The more the bourgeoisie then sought to emancipate itself economically and politically, the more loudly it emphasized its autonomy and freedom of action and sought to partially push back the state. That goal was served by the rights of freedom that were now demanded ever more insistently.[20] Eventually a revolutionary opposition formed against absolutism and used natural law as a reservoir to delegitimize the monarchies. The rulers mutated into tyrants who had to be overthrown because they had violated the fictitious social contract. In this final phase, natural

[18] Notker Hammerstein, "Samuel Pufendorf," in Stolleis (Note 3), pp. 172–96; Klaus Luig, "Christian Thomasius," in ibid., pp. 227–56; Marcel Thomann, "Christian Wolff," in ibid., pp. 257–83.

[19] Wolfgang Naucke, "Kant," in *HRG*, 2nd edn., vol. 2 (Berlin, 2012), cols. 1580–5.

[20] Diethelm Klippel, *Politische Freiheit und Freiheitsrechte im deutschen Naturrecht des 18. Jahrhunderts* (Paderborn, 1976).

law—as the legal mantle for the outrage of the oppressed—in a sense destroyed the state form itself.

After the revolution had waned and been "tamed," and "constitutional monarchy" had established itself as the basic mediating model of the nineteenth century, beginning with the French Charte constitutionnelle of 1814, the political function of natural law also came to an end. The demands of liberalism could still employ natural law, for example, in the constitutional debates in southern Germany after 1818, in which claims beyond positive law were also raised. Occasional offshoots can still be found well into the nineteenth century, quite apart from the stable internal tradition of the Roman Church. But natural law as a whole was finished when it came to the standardization of the law by absolutism; it had laid the groundwork for the great codifications, had lived off the rationalism of the Enlightenment, and had eventually inspired the human rights pathos of the revolution. But as the theoretical blueprint of an ideal society, it was swept away by the Napoleonic Wars, Romanticism, and historicism. Immanuel Kant, with his critique of knowledge and his opposition to "eudaemonism," had destroyed the confidence of the seventeenth and mid-eighteenth centuries that one could construct the social world from one vantage point and in this way create the "happiness of all" through direct action.

4. *GUTE POLICEY*

The overview so far of the constitutional law of the empire and the territories (*ius publicum*), of international law (*ius gentium*), and of natural law (*ius naturae*) and its special manifestation in general state theory (*ius publicum universale*) has not yet touched upon administration and its "law."

If we go back once more to the late Middle Ages, one can speak of administration only in a very limited sense, and of administrative law not at all. The centralization of governance in a fixed residence, the development of the apparatus of officials and agencies, of the tax system and financial administration, progressed only gradually and regionally in very different ways. What the princes and their councilors, as well as the doctrine of "politics," had in mind were the guiding principles of *gute Policey*. This meant orderly structures of governance, the food supply and prosperity, provisions to ward off dangers, a partly caring and partly repressive social policy, the building of a school system, and medical care, but also the fight against "immorality" and the cultivation of church life. Watching over all of this was—as an ideal type—the territorial lord (*Landesvater*), just as the good "housefather" was supposed to do in his own house.

The regulation of these spheres of life by the city authorities had already begun in the Middle Ages. The tight spaces in the cities necessitated multifarious commandments and prohibitions, always in the name of *gute Policey* ("good policing"). Defences, the threat of fire, the water supply, cleanliness, health, morality, the prevention of waste, preserving the distances between the "estates," and much more were regulated in urban "codes," repeatedly inculcated, adjusted to new needs, and overseen. The territorial lords did likewise and boosted the multiplicity of regulations and the intensity of their enforcement between the sixteenth and eighteenth centuries, parallel to their monopolization of power. The empire, too, issued an Imperial Police Code in 1530 and updated it step by step.[21] But since there was no executive of the empire, this Imperial Police Code was more of a "blueprint" for the territories, which, in turn, adopted it as territorial codes and added to it.

The literature on the wide field of *Policey*—that is, on the good internal ordering of the polity as a whole—is extraordinarily rich. Since the belief at the time was that good public order began at home, there were, first of all, "marriage booklets," "marriage mirrors," indeed prescriptions for a good "domestic *Policey*." These were followed by the widely disseminated books about the good housefather and the good housemother, which grew from modest beginnings into enormous works on domestic economy. Scaled up, these then gave rise to the handbooks on state economy, which later led to (national) economics.

Since a well-ordered state presupposed a well-educated prince or wise counselors, the old genre of the so-called "mirror of princes" flourished again: this mirror could be held up to the prince to admonish him to pursue a virtuous life. Corresponding "mirrors" existed for city officials, alongside manuals on the virtues and duties of the

[21] Karl Härter, ed., *Deutsches Reich und geistliche Fürstentümer (Kurmainz, Kurköln, Kurtrier)* (Frankfurt, 1996) (vol. 1 of Karl Härter and Michael Stolleis, eds., *Repertorium der Policeyordnungen der frühen Neuzeit*).

good courtier (*bonus aulicus*) or the good envoy, as well as an abundance of works on the ethics of public officials. This material gave rise increasingly to the tractates on rules (*Regimentstraktate*), which not only contained ethical guidelines or pious admonishments, but also became more substantive by dealing with the structure of the administration, the recruitment of good officials, questions of remuneration, and problems of rank and delegation. The high point of this genre was the work *Teutscher Fürstenstaat* (Germany Princely State) from the pen of Veit Ludwig von Seckendorff (1626–92), first published in 1656.[22] It is a compendium of knowledge about statistics, jurisprudence, *Policey*, financial management, politics, and ethics—all from the perspective of the small state of Saxony-Gotha, but laid out in such general terms that it remained authoritative for several generations.

During the seventeenth century, and especially after the Thirty Years War, the administration of the territories was reorganized. Standardized formularies for courts and chanceries were published, along with sample books for lawyers and notaries. Officials no longer recorded the legally important facts on documents of parchment that were kept in "archives," but processed uniformly arranged files on paper, which recorded copies of the decrees of the authorities. Only now was an effective administration with monitored enforcement possible, in that officials requested reports or dispatched visitators.[23]

In this climate of rationalization and normatization, the "police codes" (*Policeyordnungen*)—produced in great numbers via the printing presses—were now also sent out to the *Amtmänner* (bailiffs) and local authorities. Locally they were published orally or in writing and their implementation was monitored. They had various names: *Ordnung, Anweisung, Befehl, Mandat, Reskript, Gesatz,* or *Satzung*. Since official law gazettes did not yet exist, one used the "news-sheets" and other newspapers, bill postings, and public readings, but officials soon found themselves compelled to publish the current material in separate compilations.

In the eighteenth century the normatization of the various branches of the administration continued to grow to the extent that

[22] Michael Stolleis, "Veit Ludwig von Seckendorff," in Stolleis (Note 3), pp. 148–71.
[23] Cornelia Vismann, *Akten: Medientechnik und Recht* (Frankfurt am Main, 2000).

new sub-agencies evolved out of the narrow circles of officials (the "court councilors") originally in charge. Responsibility for the actual activity of governing lay with the Privy Council, for the administration of church affairs with the Spiritual Council or the Consistories, for the administration of justice with the judicial councils, for military matters with the war councils. The economic, finance, and tax administrations oversaw revenues and expenditures (cameral matters); the departments saw to the construction of roads, canals, and fortifications; and *Armenpolicey* (regulations governing the poor) was in charge of the poor; while other regulatory codes governed trade and crafts, forestry, hunting, fishing, and more.

It was not long before the growth of administrative bodies and of the material they oversaw (laws, ordinances, or directives) created two needs: first, the acquisition of ever more specialized knowledge; second, the separation of legal questions from other technical matters. What had once been simple basic knowledge about "good order," pervaded by moral and religious norms, thus gave rise in the eighteenth century to a whole web of individual specialties the content of which a single official could no longer grasp on his own. The universities soon offered special courses on agriculture, forestry, mining, trade, factory-like commercial enterprises (proto-industry), finances, and statistics. It made sense to set up separate chairs for these subjects. The Prussian government, for example, created two chairs for economics, police, and cameral matters in Halle and in Frankfurt an der Oder in 1727. Many other universities soon followed suit, also in Austria. In some cases the new subjects were incorporated into the philosophical faculties; in some cases "cameral schools" were established. Subsequent processes of differentiation gave rise to centers for economics, financial sciences, agriculture, forestry, veterinary medicine, mining, and other disciplines, which were then distributed among the universities and technical colleges in the nineteenth century. With the separation between state and society that was increasingly evident in the eighteenth century, there also arose a differentiation of groupings of subjects: policing, finances, and the state economy remained with the state, while the "private economy" and expertise about non-state life were assigned to the social sciences.[24]

[24] Hans Maier, *Gesammelte Schriften*, vol. 4 (Munich, 2009), especially 222 ff.

Questions about the law that appeared in both spheres formed a cross-sectional subject matter that had to be clearly set apart. The clearer it became that the indicated regimes, mandates, and orders belonged to the category "law," the more sense it seemed to make that jurists were also called upon to come to terms with the new developments. The previously taught subjects (common law, feudal law, criminal law, imperial constitutional law, natural law, international law) were no longer adequate. At best, some of the new material could find a home in the discussion on "territorial sovereignty in police matters." It was therefore something new when the Würzburg professor Johann Adam Ickstatt began to lecture on *ius civile oeconomico-camerale*, or when other experts on public law began to integrate *Policey* into their systems.[25] Johann Heumann von Teutschenbrunn was probably the first to present a separate "police law" (law of internal administration) in 1757.[26] Others followed, resulting in the gradual emergence of the subject matter of "police law" (*Policeyrecht*), which was then called *Administrativrecht* ("administrative law") around 1800, and *Verwaltungsrecht* ("administrative law") from the 1830s on. It made sense to structure this diverse material according to subject areas, with those areas once again following the competencies of the various ministries that were now taking shape in the transition to the constitutional state of the nineteenth century. In accordance with the departmental principle, contemporaries initially distinguished the ministries of the exterior, interior, justice, finances, and education and the arts. But the bulk of the emerging administrative law rested within the sphere of authority of the ministries of the interior.

The great account of police law around the year 1800 came from the pen of Günter Heinrich von Berg (1765–1843),[27] who also—and this was typical of his time—engaged in the first reflections on the limits imposed on administrative activity by the rule of law. A generation later, these reflections were then carried out systematically by Robert von Mohl.[28]

[25] Peter Preu, *Polizeibegriff und Staatszwecklehre* (Göttingen, 1983), pp. 123 ff.

[26] Johann Christian Pauly, *Die Entstehung des Polizeirechts als wissenschaftliche Disziplin* (Frankfurt am Main, 2000).

[27] Günter Heinrich von Berg, *Handbuch des Teutschen Policeyrechts* (Hannover, 1799 (parts 1 and 2), 1800 (part 3), 1803 (additions), 1804 (part 4), 1806 (parts 5 and 6.1), 1809 (parts 6.2 and 7).

[28] Robert von Mohl, *Polizei-Wissenschaft nach den Grundsätzen des Rechtsstaates*, 2 vols. (Tübingen, 1832–3), 2nd edn., expanded with the addition of "System der

5. SUMMARY

The emergence of public law as a distinct pattern of thought and argumentation within the framework of the legal sciences in early modern Europe is a process through which a new reality constituted itself thanks to new labels. Because the Holy Roman Empire and its constituent parts (emperor, Imperial Diet, Imperial Aulic Council, Imperial Chamber Court, imperial districts), along with the territorial states and their jurisdictions and administrations, were assigned to the normative complex of *ius publicum*/"public law," they all transitioned into a new aggregate state and were seen and conceptualized in a new way. The teaching that began at the university around the year 1600 and the wealth of publications on *ius publicum* were an expression of the political situation that had arisen after 1555, but they also shaped the consciousness of the new generation of jurists.

The learned councilors, judges, princely tutors, diplomats, textbook authors, and legal experts who were professionally involved with public law formed the backbone of the administrative branches that emerged under absolutism. They administered the "good police" internally, passed "police ordinances," developed the legal maxims for foreign relations in international law, and worked on codifying entire fields with the help of the creation of a system of natural law and on the basis of common law—in other words, they were seeking to "juridify" the entire polity.

Four primary tendencies became apparent in their labors: (1) the liberation of political action from religious constraints; (2) the transformation of the medieval feudal state (personal union) into the modern, centralized institutional state; (3) the collapse of the occidental idea of the unity of the empire and the church and the advance of competing, dynastic, and (increasingly) national individual states; (4) and, finally, the ossification and dwindling cohesive force of the imperial constitution after the Peace of Westphalia in 1648, which prepared the way for the duality of Prussia and Austria in the eighteenth and nineteenth centuries.

Each of these four tendencies led to the cultivation of public law on the imperial or territorial level. On the imperial level there arose the imposing edifice of the *ius publicum Imperii Romano-Germanicum*,

Präventiv-Justiz oder Rechts-Polizei" (Tübingen, 1844–5); 3rd, extensively revised, edn. (Tübingen, 1866).

which culminated in the eighteenth century in the imposing work of Johann Jacob Moser and of Johann Stephan Pütter at the University of Göttingen, the dominant institution in this area.[29]

The university landscape likewise produced a wealth of works on natural law: for example, by Samuel Pufendorf, Christian Thomasius, and Christian Wolff, but also the sub-field of *ius publicum universale* according to the Dutch model. The law of nations, in the seventeenth century fully under the influence of Hugo Grotius, gained less importance overall, because the empire neither participated in colonial expansion, nor—for structural reasons—was able to pursue a forceful foreign policy. Internally, however, the territories, which were nearly sovereign after 1648, participated in the "state-building process of the modern age." The property-like control of the dynasties over "land and people" developed gradually into the institutional state, which assumed its own legal personality initially as an exchequer,[30] but then as an entity overall. This state reduced the medieval legal diversity and turned increasingly into a commanding lawgiving state. The abundance of early modern "police codes" that emerged and the differentiation of the subjects of state science at the university led in the second half of the eighteenth century to the separate cultivation of the legal side of "policing"; that is, to a "police law." As a counterpart to "constitutional" law, it was called *Administrativrecht* around the year 1800, and was soon after germanicized into *Verwaltungsrecht*.

[29] Adolf Laufs, "Johann Jacob Moser," in Stolleis (Note 3), pp. 284–93 (1995); Wilhelm Ebel, *Der Göttinger Professor Johann Stephan Pütter aus Iserlohn* (Göttingen, 1975); Christoph Link, "Johann Stephan Pütter," in Stolleis (Note 3), pp. 310–31 (1995).

[30] As soon as the exchequer acted as a legally independent manifestation of the state, subjects could sue it in court without treading too close to the state as a whole or to the ruler (theory of the Fiskus).

5

Public Law between Revolution and Restoration

1. THE TRANSFORMATION OF THE POLITICAL WORLD

The twenty-five years between the outbreak of the French Revolution and the Congress of Vienna was a period of unparalleled drama. The overthrow of social and constitutional orders was followed by a series of European wars. With the last imperial law, the Final Imperial Recess (*Reichsdeputationshauptschluss*) of 1803, Germany witnessed a great territorial consolidation that saw the disappearance of 112 imperial estates. Shortly thereafter came the secession of the Confederation of the Rhine and the abdication of the emperor; even though these moves were made unilaterally and without the imperial estates, they meant the end of the Old Empire. The imperial officials, including the judges at the Imperial Chamber Court in Wetzlar, lost their positions. In 1806, Napoleon inflicted a humiliating defeat also on Prussia, thus forcing it indirectly onto a path of fundamental reforms. Comparable reforms had already begun in Bavaria with the change of government in 1799, in Württemberg and Baden with the acquisition of new territories after 1803. The period closed with the establishment of a somewhat stable order of peace and the beginning of the "era of Metternich" at the Congress of Vienna in 1814–15.[1] All of these events touched directly on public law and its scholarly treatment. The "constitutional law" of the Old

[1] A detailed account in Ernst Rudolf Huber, *Deutsche Verfassungsgeschichte seit 1789*, vol. 1 (Stuttgart, 1957); Dietmar Willoweit, *Deutsche Verfassungsgeschichte*, 7th edn. (Munich, 2013).

Empire had vanished, and new medium-size states had emerged and were making great efforts to integrate the new territories. Their monarchs enjoyed new royal or grand-ducal honors. The House of Habsburg did not lag behind, and, like Napoleon earlier, it claimed the imperial crown.

For the universities this period initially led to severe contraction around 1800. About half of the approximately forty universities in the empire closed their doors, in part because they were ecclesiastical institutions or small universities with professorial dynasties and incapable of reform, in part because it made economic sense to shut them down. The legal faculty in Basel, for example, had only six students and two professors around 1817. Other universities flourished, however—among them the University of Munich (which had been moved from Landshut), the newly established University of Berlin, and liberal Heidelberg University.

2. GERMAN CONFEDERATION (*DEUTSCHER BUND*)

The experts on public law at these universities thus had to thoroughly reorient themselves. "The book collections of the *Reichspublicist*," wrote Robert von Mohl looking back, "became mostly useless in 1803 and 1806, his learnedness a skill with no prospects."[2] That is true, as long as one is talking about positive public law, but it does not apply to methodology. As soon as the Treaty of the Confederation of the Rhine had been published in 1806, professors came forward to systematize this new and unfinished entity in the same way Pütter in Göttingen had done with the imperial constitution. And so a public-law "literature on the Confederation of the Rhine" emerged within a few years, along with a journal, *Der Rheinische Bund* (The Confederation of the Rhine) (1806–13).[3] What preoccupied the authors were the questions

[2] Robert von Mohl, *Die Geschichte und Literatur der Staatswissenschaften*, 3 vols. (Erlangen, 1855–8), vol. 2, p. 239.

[3] Gerhard Schuck, *Rheinbundpatriotismus und Politische Öffentlichkeit zwischen Aufklärung und Frühliberalismus* (Stuttgart, 1994); Naoko Matsumoto, *Polizeibegriff im Umbruch: Staatszwecklehre und Gewaltenteilungspraxis in der Reichs- und Rheinbundpublizistik* (Frankfurt am Main, 1999).

of how much sovereignty the "protector" Napoleon would leave to the members of the Confederation, what the internal organization should look like, and whether the confederation was to be a federation of states or a federal state. But all of this became moot soon enough, and beginning in 1815 the authors could turn their attention to interpreting the constitution of the German Confederation (*Deutscher Bund*).

This construct of state law overarching the German states and four free cities (Lübeck, Frankfurt, Bremen, Hamburg) was created on June 8, 1815. Members included not only the rivals Prussia and Austria, but also Denmark (on account of Holstein) and the Netherlands (on account of Luxembourg). The German Confederation with its thirty-eight "sovereign" members was hardly capable of acting politically. Austria, under its Chancellor Metternich, established itself as the leading power, and henceforth, flanked by Prussia, it also determined the politics of the individual states, especially in regard to the suppression of national and liberal aspirations with the Carlsbad Decrees of 1819.[4]

The professors of public law who taught at the universities and published between 1815 and 1848 had to fulfill several tasks side by side. They were, to begin with, obligated to present the "public law of the German Confederation"; that is, the constitutional law that was valid and applicable to the states of the confederation. But since this could not be exhausted in commentary on the Act of Confederation of 1815 and the detailed and complementary Final Act of Vienna in 1820, they simultaneously undertook a second and more important task by providing information also about the constitutional law of the individual states. The lectures and resultant books thus for the most part bore the title "The Law of the German Confederation and of the States of the Confederation." As such they offered a broad overview of the German constitutional situation. Among the constitutions of the confederation states, one usually finds an average picture of the "general state law" of the constitutional monarchies. This was therefore not a "general theory of the state" constructed from

[4] Confederation decrees concerning the universities, the press, and the creation of a central authority to examine "the revolutionary machinations uncovered in several states of the Confederation" were all dated September 20, 1819. Texts in Ernst Rudolf Huber, ed., *Dokumente zur Deutschen Verfassungsgeschichte*, vol. 1 (Stuttgart, 1961), Nos. 31–3. English translation in Louis L. Snyder, *Fifty Major Documents of the Nineteenth Century* (Princeton, 1955).

propositions of natural law, but a cross-summation of the positive constitutional law that was valid in most states. It also contained an indirect warning to those states whose constitutional state of affairs lagged behind the average. Where relatively progressive conditions prevailed, for example, in the three southern German constitutional states of Bavaria, Baden, and Württemberg, the third task was commentary on the constitutions of one's own territory. But since this occasionally carried the risk of clashing with the territorial government, accounts of the territorial constitutional law of larger individual states came only incrementally. It was not until the second half of the nineteenth century that all states of the German Empire were covered in terms of state law in a series of monographs.

The leading survey in the first half of the nineteenth century came from the pen of Johann Ludwig Klüber (1762–1837). He had already written a "State Law of the Confederation of the Rhine" in 1808, followed by a sourcebook on the Congress of Vienna, which made him the most knowledgeable expert on the creation of the German Confederation. This provided the basis for his 1817 *Oeffentliches Recht des Teutschen Bundes und der Bundesstaaten* (Public Law of the German Confederation and the Confederation States),[5] a positivistic but in its basic tenor liberal account of the constitutional law of the constitutional monarchies down to 1830.

After Klüber's death, the field was dominated by corresponding accounts by Heinrich Zöpfl (1807–77) and Heinrich Albert Zachariä (1806–75). All three books combined the law of the German Confederation with the aggregate of the state law of the individual states. Along the way, as time passed, the grounding in the *ancien régime* still palpable in Klüber receded and was replaced by an increasingly positivistic perspective. But there was certainly no rigid restriction to "purely legal" points of view. The authors argued historically, invoking prevailing law but also organizing principles and "essential concepts." Politically they were neither revolutionary republican democrats nor zealous defenders of the principle of monarchy. Instead, they sought to "organically" combine the traditional monarchies with the new parliamentary, representative bodies

[5] 4th, posthumous edn. (Frankfurt am Main, 1840), overseen by Karl Eduard Morstadt.

of the people. The state was to be "constitutionally" ordered; that is, it should have a constitution that sought a balance between the right of the people and the right of the monarch. On the one hand, it should proclaim basic rights, and, on the other hand, guarantee central rights for the monarch: inviolability, control over the bureaucracy and the military, and in Protestant states continued authority over the churches, which was nominally exercised by the territorial lord. In the bicameral system, there existed alongside the parliaments (assembly of estates, chamber of deputies or popular chamber, second chambers) also a first chamber that was appointed by the monarch and was supposed to form a conservative counterweight to the second chambers.[6] In some places "state councils" were set up following the Napoleonic model, another instrument of the monarch to deliberate legislation and, if need be, restrain the legislating of the second chamber.[7]

3. GERMAN CONSTITUTIONAL LAW (*ALLGEMEINES STAATSRECHT*)

The theory of state law in the *Vormärz* period—broadly understood as extending from the Congress of Vienna to the Revolution of 1848—was thus moving on unsteady ground. The constitutional law of the German Confederation attracted relatively little attention, and as the legal expression of Metternich's politics it was also perceived as oppressive. The "general" German constitutional law of the individual states was a construct that was supposed to be a kind of bracket for the non-existing national state. It shows the constitutional monarchy as an unstable compromise between princely sovereignty and popular sovereignty. The way out of this inherent dilemma was, then, an idea that had been discussed for some time: to make neither the prince nor the people but the "state" the locus of sovereignty and declare the

[6] Michael Stolleis, "Zweikammersystem," *HRG*, vol. 5 (Berlin, 1998), pp. 1833–5; Joachim v. Wedel, *Zur Entwicklung des deutschen parlamentarischen Zweikammersystems* (Berlin, 2011).

[7] See, for example, Hans Schneider, *Der Preussische Staatsrat 1817–1918* (Munich and Berlin, 1952); overview in Patricia Conring, "Staatsrat," in *HRG*, vol. 4 (Berlin, 1990), pp. 1832–6.

prince and the parliament its "organs." The abstraction of the "state" now became a legal person.[8]

Normatively this state was held together by the constitution, which rested almost entirely on sovereign concession rather than the popular will articulated in revolutionary fashion. The popular assemblies were still a long away from a franchise that was egalitarian and also included women. Men were subject to a census suffrage that favored the propertied and educated bourgeoisie. Rural and industrial workers who had no taxable possessions remained excluded. Census suffrage was dismantled in the separate states only when the egalitarian male franchise was established in the North German Confederation in 1867 and in the empire in 1871. Prussia retained the increasingly anachronistic three-class franchise until 1917.

If the monarch—in keeping with the "monarchic principle" championed by the conservative camp—thus stood in the traditional manner theoretically and practically at the head of the state, and if parliaments were granted merely a right of "participation" in lawmaking and in the preservation of the declared basic rights, then all the more importance was attached to inherent counterweights. In contrast to absolutism, the ultimately all-commanding and untouchable monarch who kept the machinery of the state running no longer existed. Instead, the monarch now functioned as the "organ" of the legal person of the state. He should no longer govern directly, but represent the state as a whole. The government was led by a prime minister appointed by the monarch and sustained by his confidence; the prime minister in turn selected the ministers in charge of their "departments." Politically this took some of the burden off the shoulders of the monarch, but it also made any minister open to parliamentary attack if he had signed off on a sovereign act issued in the name of the monarch (countersignature).[9] This led to a slow growth in the powers of the parliaments. Once they had established themselves, these parliaments no longer thought of themselves as "territorial estates" in the sense of the *ancien régime*, but as legitimized, representative organs of the entire people charged with protecting its (basic) rights. At first the parliaments were thus granted only monitoring rights in the legislative process, then

[8] Henning Uhlenbrock, *Der Staat als juristische Person: Dogmengeschichtliche Untersuchung zu einem Grundbegriff der deutschen Staatsrechtslehre* (Berlin, 2000).

[9] The classic work is by Robert von Mohl, *Die Verantwortlichkeit der Minister in Einherrschaften mit Volksvertretung* (Tübingen, 1837).

participatory rights, and eventually rights of initiative. Central in this process—as the constitutional conflict in Prussia in 1862 would show—was the struggle over the budgetary powers; that is, control over the approval of taxes and state spending.

Given the myriad restrictions on political participation by the people via the parliaments, the interest of liberal jurists shifted to the possibility of restraining the power of the state through the judiciary. Within the European framework, this was a crucial aspect of developments in Germany. Where the theory and practice of absolutism had still seen the judge strictly as a servant of the state tied to the will of the monarch, the doctrine of the "division of powers" now created the first separations. The demands for the *Rechtsstaat* (a state under the rule of law) that were raised beginning around the year 1800 included the (personal and functional) independence of the judiciary.[10] Judges, guided by this model through their training, now occasionally ventured—by invoking the new constitutions—to declare actions by the government "unconstitutional." The governments responded with disciplinary measures,[11] but in the end they were unable to halt the progressive emancipation of the judiciary. The final question that arose was whether it was possible for the individual citizen to seek recourse in the courts against administrative measures. While the conservatives advocated merely internal administrative oversight, the liberals—especially in the National Assembly of 1848–9—championed the authority of the regular judicial apparatus. The final result was a compromise which, beginning in 1863, opened the way for the administrative jurisdiction of today.[12]

4. CONSTITUTIONAL LAW OF THE TERRITORIAL STATES AND ADMINISTRATIVE LAW

Depending on their constitutional situation, the need for accounts of the state law of the territorial state under the new

[10] Dieter Simon, *Die Unabhängigkeit des Richters* (Darmstadt, 1975).

[11] Thomas Ormond, *Richterwürde und Regierungstreue: Dienstrecht, politische Betätigung und Disziplinierung der Richter in Preußen, Baden und Hessen 1866–1918* (Frankfurt am Main, 1994).

[12] Michael Stolleis, "Hundertfünfzig Jahre Verwaltungsgerichtsbarkeit," *Deutsches Verwaltungsblatt* (2013), 1274–80.

constitutional conditions varied in the individual states of the German Confederation. Some territories were too small to justify such an account; some had no constitution, in which case only a collection of laws was conceivable. That is why the southern German constitutional states were clearly in the lead when it came to their own public law. In Württemberg the work of Robert von Mohl was pre-eminent from 1829;[13] Bavaria had no fewer than five textbooks on state law (Schmelzing, Schunck, Cucumus, Moy, Pözl); Baden, meanwhile, lacked a textbook, but here the great State Lexicon by Rotteck and Welcker and several journals worked to consolidate public law.

Compared to these states, one can hardly speak of a cultivation of public law in Electoral Hesse, Hesse-Darmstadt, Nassau, Hanover, Brunswick, and Mecklenburg prior to 1848. In Saxony, too, state law slowly got under way only after the Constitution of 1831. Schleswig-Holstein could not settle down for political reasons; in the free cities of Bremen, Hamburg, Lübeck, and Frankfurt am Main the space was too constricted; in Mecklenburg the two grand duchies persisted in pre-constitutional conditions.

That left as large states only Prussia and Austria, and although neither one was a constitutional state, both had strong, centralized administrative apparatuses. The pertinent works skirted constitutional questions. Any kind of significant or independent literature on Prussian or Austrian state law therefore did not arise before 1848. The situation was particularly difficult in Austria, a multi-ethnic state threatened by nationalisms. As long as the "Metternich system" was in place, which sought to suppress liberal and nationalistic aspirations, free academic debate was not possible. Instead of state law one read "statistics" (*Staatenkunde*), instead of "general theory of state law" there was "legal studies" (*Gesetzeskunde*). Perhaps the intensive flourishing of legal theory and public law that could be seen there in the last quarter of the nineteenth century and the first third of the twentieth was due to the fact that the relevant intellectual energies had been bottled up for decades.

The scholarly attention to state and administrative law in the period between the Congress of Vienna and revolutionary year 1848 thus depended in large measure on the constitutional situation. Those

[13] Robert von Mohl, *Staatsrecht des Königreichs Württemberg*, 2 vols. (Tübingen, 1829), 2nd edn. (Tübingen, 1840).

states in the German Confederation who had established themselves first as constitutional states (Bavaria, Baden, Württemberg, somewhat Hesse-Darmstadt, and Nassau) were also the earliest to organize their administrative law. The constitutions that emerged in the wake of the French July Revolution of 1830 (Electoral Hesse, Hanover, Saxony) could, in principle, have likewise exerted an invigorating effect, but the external conditions were too unfavorable: Electoral Hesse was entangled in internal conflicts, as was Hanover in 1837, and Saxony, which did not find its way to a genuine liberalization, could not go beyond some initial beginnings. And so when it comes to administrative law before 1848, the pre-eminent work was that by Robert von Mohl: *Die Polizei-Wissenschaft nach den Grundsätzen des Rechtsstaats* (Police Science on the Principles of the *Rechtsstaat*) (Tübingen, 1832–3). This was the first time that the word *Rechtsstaat* appeared in the title of a book. The wealth of "policing" subject matter, which also encompassed the goals of public welfare, was to be cast into legal form. Mohl assigned all matters of domestic politics to constitutional purposes, although he demanded a legal basis only for interferences in the liberty and property of citizens; he came out against retroactive impositions and demanded, as was long since customary, compensation for expropriations.

Apart from that, the administration was permitted to act at its discretion, though not arbitrarily. For Mohl, *Polizei-Wissenschaft* was part of the comprehensive sciences of the state. He was still a long way from a reduction to formal "law" or to a "General Part" of administrative law. What he had in mind was the well-ordered liberal constitutional state, one that was receptive to the social problems that were now emerging. In this regard he urged greater exertions by the state. It is therefore no coincidence that Tübingen was given the first regular chair for administrative law in 1842 and was the founding location for the *Zeitschrift für die gesamte Staatswissenschaft* (Journal for State Science).

6

St. Paul's Church (*Paulskirche*)

> In all German assemblies of the estates one finds a very strong influence of legal scholars. But the number of the same, and the legal spirit that prevails in the deliberations, are not coincidental. The entire political education of the German nation emanated from the training of the legal sciences ... That is why the universities have an importance in the history of German civilization that is far greater than in any other nation ...

So wrote the Hanover politician Rehberg (1757–1836).[1] It is in fact true that before 1848, all professors of public law were more or less also "political professors." They appeared as speakers at "constitutional celebrations," were carefully watched in lecture halls, wrote expert opinions on constitutional questions, were candidates for parliaments, or were sent by their universities as representatives to the first chambers. A number of them also lost their positions because of excessively liberal statements. Freedom of the press, of academic research, and of association was the subject of constant agitation. The punishment meted out to the seven Göttingen professors in 1837 for protesting the suspension of the constitution by the new ruler resonated in among public for a long time. Moreover, the nineteen German and four Austrian universities were in any case political trouble spots during the years of the "Metternich system," with *Burschenschaften* and *Landsmannschaften* (forms of student fraternity) playing a large role. Everywhere people were discussing human and civil rights, suffrage, the separation of powers, the openness of legal proceedings, or administrative supervision.

[1] August W. Rehberg, *Die Erwartungen der Teutschen von dem Bunde ihrer Fürsten* (Jena, 1835), pp. 43–63.

And thus a number of renowned jurists also became part of the Pre-Parliament and the National Assembly in St. Paul's Church in Frankfurt am Main, which opened on May 18, 1848: among them the constitutional jurists Wilhelm Eduard Albrecht, Konrad Cucumus, Sylvester Jordan, Heinrich Albert Zachariä, Robert von Mohl, and Karl Theodor Welcker. Especially in the early phase, they were very actively involved in the central questions: the form of the state, a unicameral or bicameral system, hereditary or elective monarchy or republic, suffrage, the rules of parliamentary procedure, basic rights. All this was reflected in the ultimately failed imperial constitution of March 28, 1849. Its Section VI, "The Basic Rights of the German People," remained influential for the Weimar Constitution of 1919 and the Basic Law of 1949.[2]

The failure of the efforts by the National Assembly, the return of conservative forces, military suppression, and the trials of the revolutionaries led to a depressed mood among the bourgeoisie and to a shift toward the industrial revolution that was now picking up steam. The focus was on the elimination of trade barriers, on a common law governing bills of exchange and commerce, and on the perfection of the *Rechtsstaat*. The new slogan was *Realpolitik*.[3] Under its banner it became more apparent that alongside the civic revolution of 1848 there had also been a social revolution, carried by journeymen and the growing workers' movement. The latter organized itself into unions and merged into social democracy on the level of the parties.

For the theory of state and administrative law, the post-1848 landscape meant having to regroup. On the level of Germany as a whole, one could observe the attempts to create a union between the Austrian monarchy and the German federal state (the Constitution of the Erfurt Union), the conflict in Electoral Hesse between the land and its authoritarian monarchic head, the hotly contested question between Denmark and Germany over the affiliation of Schleswig and Holstein, and the restoration of the German Confederation on May 10, 1850. In the individual states the issue revolved around the revocation of the concessions made in 1848, and in Prussia around the content of

[2] Jörg-Detlef Kühne, *Die Reichsverfassung der Paulskirche: Vorbild und Verwirklichung im späteren deutschen Rechtsleben* (Frankfurt am Main, 1985), 2nd edn. (Frankfurt am Main 1998).

[3] August Ludwig v. Rochau, *Grundsätze der Realpolitik: Angewendet auf die staatlichen Zustände Deutschlands*, 1. Teil (Stuttgart, 1853), 2. Teil (Stuttgart, 1869).

the first constitution, which came about in 1851. All in all, this was a shaky period of transition, in which a turn toward *Realpolitik* took place also methodologically. The place of political commitment was taken by the ideal of legal scientificity.[4] The hope was that in this way one could also achieve in public law the systematization and conceptual clarity of civil law. The law of the state and the slowly emerging administrative law were to be freed from non-legal (historical, political, and moral) elements and presented in a "purely juristic" manner. This promised to create distance from day-to-day politics and a boost in standing—not only within jurisprudence, but also in competition with the triumphal march of the natural sciences. Whoever dealt with the dogmatics of the prevailing law within the methodical prohibitions could feel secure in terms of politics and of one's scientific approach. The depoliticization of legal science found its form in the demand for "autonomy."[5] It fortified the law against revolutionary interferences from below and against autocratic interferences from above; it was implicitly a position of the bourgeois middle, but at the same time also a claim to a position by legal science itself.

On the whole, state law of the period after 1850 moved within the main current of European, multifaceted "positivism"; that is, within the endeavor to dispense with all speculative and ideological premises and work with the material that was thus rendered positive. Applied to jurisprudence, this could mean the orientation toward the law or at least positive law, but also a legal science freed from non-positive preconditions. In public law the issues revolved concretely around the interpretation of the new, sometimes fluctuating, constitutional conditions, the resumption of the "common German state law," which was now once again seen as the intellectual clamp for a national state which had still not been achieved—as unconvincing as this may have been. The textbooks about territorial state law (*Landesstaatsrecht*) stagnated. Robert von Mohl noted in 1867 that "for many years no work about territorial state law has appeared in

[4] The terminological transition from "jurisprudence" (*iuris prudentia*) or legal learnedness to "legal science" (*Rechtswissenschaft*) took place around the year 1800 under the influence of Kant's philosophy and the now rising natural sciences. See Benjamin Lahusen, *Alles Recht geht vom Volksgeist aus: Friedrich Carl von Savigny und die moderne Rechtswissenschaft* (Berlin, 2013), pp. 85 ff.

[5] Joachim Rückert, *Autonomie des Rechts in rechtshistorischer Perspektive* (Hannover, 1988), pp. 56 ff.

Germany."[6] Disappointment about the failed Revolution of 1848 and uncertainty about the progress of national unification had a paralyzing effect. The momentum of natural law and of the idealistic philosophy had evaporated. Between 1850 and 1860, public law was either in the doldrums or incubating for a new era.

[6] Robert von Mohl, "Bemerkungen über die neuesten Bearbeitungen des allgemeinen deutschen Staatsrechts," *Aegidis Zeitschrift* 1 (1867), 354–84, 365.

7

Imperial State Law

1. *RECHTSSTAAT* AND LEGAL METHODOLOGY

What announced this new era was the publication, within a very short time, of a whole host of works that showed, in retrospect, how the lines of development sketched above condensed—eventually producing what is usually called a paradigm shift. It began with the treatise by the private-law expert Carl Friedrich von Gerber, *Über öffentliche Rechte* (On Public Rights) (1852), followed by the programmatic essay of his friend and companion Rudolf von Jhering, *Unsere Aufgabe* (Our Task) (1857). At the same time, a nearly unknown Württemberg practitioner, Friedrich Franz (von) Mayer, penned the first attempt to formulate a General Part in administrative law (1857–62). In 1864, the Hessian judge Otto Bähr published the important book *Der Rechtsstaat: Eine publicistische Skizze* (The *Rechtsstaat*: A Sketch on Public Law). Hermann Schulze's *Einleitung in das deutsche Staatsrecht* (Introduction to German State Law) appeared in 1865; while 1867 saw the publication of the first and only issue of the *Zeitschrift für Deutsches Staatsrecht und Deutsche Verfassungsgeschichte* (Journal for German State Law and German Constitutional History) with important articles.

At the same time, important political events came in rapid succession: Bismarck survived the Prussian constitutional conflict and ended the Prussian–Austrian dualism successfully, but also moderately; he extended Prussia all the way to the Main, created the North German Confederation, and for the first time offered a real chance to establish a smaller German state. The situation was tense, because the foundations of state law were again in flux. Jhering sneered in 1866 that it was an art to know anything about state law now:

> law of the federal state, the state law of Hanover, Electoral Hesse, and of Nassau—it has been lost overnight. Only the booklets of the professors are remaining. They lie idly in the desk drawer and grumble at the evil Bismarck; perhaps they are also dreaming of a happy resurrection, where the world that has slipped from their hands returns penitently to their booklet, and the dispossessed sovereigns return again to their "realms" and to their "peoples."[1]

From the supposedly secure throne of the ever unchanging private law—which Jhering himself, however, had already left after 1859—it might have appeared that way. But public law was always political law and endangered in its substance. Hermann Schulze, at any rate, wrote this: "The year 1866 was as profoundly important for the practice and theory of German state law as was the year 1806."[2] The German Confederation had disappeared, and with it the previous accounts (of H. Zöpfl, H. A. Zachariä) had become obsolete. The state law of the states annexed by Prussia had likewise been abolished. All publications that appeared during this state of limbo sought stability from the outside, either in history or precisely in the expulsion of history from the formation of theory, which was to be untroubled by historical diversity.

After 1848, all of nineteenth-century German legal science went the path of an ever-stronger emphasis on the "real," on what was "positively given"—relying either on the stability of the ordinary law or on a theoretically more demanding philosophical, scientific positivism, which regarded the essence of a concept concealed in the material as more reliable. The Pandectists who dealt with "common law" gradually disconnected themselves from the postulates of the historical school and cultivated primarily the logical coherence of the leading doctrinal personalities (Puchta, Vangerow, Brinz, Bekker, Regelsberger, Arndts, Dernburg, Windscheid). Experts on criminal law were aiming at a pan-German, precise statute law, and they called for "clear, distinct concepts and a self-contained system."[3] The experts on public law moved along

[1] Rudolf von Jhering, *Vertrauliche Briefe über die heutige Jurisprudenz*, 6. Brief, in *Deutsche Gerichtszeitung* 5 (1863), pp. 141–7.

[2] Hermann Schulze, *Die Krisis des Deutschen Staatsrechts im Jahre 1866: Nachtrag zur Einleitung in das Deutsche Staatsrecht* (Leipzig, 1867), Preface, unpaginated.

[3] Franz von Liszt, *Lehrbuch des Strafrechts* (Berlin and Leipzig, 1881), Preface, unpaginated. For the opposite view, see Daniela Westphalen, *Karl Binding (1841–1920): Materialien zur Biographie eines Strafrechtsgelehrten* (Frankfurt am Main, 1989).

in this current and now also began with an "analysis and construction of the purely juristic element."[4] The protagonist was Carl Friedrich von Gerber (1823–91), who presented an entirely new system derived from the power of the state as a "power of the will."[5]

He set aside historical and philosophical reflections about the state, as he did administrative law. What remained was "the naked and fixed juristic skeleton":[6] the state power exclusively in charge, the state organs, the state functions, legal protection. Even though this outline rested on conservative monarchist convictions, it also determined the shape of other currents. Henceforth, the informational but methodologically unclear or merely additive account of the political sciences lost ground, and those involved tried to construct their systems in a "purely juristic" manner.

The new material for such constructions was quickly at hand again. The founding of the empire and its new constitution were greeted with enthusiasm. Experts on constitutional law offered a wealth of opinions, whether in commented descriptions or in newspaper articles. The most important work, and one that initially displaced all others, came from the pen of a then little-known legal historian and expert on commercial law, Paul Laband (1838–1918), who had been given a chair in Königsberg in 1864.

After he had for the first time drawn a clear distinction between the law in the formal and the material sense in a treatise on budget law, he switched to state law. From his post in Strasbourg after 1872, he wrote a monumental *Staatsrecht des Deutschen Reiches* (State Law of the German Empire), which was published beginning in 1876.[7] It dominated the field. Laband proceeded on the basis of positive constitutional law, but he also believed that the formation of "concepts"

[4] Dietrich Tripp, *Der Einfluß des naturwissenschaftlichen, philosophischen und historischen Positivismus auf die deutsche Rechtslehre im 19. Jahrhundert* (Berlin, 1983), pp. 151 ff.

[5] Carl Friedrich von Gerber, *Grundzüge eines Systems des deutschen Staatsrechts* (Leipzig, 1865), 2nd edn. (Leipzig, 1869), 3rd edn. (Leipzig, 1880).

[6] Ernst Landsberg, *Geschichte der deutschen Rechtswissenschaft*, Abteilung III/2 (Munich and Leipzig, 1910), p. 830. On this see Carsten Kremer, *Die Willensmacht des Staates: Die gemeindeutsche Staatsrechtslehre des Carl Friedrich von Gerber* (Frankfurt am Main, 2008).

[7] Paul Laband, *Staatsrecht des Deutschen Reiches*, vol. 1 (Tübingen, 1876), vol. 2 (Tübingen, 1878), vol. 3/1 (Tübingen, 1880), vol. 3/2 (Tübingen, 1882), 2nd edn. (Tübingen, 1888), 3rd edn. (Tübingen, 1895), 4th edn. (Tübingen, 1901), 5th edn. (Tübingen, 1911–). Paul Laband, *Deutsches Reichsstaatsrecht* (Tübingen, 1894), 6th edn. (Tübingen 1912; the so-called "Little Laband").

and "legal institutes" was possible, also the filling of gaps by analogies or inversions of an argument, if they could be integrated into the system without any logical contradictions. Like Gerber, Laband based his construct on the legal unit of the will of the state power and its organs. He filled in the basic framework with the rapidly created imperial law in the areas of citizenship, currency, the court system, the military, and finances. All in all, this created a clearly structured new edifice and possessed internal consistency. With that, the "juristic method" had been established in state law.

To be sure, prior to World War I there were some who found fault with this kind of positivism. One critic was Otto von Gierke (1841–1921), the last important proponent of the historical school. He opposed both the conceptual jurisprudence with its ahistorical procedures, and the reduction of the citizen to a "subject" subordinated to the institutional state. Others also rebuked Laband's distaste for "basic rights" and found fault with the distance between his conceptual world and political life. Still others disapproved of the analogy of his conceptualizations to civil law, or of the political orientation that did in fact exist under the surface. All of this notwithstanding, this imperial state law remained authoritative until 1918. And its methodological influence extended well into the Weimar era, for that period also saw experts in state law who claimed that they were deriving their conclusions from concepts in an entirely apolitical and "strictly juristic" manner.

Up to the outbreak of World War I, most of the field of state theory adhered to the notion of a constitutional monarchy, with the king and chancellor in a dominant position. Neither a parliamentary democracy with a government sustained by the majority, nor a republic, was wanted. The "political professor" of the *Vormärz* period, who desired a different state, was no longer the decisive figure. On the whole, contentment reigned, and this meant for jurists that while they might criticize statutory law politically, they did not question its legal validity, provided that its enactment had been formally correct.

Very different points were emphasized by Laband's contemporaries: for example, Georg Meyer (1841–1900) in Heidelberg; Philipp Zorn (1850–1928), an expert on state and international law; Hermann Schulze von Gaevernitz (1824–88), an expert in state law; Heinrich Rosin (1855–1927), the pioneer of social insurance law; Albert Hänel (1833–1918), a liberal professor and politician; and Heinrich Triepel (1868–1946) in Tübingen and Kiel, a young expert on state and international law. Their works displayed a broad palette in terms of both methodology and content. International law attracted more attention again after 1871, as did colonial law and the new workers' insurance law emerging since 1881, while the special private law of the princely houses tended to point backward. Heinrich Triepel alone provided three fundamental monographs on state law and international law.[8] They all noted the strong shifts within the imperial constitution, in part through amending law, in part through "silent constitutional change";[9] however, in the final analysis they all remained within its framework. The debate in the first years following the creation of the empire—whether one was dealing with a league of princes, a league of states (as Max von Seydel, an expert in state law from Munich, believed), or a federal state—was resolved in the course of time in favor of the federal state. The opposition to the theorem of the state as a legal person—initially still criticized as "soulless" or an unrealistic fiction—also died down. This state was a constitutional monarchy, but not a parliamentary democracy. Still, the Reichstag gradually acquired greater political weight.[10]

2. GENERAL THEORY OF THE STATE

The summation of nineteenth-century theory was accomplished in 1900 by Georg Jellinek's *Allgemeine Staatslehre* (General Theory of the State).[11] Following neo-Kantianism, it separated "is" and "ought" and thus offered from the factual side a "social theory of the state,"

[8] Heinrich Triepel, *Völkerrecht und Landesrecht* (Leipzig, 1899); Heinrich Triepel, *Unitarismus und Föderalismus* (Tübingen, 1907); Heinrich Triepel, *Reichsaufsicht* (Berlin, 1917). See Ulrich M. Gassner, *Heinrich Triepel: Leben und Werk* (Berlin, 1999).

[9] Georg Jellinek, *Verfassungsänderung und Verfassungswandlung: Eine staatsrechtlich-politische Abhandlung* (Berlin, 1906); Paul Laband, "Die geschichtliche Entwicklung der Reichsverfassung seit der Reichsgründung," *Jahrbuch des öffentlichen Rechts* 1 (1907), 1–46; Rudolf Smend, "Ungeschriebenes Verfassungsrecht im monarchischen Bundesstaat," in *Festgabe für Otto Mayer* (1916), later in his *Staatsrechtliche Abhandlungen und andere Aufsätze*, 4th edn. (Berlin, 2010), pp. 39 ff.

[10] Norbert Ulrich, *Gesetzgebungsverfahren und Reichstag in der Bismarck-Zeit, unter besonderer Berücksichtigung der Rolle der Fraktionen* (Berlin, 1996).

[11] Georg Jellinek (1851–1911), one of the most important experts on state law of the late nineteenth century, taught at Heidelberg from 1891 to 1911. See Klaus Kempter, *Die Jellineks 1820–1955* (Düsseldorf, 1998); Stanley L. Paulson and M. Schulte, eds., *Georg Jellinek: Beiträge zu Leben und Werk* (Tübingen, 2000).

and from the normative side a "general theory of state law." The recognition of the facticity of the state took account of the pressure for recognition that came from the empirical social sciences, while the normative side preserved the province of the law. On this legal side, the state appeared as a territorially bound legal entity that had to satisfy three requirements to exist: a state territory, a state people, and a state authority. Grasping the latter as a factual reality in the first place required a look at the psyche of individuals subject to authority. The validity of law became a phenomenon of consciousness. Thus, in certain situations, especially after revolutions, the factual developed "normative force." This was a flexible theory that accorded with external conditions. One had learned from the nineteenth century that decisions of power politics could become law by way of "acceptance."

Jellinek's *Allgemeine Staatslehre* thus marks a state of transition between the constitutional monarchy of the nineteenth century and the emerging democratic industrialized society. The "monarchic principle" remained intact in both the Wilhelmine and the Habsburg state, even though in veiled form. The bourgeois constitutional state stopped halfway. Contemporaries were satisfied with the guarantees of the *Rechtsstaat*, and the national movement had found its fulfillment in 1871. There was little interest in expanding political participation, for example, through suffrage for women or the elimination of the three-class franchise, also because no one wanted to endanger their own position.

While the imperial constitution did not know basic rights, these were found in the constitutions of the states; moreover, essential areas of basic rights were secured by ordinary law (freedom of the press, freedom of association, freedom of assembly, citizenship). The theoretically recognized separation of state and society was an invitation also to public law to develop an equivalent to the "claim" or "entitlement" in private law. This was "subjective public law," de facto similar to basic rights and also actionable, provided it had a statutory basis. After all, the Reichsjustizgesetze (Imperial Judiciary Laws) of 1877 had created legal unity in procedural law (Law on the Organization of Courts, Code of Civil Procedure, Code of Criminal Procedure, Bankruptcy Code, Attorney's Code, Law on Court Costs). Administrative jurisdiction existed from 1875—with a precursor in Baden in 1863—in the larger states (Prussia, Bavaria, Württemberg, Austria), though not at the level of the empire. Legal disputes about social insurance law were settled within the Reichsversicherungsamt

(Imperial Insurance Office); that is, within the executive. A special labor court did not exist yet. But all in all, a *Rechtsstaat* had been created, one that was generally trusted and trustworthy, especially since administration and the judicial system, which were important to daily life, were in the hands of the states.

The Wilhelmine state undoubtedly had its unpleasant traits, beginning with the emperor and his mercurial and arrogant "personal rule."[12] The imperialist colonization movement, the unwise naval buildup, and upstart-like behavior damaged foreign relations. At home there was the much-lamented censorship—both prudish and politically motivated—of art and literature;[13] the inadequate integration of the labor movement, whose representatives were also deliberately kept from governing responsibly; and, finally, the anti-Semitism that was slowly becoming academically and politically reputable, and which was threatening to destroy what the Jews had achieved in terms of equality and toleration in the nineteenth century. On the other side, the industrial revolution created growing prosperity, in which the working class, too, slowly shared. The unions and social democracy changed course to a reformist line. The intensity of labor struggles eased. The unions and the large advocacy groups faced off, exerted influence on legislation, and turned the liberal state from the mid-century into the highly active interventionist state. The latter, now driven by reasons of social and economic policy, increasingly took steps on behalf of consumer protection, intervened in contractual relationships, issued prohibitions and qualified approvals, or exerted guidance through tax and corporation law. Cartels and trusts expanded, combined with intensive industrial financing by the banks. The legislature responded to this development on all levels of private and criminal law, but above all through the especially relevant legal concepts of public law.[14]

[12] C. G. Röhl, *Wilhelm II.*, 3 vols. (Munich, 1993–2008), is considered the standard work in this area.

[13] Michael Stolleis, "Der *Mordfall Heinze* und die *Lex Heinze*," in Bernhard Greiner, Barbara Thums, and Wolfgang Graf Vitzthum, eds., *Recht und Literatur* (Heidelberg, 2010), pp. 219–35.

[14] Michael Stolleis, "Die Entstehung des Interventionsstaates und das öffentliche Recht," in Michael Stolleis, *Konstitution und Intervention: Studien zur Geschichte des öffentlichen Rechts im 19. Jahrhundert* (Frankfurt am Main, 2001), pp. 253–82.

8

Administrative Law in the State of the Early Industrial Society

1. CHANGE OF PERSPECTIVES

After the end of the German Confederation (1866) and the founding of the empire (1870–1), administration remained a domain of the states. An imperial administration was slow to develop. The imperial offices initially established by Bismarck gradually evolved into full ministries, which then, in turn, generated imperial law via the legislature. The pages in the Imperial Law Gazette (*Reichsgesetzblatt*) multiplied accordingly.

And so the scholarly cultivation of administrative law that was slowly emerging in the second half of the nineteenth century was initially also tied to the state administrations and to the journals created in the states. A *Zeitschrift für Rechtspflege und Verwaltung* (Journal for Judiciary and Administration) had been published in Saxony since 1838, while the supra-regionally conceived *Zeitschrift für die gesamte Staatswissenschaft* (Journal for State Science) appeared in Württemberg (Tübingen) beginning in 1844. Its preface stated, "We intend to pay special heed to what is otherwise often neglected by scholarship, namely administrative law, seeing as the application to life is also worthy of attention, not only the fundamental ideas." Bavaria had the *Blätter für administrative Praxis* (Journal for Administrative Practice) starting in 1851, Baden the *Zeitschrift für badische Verwaltung und Verwaltungsrechtspflege* (Journal for Administration and Administrative Law Doctrine in Baden) from 1869, and Prussia the *Preußisches Verwaltungsblatt* (Prussian Administrative Journal) from 1879. All of these journals had a strong orientation to praxis.

After 1850, the universities offered barely any administrative law. It was not tested in examination. The necessary knowledge was acquired by practicing it. Still, under the key word *Rechtsstaat*, it became increasingly important to grasp what was specifically legal about administration. And so the first attempt was made in Württemberg to do a comparative study of administrative law in Württemberg, Prussia, and Bavaria, and to develop those "basic principles" from which a "General Part" of administrative law subsequently arose.[1] Wherever administration existed, there had to be comparable basic principles, as well as basic doctrinal concepts. One such basic concept was the unilateral sovereign interference in the rights of the citizen, the "administrative act."[2] Next to Württemberg, it was above all Bavaria that distinguished constitutional and administrative law early on and thus came to have separate textbooks on administrative law (E. v. Moy, J. Pözl, M. v. Seydel).

If we leave aside regional peculiarities, one can identify a few general traits in the emergence of administrative law and the science of administrative law for the period between 1850 and about 1895. The domain from which administrative law originated involves the policy ordinances of the early modern era, which were passed by the authorities to regulate the internal spheres of the community's life with commands, precepts, or prohibitions. The community should be "well-ordered," and subjects should be protected, controlled, and encouraged to live a "good life." Which legal forms were used in the process was secondary, because in the final analysis all forms sprang from the command authority of the sovereign. The matter to be regulated, the practical fields and scholarly branches involved, and the law deployed in the process were still closely associated.

The increasing specialization of scholarly fields in the eighteenth and nineteenth centuries led within the state sciences to the formation of separate segments within the sciences of policing, cameralistics, or finances. One of those segments was law, which transmuted from police law into *Administrativrecht* and from there into *Verwaltungsrecht*.

[1] Toshiyuki Ishikawa, *Friedrich Franz von Mayer: Begründer der "juristischen Methode" im deutschen Verwaltungsrecht* (Berlin, 1992).

[2] Walter Pauly, "Verwaltungsakt," in *HRG*, vol. 5 (Berlin, 1998), pp. 875–7; Markus Engert, *Die historische Entwicklung des Rechtsinstituts Verwaltungsakt* (Frankfurt am Main, 2002).

The constitutional movement and the interests of a society that was becoming more autonomous economically and politically gave rise to the call for the *Rechtsstaat*. Concretely, it meant that the administration should act in accordance with the rules of the law, and that it should be subject to oversight by the courts in this regard. In Germany, following a longer debate, one opted after 1863 for courts specializing in public law: the administrative courts.

The gradual emergence of a material administrative law and that of administrative jurisdiction were mutually reinforcing processes. The universities, too, began to offer courses on administrative law between about 1865 and 1885, and textbooks were written. At first, the authors added administrative law to state law in a second volume as "state administrative law," organized the material additively according to the departmental principle, and thus offered an overview that followed the system of ministries.

As the material continued to grow, it became more and more urgent to structure it by bringing out the connecting legal elements and basic doctrinal concepts, cutting across departments. In this way, an overarching "General Part" of administrative law began to slowly emerge. Its intellectual background were the general turn toward legal positivism, toward "strictly legal" procedures, the role-model effect of civil law, and the depoliticization that began after 1850.

However, the result of this act of drawing the legal elements out of the administration was that connecting threads were severed in two directions: first, to the non-legal disciplines of *Polizeiwissenschaft* (science of policing), which now took on the name *Verwaltungslehre* (administrative theory); second, for the sake of the autonomy of the discipline, to constitutional law, from which at the time only the postulates of the *Rechtsstaat* and of the separation of powers could be derived.

2. IMPORTANT AUTHORS

The various stages of this process have been well studied by now. Here I would like to single out only the later almost forgotten pioneer Friedrich Franz von Mayer, who compared the administrative legal norms of Prussia, Bavaria, and Württemberg in 1857 in an effort to arrive at common "principles."[3] He did this contemporaneously with the publication of the second edition of Gabriel Dufour's *Traité général de droit administratif* (General Treatise of Administrative Law) in seven volumes (1854–7); of course, Dufour followed a centralistic model that scholars in Germany, fragmented as it was in terms of state law, could only look upon in admiration. A brief *Verwaltungsrecht* with a historical and comparative focus appeared for the first time in 1870.[4] In 1875, Georg Meyer, an expert in public law from Jena, called for the separation of administrative theory and administrative law, and recommended "the legal permeation of the material and a juristic construction of the institutes of administrative law."[5] In 1881, the subject of administrative law became an obligatory subject at Prussian universities, and a series of general works by Georg Meyer (1883), Otto Sarwey (1884), Edgar Loening (1884), and Karl Stengel (1886) followed in rapid succession. The authors shared the stronger orientation toward the legal element, but differed on the questions of how much one had to break with the traditional account of the political sciences, and what practical value the "constructive method" practiced in civil law might have in administrative law.[6]

It was part of the intrinsic logic of this development that the Strasbourg professor Otto Mayer, who had published a *Theorie des französischen Verwaltungsrechts* (Theory of French Administrative Law) in 1886, now took on the task of doing the same for Germany.

What his faculty colleague Paul Laband had done for imperial state law, so his thinking went, could succeed also for administrative law, if one applied the French (and Italian) models constructively.[7] Otto

[3] Friedrich Franz von Mayer, *Grundzüge des Verwaltungs-Rechts und -Rechtsverfahrens* (Tübingen, 1857); Friedrich Franz von Mayer, *Grundsätze des Verwaltungs-Rechts: mit besonderer Berücksichtigung auf gemeinsames deutsches Recht, sowie auf neuere Gesetzgebung und bemerkenswerthe Entscheidungen der obersten Behörden zunächst der Königreiche Preußen, Baiern, und Württemberg* (Tübingen, 1862). On von Mayer, see Ishikawa (Note 1).

[4] Ernst von Meier, "Das Verwaltungsrecht," in Franz von Holtzendorff, ed., *Encyklopädie der Rechtswissenschaft* (Leipzig, 1870), pp. 693–746.

[5] Georg Meyer, *Das Studium des öffentlichen Rechts und der Staatswissenschaften in Deutschland* (Jena, 1875), p. 17.

[6] Edgar Loening, "Die konstruktive Methode auf dem Gebiete des Verwaltungsrechts," *Schmollers Jahrbuch* 11 (1888), 117–45.

[7] Vittorio E. Orlando, *Principi di diritto amministrativo* (Florence, 1891); Vittorio E. Orlando, *Primo trattato completo di diritto amministrativo italiano* (Milan, 1897).

Mayer was well versed in administrative praxis, and his formulations were direct and catchy, but most of all he brought out—in a process of abstraction—the basic concepts that kept reoccurring. At the top he placed the administrative act, the law-shaping command of the state, which was supposed to tell the citizen "what is lawful for him." Equally fundamental seemed to him the distinctions between common use and special use, between the general and the special relationship of authority between the state and its citizens; between corporation, foundation, and institution; between tax, fees, and dues. But Mayer had no success with his attempt to establish an independent public property, nor with his opposition to the public-law contract, because he felt that the state should not enter into agreements with citizens. On the whole, though, he was so successful that one still debated in the 1970s how far one should deviate from his concepts.[8] He had great influence on his contemporaries Karl Kormann, Paul Schoen, Walter Jellinek, Richard Thoma, Ottmar Bühler, Otto Koellreutter, and others. Through the Swiss Fritz Fleiner and the Swede Carl-Axel Reuterskiöld, his thinking radiated abroad.

In spite of this recognition, there were also objections, for example, against the expulsion of history and administrative theory; against the unilaterally sovereign perspective, which perceived only the "subject" (the recipient of commands) but not the citizen; and against the faith in conceptual jurisprudence. The latter concerned also civil jurisprudence, ever since Jhering had made the *Zweck im Recht* (law as a means to an end) central to civil jurisprudence, ever since the *Freirechtsschule* (doctrine advocating freedom in interpreting and adapting the law) had appeared and *Interessenjurisprudenz* (jurisprudence of interests) was gaining adherents. Behind these movements stood the emerging industrial mass society, with entirely new power relationships and dependencies. Labor law, social law, association law, corporate law, industrial law, and technology law pushed to the fore, and this made it seem ever more urgent to reconnect "constructional jurisprudence"—which seemed so far removed from the realities—once again with the historical, economic, and political momentum. But these trends did not fundamentally shake the only recently

[8] Otto Bachof and Winfried Brohm, "Die Dogmatik des Verwaltungsrechts vor den Gegenwartsaufgaben der Verwaltung," *Veröffentlichungen der Vereinigung der Deutschen Staatsrechtslehrer* 30 (1972), 193 ff.

erected edifice of administrative law, at least not before the outbreak of World War I.

The real turning point occurred on August 1, 1914. It spelled the end not only of the "good old days," but also of the era of classic international law, which had just recently celebrated a triumph in the Hague peace conferences of 1899 and 1907. The war transcended the laboriously achieved boundaries; it became a war of propaganda, national economies, and military technology. The Enabling Act that was passed as early as August 4, 1914, created a temporary civilian and military dictatorship, which governed the country with a total of 825 *Bundesrat* ordinances, while parliamentary legislation lost importance—as did the monarch himself. The land was covered with detailed military administration law, which rendered the distinction between private law and public law nearly unrecognizable. What had started to emerge since the 1880s now unfolded with the utmost speed in the pressure-cooker atmosphere of the war. Civil class society was mutating into an industrial mass society, and state and administrative law were mutating right along with it.

The theory of state law and administrative law, as well as international law, were not only flooded with a multitude of problems by the war; they also experienced a considerable increase in practical importance. The transition to the parliamentary system, the abolition of the Prussian three-class voting system, the threat to the *Rechtsstaat* and self-administration through wartime emergency law, and the multiplication of administrative legal norms had to be digested. The events of the war themselves, especially the controversial submarine warfare along with the illegal torpedoing of the British ship *Lusitania* in 1915, revealed the lack of institutional research and consultation on international law. The reactions within the disciplines during the Weimar Republic—for example, making state law and administrative law a greater part of legal training, the multiplication of relevant professorships, and the creation of institutes for international law in Kiel and Berlin—were largely based on the experiences that had been made in the world war.

9

The Theory of State Law and Administrative Law under the Weimar Constitution

1. THE DEPARTURE TOWARD "POPULAR SOVEREIGNTY"

The revolution of 1918 ended the era of constitutional monarchies in the nineteenth century and established popular sovereignty as the legitimizing foundation of the new polity. This happened nearly contemporaneously at the levels of the empire and the states. Everything that had been handed down was up for grabs: the *Reichstag* with a franchise that needed to be renewed (and for the first time included women), the structured federal state and the representation of the *Länder* on the level of the empire, a unitary or binary leadership at the top (chancellor, president), the authority of territorial rulers over the churches,[1] the classification of the civil service and the military. Internally the issue revolved around the creation of a new "unity," externally around the defeat in the war and the Treaty of Versailles. Serious domestic political problems as well as the national humiliation from the burden of "war debt" and reparation demands made the transition all the more difficult.

But this transition was also made possible in the first place by the fact that the civil servants, the judiciary, and the military did not resist the change, but rather engaged in a more or less loyal collaboration. The statehood of the German Empire (founded in 1871) was preserved; on this point there was a consensus, but the

[1] Christoph Link, *Kirchliche Rechtsgeschichte*, 2nd edn. (Munich, 2010) §26; Michael Stolleis, "Kirchenregiment, landesherrliches," in *HRG*, 2nd edn., vol. 2 (Berlin, 2012), pp. 1826–8.

form of the state had to be changed from the ground up. That was now done in the constitution-creating process between the winter of 1918–19 and the summer of 1919, far from Berlin, in classical Weimar; the "Weimar Constitution" went into effect on August 14. The first concept, created by the left-liberal state law expert Hugo Preuß (1860–1925), got caught in the crush of interests between parties and states, especially Prussia, which fought against being split into several middle-sized states. The planned unitary state became once again a federal state with a strong Prussian preponderance; the Reich president became the "substitute emperor," endowed with potent (and vaguely defined) emergency powers; the Reich chancellor headed a government answerable to parliament; and above all a catalog of basic rights and duties (based largely on the model of the constitution of the Frankfurt St. Paul's Church in 1848) was created. For the workers' movement the constitution contained a social program and the promise of a participatory voice in the workplace; for the churches there were autonomy, certain privileges for the national churches, and material guarantees. All told, it seemed an acceptable compromise, though it naturally included also "dilatory compromise formulas."

But the Weimar Constitution was only truly operative for ten years. After barely surviving the first crisis in 1923, the parliamentary form of government ended in 1929 and transitioned to an emergency regime, which functioned through the interplay between the Reich chancellors (Brüning, von Papen, von Schleicher) and the Reich president. The real or alleged flaws in its construction could probably have been remedied under more favorable conditions. And the necessary reform of the Reich might also have succeeded. But the trust in parliamentary democracy and in economic liberalism had been politically and intellectually exhausted. The leading classes turned against the "system," as did the masses attracted equally by extreme left-wing and extreme right-wing positions.

2. THE ROLE OF *STAATSRECHTSLEHRE* (STATE LAW THEORY)

Staatsrechtslehre found itself confronted by a wealth of tasks under the new constitution. The professors of public law had been educated during the monarchy. They advocated a strong state that stood above societal conflicts and should also have a representative who stood above the parties. Following the end of the monarchies, such a representative could only be a Reich president directly elected by the people. The theorists of state law (Fritz Stier-Somlo, Hermann Heller, Ernst Fraenkel, in Austria Hans Kelsen) lamented that parties were invading the shaping of the public will outside parliament, and they reaffirmed Article 130 of the new constitution, which declared that officials "serve society in its entirety, not a specific party." Politically, they fell along the continuum from "German national" to "national liberal," while social-democratic positions or party membership were a rarity. But even the conservative majority believed that a new, valid order had been created by the "law-establishing power of the revolution." Even those who railed against the "November criminals" and mocked the new national colors ("black–red–mustard") in the lecture halls did not deny the validity of the constitution adopted by the Weimar National Assembly. The de facto holding of state power, the formal process of summoning a National Assembly, and the finalization of the text by its decision—all of these things were sufficient, as soon they were joined by recognition on the part of those subject to the norms. All later attempts to qualify the existing text of the constitution by invoking a "true constitution" or its spirit changed nothing.

The authors thus wrote their first textbooks and commentaries on this new basis. Among the latter, the most prominent was soon the commentary on the Reich Constitution by Gerhard Anschütz (1867–1948), a theorist of state law at Heidelberg.

The work went through fourteen editions by 1933 and acquired great authority.[2] Anschütz defended the constitution and the republic against the anti-positivist voices that grew ever louder after 1926. In 1930–2, he and his former Heidelberg colleague Richard Thoma—also a committed supporter of parliamentary democracy[3]—compiled the entire state law of the Weimar Republic once more into a two-volume *Handbuch des Deutschen Staatsrechts* (Handbook of

[2] Gerhard Anschütz, *Die Verfassung des Deutschen Reichs vom 11. August 1919*, 14th edn. (Berlin 1933; reprint, Darmstadt, 1960). On this, see also his *Aus meinem Leben*, edited and with an introduction by Walter Pauly (Frankfurt, 1993).

[3] Richard Thoma, *Rechtsstaat—Demokratie—Grundrechte*, edited and with an introduction by Horst Dreier (Tübingen, 2008).

German State Law).[4] If one adds the commentary *Die Grundrechte und Grundpflichten der Reichsverfassung* (The Basic Rights and Basic Obligations of the Reich Constitution),[5] the work of Hans Carl Nipperdey (1895–1968), an expert on labor law, one has the sum of the pronouncements on the positive state and constitutional law of the Weimar era.

3. VERSAILLES AND INNER UNITY

Domestic politics and international law revolved around "Versailles." This treaty, a deliberate, humiliating *Diktat* by the victors, stirred up everyone's emotions. It excluded Germany from the newly created League of Nations; enshrined the territorial changes to the borders with Belgium, France, Denmark, Poland, and Czechoslovakia; and prohibited the annexation of Austria. Germany's colonies were placed under the mandate of the League of Nations, and the country was demilitarized and had reparations of undetermined size imposed on it. Above all, Article 231 of the treaty defined the "war guilt." The German and Austrian experts on international law, who had been organized into their own association since 1917 and had two research institutes (Kiel, Berlin), wrote commentaries on the Versailles Treaty; published documents; and dealt with various territorial issues, the plebiscites, the protection of minorities, and reparations. The basic line in all of this was that everything should be done to strengthen one's own position and to reverse the country's international ostracism, which was also having negative academic effects. Within this consensus, the positions ranged from "German national" (Axel von Freytagh-Loringhoven, Erich Kaufmann, Heinrich Triepel) to "pacifist" (Walther Schücking, Hans Wehberg), though with a strong preponderance of the nationalist tones—as it was the case throughout society during the interwar period.

[4] Gerhard Anschütz and Richard Thoma, eds., *Handbuch des Deutschen Staatsrechts*, vol. 1 (Tübingen, 1930), vol. 2 (Tübingen, 1932). Reprinted with an introduction by Walter Pauly (Tübingen, 1998).

[5] Hans Carl Nipperdey, *Die Grundrechte und Grundpflichten der Reichsverfassung*, 3 vols. (Berlin, 1929–30; reprint, Kronberg, 1975).

State law was less concerned with territorial unity, since Germany, in spite of the loss of territory, had not been divided as it would be after 1945. The real issue was internal unity. Already the balance between the Reich and the constituent states had shifted in favor of the Reich compared to the constitution in 1871, though a unitary state did not emerge and the mighty bloc of Prussia was not broken up. But there were the worrisome separatist movements in the Rhineland and the Bavarian Palatinate on the left side of the Rhine, the Hitler Putsch in Bavaria, a conflict with Thuringia, and finally the forceful deposition of the Prussian government on July 20, 1932 by Reich Chancellor Franz von Papen, the unconstitutional so-called "Prussian coup" that already laid the groundwork for the assumption of power by the National Socialists.[6] The discipline of state law raised its voice on all of these events, also in an admonitory and mediating way, though without being able to exert any meaningful influence. In the proceedings before the *Staatsgerichtshof* (constitutional court), it was not only the Reich government and Prussia that confronted each other, but also the camps of state law experts: on the side of the Reich, for example, Carl Schmitt, Erwin Jacobi, and Carl Bilfinger, on the side of Prussia Arnold Brecht, Gerhard Anschütz, and Hermann Heller.

The "internal unity" of the young republic was the still more urgent problem. Society felt torn and directionless. The workers' movement had split with the outbreak of the war, and social democracy was now governing the Reich and Prussia, while the communists (the Unabhängige Sozialdemokratische Partei, later the Kommunistische Partei Deutschlands or KPD) were invoking class struggle. The bourgeoisie, materially weakened by the inflation of 1923, feared extremism on the left and the right, but also the dissolution of the substance of the state by the new power of the parties and organizations. The instability of the cabinets destroyed confidence in the ability of the governments and the Reichstag to act. "State authority derives from the people," declared the Weimar Constitution in classic simplicity (Article 1 (2)), but the line that connected state power back to popular sovereignty branched out in multiple ways. The Reich president, "elected by the entire German nation" (Article 41 (1)), had his own

[6] The classic study on this topic is Karl Dietrich Bracher's *Die Auflösung der Weimarer Republik: Eine Studie zum Problem des Machtverfalls in der Demokratie* (Stuttgart, 1955), 5th edn. (Stuttgart, 1971).

legitimation and dictatorial powers in case of a crisis (Article 48). The members of the Reichstag represented "the entire nation" (Article 21 (1)). The members of the Reichsrat were indirectly legitimated through elections in the federal states (Article 63 (1)). Alongside the Reichstag there were several ways of holding a "plebiscite" about a law (Article 73). The governments of the federal states, in turn legitimated by elections, could also take dictatorial measures in case of a crisis (Article 48 (4)). All in all, then, there were many possibilities of exercising state authority without direct legitimation by the will of citizens. State and society were not sufficiently related to one another. The historical reserves were too weak to allow the necessary slow growth of confidence in the functional capacity of democratic institutions. When the presidential dictatorships began in 1932, the chances of restoring "internal unity" had already been gambled away.

10

Controversies over Method and General Theories of the State

1. SHAKING OF THE FOUNDATIONS

The grave crises of the Weimar Republic are marked by the years 1923 and 1929. Inflation, the Hitler Putsch, and the Rhineland crisis dominated 1923. The years 1929 to 1932 saw the global economic crisis, the paralysis of the parliamentary system, and the coup of the Reich government against Prussia. The doctrine of state law was deeply unsettled by all of this and searched for new theoretical foundations. What was holding the state together, and where should development lead? This was a debate about the form of political life, and it was carried on with passion and existential seriousness.[1]

Already before 1914, there had been voices declaring the prevailing positivism in the theory of state law inadequate. They criticized the formal exclusion of the political, economic, and historical elements, preferring to see them openly integrated rather than have them enter through methodological back doors. Moreover, customary constitutional law and "quiet constitutional change" seemed hard to grasp from the perspective of legal positivism. But there was more. Industrial and

[1] Rudolf Smend, "Die Vereinigung der Staatsrechtslehrer und der Richtungsstreit," in H. Ehmke, J. H. Kaiser, W. A. Kewenig, K. M. Meessen, and W. Rüfner, eds., *Festschrift für Ulrich Scheuner* (Berlin, 1973), pp. 575–98; Manfred Friedrich, "Der Methoden- und Richtungsstreit; Zur Grundlagendiskussion der Weimarer Staatsrechtslehre," *AöR*, 102 (1977), 161–209; Klaus Rennert, *Die "geisteswissenschaftliche Richtung" in der Staatsrechtslehre der Weimarer Republik: Untersuchungen zu Erich Kaufmann, Günther Holstein, und Rudolf Smend* (Berlin, 1987); Dian Schefold, "Geisteswissenschaften und Staatsrechtslehre zwischen Weimar und Bonn" (1998), in Dian Schefold, *Bewahrung der Demokratie: Ausgewählte Aufsätze* (Berlin, 2012), pp. 175–205.

mass society, which was now intensely palpable, changed the entire situation, politically and economically, but also in the humanities.

In philosophy, the neo-Kantianism of the turn of the century persisted, but it had long been overlaid by a variety of new schools (phenomenology, material ethics of values, existential philosophy). Sociology and legal sociology were established by their famous founding fathers (Max Weber, Georg Simmel, Ferdinand Tönnies, Werner Sombart, Eugen Ehrlich). The science of politics, which had nearly vanished in the nineteenth century, experienced a new founding era. History had its "historians' quarrel" (Karl Lamprecht), in that the new social history was seeking to displace the classic history of politics and ideas. The historicism of the nineteenth century was encountering its limits. Then there were all sorts of semi-reputable and prophetic currents. Oswald Spengler's *Der Untergang des Abendlandes* (The Decline of the West) (1919) disseminated an eagerly received mood of depression. Parallel to this work, *Grundlagen des XIX. Jahrhunderts* (Foundations of the Nineteenth Century) (1899) by the Germanophile and anti-Semitic Englishman Houston Stewart Chamberlain (1855–1927) met with very wide reception. This was the time of self-proclaimed prophets and world redeemers, of the founding of rural communes, of political combat organizations and revolutionary communities at the margins of politics, but also of educational and social reforms, of a pan-European movement and pacifism.

Within the discipline of state-law theory, which now had to find its bearing in this field after World War I, several groups emerged which were held together by generational experiences and political convictions. The majority of the experts on state and administrative law who worked in the Weimar Republic had grown up during the "good old days" before 1914, and they now applied the classic "juristic method" to the new constitution. For the sake of the scientific nature of their own discipline, they were at pains to develop state law systematically and consistently on the basis of its own terminology. They made a point of wanting to argue in a "strictly juristic" manner, and not as politicians, ethicists, moralists, economists, or sociologists. They were "legal positivists," and to the extent that they felt a political affinity with the prevailing direction of the empire, they were "statutory positivists" who received the valid law from the hand of the legislature and limited themselves to this material. This positivism was by no means political, but its foundations originated in the relatively relaxed atmosphere at the end of the nineteenth century. Many professors might have preferred the survival of the constitutional monarchy with full parliamentarization as the more organic development of political life, as happened in the Netherlands, Scandinavia, and England, for example; however, they realized that the reserves of legitimacy for such solutions had been used up after the revolution of 1918. The liberals among them (mostly from southern Germany), therefore, shifted to a "constitutional positivism" under the Weimar Constitution. Among these scholars are found particularly eager commentators of the prevailing law (Gerhard Anschütz, Richard Thoma, Walter Jellinek, Fritz Stier-Somlo, Karl Rothenbücher, Friedrich Giese), but also representatives of the new sub-disciplines of economic law, labor law, social law, and tax law. All were loyal supporters of the republican-parliamentary democracy, which by no means ruled out a national mindset.

Methodologically speaking, positivists were often also those who were situated at the far right politically. Although they disapproved of the republic as nationalists and invoked a "higher justice" against it, their positivist education and deeply rooted confidence in the state were so potent that they did not question the binding force of the constitution in their everyday work. This is true, for example, of three conservative experts in state law who clashed with the republic over their critical statements (Hans Helfritz, Axel Freiherr von Freytagh-Loringhoven, Fritz Freiherr Marschall von Bieberstein).

2. THE VIENNA SCHOOL

The traditional legal positivism of the nineteenth century was not only beholden to the period before 1914, but also displayed theoretical inconsistencies. Hans Kelsen (1881–1973), a legal theorist and expert in state law from Vienna, uncovered these inconsistencies and dealt with them in an imposing system. Following the publication of his book *Hauptprobleme der Staatsrechtslehre, entwickelt aus der Lehre vom Rechtssatze* (Main Problems in Theory of Public Law) (1911), the debate over his theories did not cease. Within a few years there emerged from his intellectual circle books and brochures, essays and detailed reviews, countertractates and counterreviews, often in the journal he oversaw, *Zeitschrift für öffentliches Recht* (Journal for Public Law). State law, administrative law, and international law (the latter chiefly at the hands of Alfred Verdross) now appeared in an entirely new light as a self-contained normative system, which was organized by what Adolf Merkl called its "hierarchical structure" (*Stufenbau*), and which was supposed to be held together at the top by a much-discussed, hypothesized "basic norm."[2]

It was no coincidence that the efforts to lay the theoretical foundations for a methodologically "pure" legal science culminated in Vienna. This city at the intersection of Central and Southeastern Europe, overflowing with talent of every kind, spawned "schools" in economics, art history, the fine arts and music, psychoanalysis, and philosophy.[3] The circle around Kelsen, Merkl, and Verdross pursued a similar basic line as the "Vienna circle" of philosophy around Moritz Schlick, Otto Neurath, and Rudolf Carnap, with Ludwig Wittgenstein and Karl R. Popper also working at its margins: empiricists, logicians, mathematicians, philosophers of language, and theorists of science, who, for all their differences, were all searching together for the scientific foundations of thinking and for a way to grasp the world without ontologies and without metaphysics.[4]

Another reason why Vienna was the place for a consistently elaborated legal positivism was the positivist tradition of Austria's legal training and a professional civil service oriented toward the state and the law. The Habsburg multi-ethnic state was held together by its legal system and its administration. On the one hand, it inspired the development of legal sociology; that is, the study of the de facto creation and implementation of legal norms (Eugen Ehrlich). On the other hand, however, it led to the very goal of a "pure" normative order freed from causal sciences like metaphysics, which would make it possible to claim the status of a science also for jurisprudence. That is to say: jurisprudence should not only strive for purity and the logical consistency of its premises in terms of method, but it should also be immune to nationalist ideologies of the multi-ethnic state and to the moral and theological (i.e., metaphysical) arguments advanced by the church. For a group of scholars who were often of Jewish

[2] Horst Dreier, *Rechtslehre, Staatssoziologie und Demokratietheorie bei Hans Kelsen* (Baden-Baden, 1986), 2nd edn. (Baden-Baden, 1990); Stanley L. Paulson and Michael Stolleis, eds., *Hans Kelsen: Staatsrechtslehrer und Rechtstheoretiker des 20. Jahrhunderts* (Tübingen, 2005); Matthias Jestaedt and Oliver Lepsius, eds., *Hans Kelsen: Verteidigung der Demokratie* (Tübingen, 2006).

[3] Allan Janik and Stephen Toulmin, *Wittgenstein's Vienna* (New York, 1973).

[4] For an initial overview, see Manfred Geier, *Der Wiener Kreis* (Reinbek, 1992).

background—and thus tended to opt for democracy, rights of liberty, emancipation, and social equity—a "scientific character" was also a suitable platform on which to oppose an anti-Semitism that had long since become virulent in Austria and a clericalism that was in part parallel to it.

Apart from the specific Austrian environment, the rise of the pure theory of law also expressed a general shift in circumstances. The splendid successes of the natural sciences heightened the pressure on jurisprudence, which had always operated in a rather pragmatic and eclectic manner. The pure theory of law was a radical challenge to the traditional positivism to relinquish the syncretism of methods in favor of a uniform system of knowledge and to employ more precise instruments. That this would also make it possible to exclude a priori political and moral stipulations that had been imported into jurisprudence seemed only desirable. The stereotypical charges leveled against the pure theory of law were that it ignored real life, offered only empty abstractions and no moral footing, and misunderstood the nature of the law. But it was also very openly condemned politically, from the right and the left equally. In his philosophical polemic of 1921, Erich Kaufmann declared that there was really no need to read Kelsen's big books, and that the neo-Kantian theory of law was unsuited to "paralyzing the dangerous materialistic and utopian poison of Marxism."[5] Four decades later one heard analogously from the GDR that the pure theory of law was an ideology that concealed bourgeois interests precisely because of its "emptiness."[6]

3. THE CONTROVERSY OVER METHOD OR DIRECTION

The pure theory of law was a radical and incisive answer, but it did not accord with the prevailing psychological need in Germany for a metaphysical grounding, for a fusion of law and morality, for the

[5] Erich Kaufmann, "Kritik der neukantischen Rechtsphilosophie: Eine Betrachtung über die Beziehungen zwischen Philosophie und Rechtswissenschaft" (1921), in Erich Kaufmann, *Gesammelte Schriften*, vol. III (Göttingen, 1960), pp. 176 ff., 193 f., 242.

[6] Hermann Klenner, *Rechtsleere: Verurteilung der Reinen Rechtslehre* (Berlin and Frankfurt am Main, 1972).

overcoming of the separation between Is and Ought. In fact, the pure theory of law as a legal theory did *not* answer precisely the vital problems of orientation at the time. The German theory of state law did not long for a heightening of its "scientific character," but for inner cohesion in a turbulent time. That cohesion could be offered only by a system of values, such as began to emerge in the second main part of the Weimar Constitution concerning basic rights and obligations. Even if its pronouncements reflected compromise and were inconsistent, the basic rights did offer a new point of departure. They attracted intense interest for the first time from about 1925, and scholars began to systematize them and expand them into a value system.[7] The legislator, too, was now supposed to be bound by this value system—a novel idea at that time, but today prevailing constitutional law (Article 1 (3) of the Basic Law).

Some scholars thus opted for a strict separation of Is and Ought, law, and morality, as a way of making possible a theoretically "pure" treatment of the legal norms. Others did the opposite, opting for "values," for a "real constitution" that surpassed the simple constitutional texts, and for a close connection between constitutional law and the social sciences. Thus the front lines of the emerging controversy over method were visible early on.

The "controversy over method" (*Methodenstreit*) that became famous within the theory of state law was outwardly inconspicuous. It is found in the talks at the meetings of the Association of German Professors of State Law between 1925 and 1929, as well as in the discussions and in a few accompanying essays.[8] On the surface, the dispute there was over whether one should stick with the traditional "juristic method" (possibly in an intensified form courtesy of the Vienna school) when interpreting the constitutional text, or whether one could make use of the "humanistic [*geisteswissenschaftliche*] method." The latter took its orientation from the tradition of hermeneutic understanding stretching from Schleiermacher to Dilthey, the precondition of which was the incorporation of the societal context with the relevant "variations in meaning." Behind this approach stood diverse views of the state and political options.

[7] Carl Schmitt, "Inhalt und Bedeutung des zweiten Hauptteils der Reichsverfassung," in Gerhard Anschütz and Richard Thoma, eds., *Handbuch des Deutschen Staatsrechts*, vol. 2 (Tübingen, 1932), §101.

[8] Smend (Note 1), pp. 575–89.

At the meeting in Münster in 1926, the anti-positivist and positivist camps clashed head-on in the persons of Erich Kaufmann and Hans Nawiasky. That probably had something to do with the topic (the equality clause, Article 109 of the Weimar Constitution), and with the extremely contrasting speakers. The backdrop was the experience of inflation and the hitherto negated question of whether legislating was also bound by the equality clause. If it was, then nearly every law that was relevant to social policy could be challenged for "violating equality." Another confrontation between methodological approaches occurred in 1927 in the discussion over the scope of the basic right of freedom of opinion (Article 118 (1) of the Weimar Constitution). Karl Rothenbücher championed a statist–positivist position, while Rudolf Smend regarded the basic right as part of a stock of cultural values above the individual, thereby relativizing the primacy of the "general laws"—to which this basic right should also be subject—in the light of the value to be protected. One faction of state-law experts agreed emphatically with Smend, another criticized the softening of the legal boundaries.

Finally, the opponents met in Vienna in 1928 during the debate over the usefulness and future of constitutional jurisdiction. The talks were delivered by Heinrich Triepel and Hans Kelsen. Triepel emphasized the dialectical interplay of law and politics, denied that politics could be completely juridified, and advocated a constitutional jurisdiction that was separate from normal jurisdiction in procedure and character. Kelsen also did the latter, but in a very different sense. He insisted that the constitution had the character of law, and he saw the primary task of constitutional jurisdiction in annulling unconstitutional sovereign acts, including statutes. Based on his experiences in Austria, the work of an independent court that was largely free from the influence of party politics was possible and desirable. Where he disagreed with Triepel was in his concept of the constitution. To him the difference appeared as one of worldview; that is, it could not be resolved by scientific means. The same was true in reverse for Hermann Heller, who saw himself in "metaphysical–ethical opposition" to Kelsen, because the pure theory of law, as he put it, "is not capable of abiding the political with its formalistic and rationalistic ideal of security." For Kelsen, in turn, the Triepel–Smendian formulas of integration were pure metaphysics, a matter of "theology." The antagonism between politics and law, as Carl Schmitt understood it, but also in Triepel's dialectical formulation, was unacceptable to him.

The far end of the method dispute is marked by the lecture given by Gerhard Leibholz on the franchise at the meeting of 1931. It shows the kind of resigned, indeed apocalyptic, mood that had already taken hold. Essentially it was already an epilogue. Like most bourgeois scholars unwilling to embrace *völkisch* (ethnic-national) irrationalism and collectivism, Leibholz saw no feasible way out. And so the fact that the meeting of 1932 was canceled, that a meeting was entirely dispensed with in 1933, and that the activity of the Association of State Law Teachers was suspended, as were the meetings of the experts on international law, can be seen as a withdrawal into silence. Communication was at an end. The "gulf of failing to understand the problem and terminology that existed between one group and the other," which Richard Thoma had talked about in 1927 in front of the teachers of state law, had now become unbridgeable for political reasons.

4. THE FORMATION OF GROUPS

Those who wished to preserve the Weimar Republic as a parliamentary democracy with its unavoidable parties within a constitutional framework considered themselves "positivists" when it came to constitutional law. They included not only the leading commentators on the Constitution, Gerhard Anschütz (Heidelberg), and Richard Thoma (Bonn), but also Karl Rothenbücher and Hans Nawiasky (both Munich), Fritz Stier-Somlo (Cologne), Fritz Giese (Frankfurt am Main), and many others. This group ended up on the losing side in the crisis of the Weimar Republic. The more the parties in the parliaments of the *Länder* and in the Reichstag blocked each other and proved incapable of constructive compromises, the more difficult it became to defend classic state-law positivism. When the presidential dictatorships began and calls for the *Volksstaat* (state of the ethnic nation), "true democracy," *Volksgemeinschaft* (national community), and the *Führer* grew ever louder, the insistence on loyalty to the Constitution had become a hopeless position.

The opposing group, gathered together under the vague name "humanistic [*geisteswissenschaftlich*] direction," was heterogeneous. Some made their way into this camp via international law roiled by the Versailles Treaty and the League of Nations; others from the borderland experiences in the Baltics, in Poland, or in Alsace; still others from the youth movement or similar group experiences with the postulates of a *Ständestaat* (corporatist state). Many were cultural Protestants, their thinking idealistic and German-national. The latter is true especially of Rudolf Smend, who hailed from the milieu of Protestant theological learnedness. At the meeting of teachers of state law in 1927, he had delivered the previously mentioned lecture on the interplay between the basic right of freedom of opinion and the statutory law that limited it, and his theses took on a semi-official character in the Federal Republic through the Lüth decision by the Federal Constitutional Court (BVerfGE 7, 198 ff.).

In a broader sense one can include in this group also the "Young Right," who began their scholarly career during the death throes of the republic and who distanced themselves most strongly from liberalism, relativism, and parliamentary democracy. If they picked a philosophical lodestar, it was more likely Hegel than Kant. They opted for a strong state, for "community," "decision," and "action." Some of them gathered around the decidedly anti-liberal Carl Schmitt, while others looked for guidance in a pointed statism or in models of "community" animated by the spirit of the youth movement. Some defined themselves as belonging to the "conservative revolution," a collective label for a multiplicity of anti-liberal and anti-democratic currents, but as jurists they were for the most part more moderate and professional than the brothers Ernst and Friedrich Georg Jünger, for example, or the journalists Edgar Jung, Heinrich von Gleichen, Hans Zehrer, Arthur Moeller van den Bruck, or Ernst Niekisch. Where the dichotomy between revolutionary posture and bourgeois existence became too great, or the young private lecturers feared for their careers, they published—revealingly enough—under pseudonyms (Ernst Forsthoff, Ernst Rudolf Huber), for example in Hans Zehrer's journal *Die Tat* (The Deed), or in Heinrich von Gleichen's *Der Ring* (The Ring).[9]

Between the two camps, and disliked by both, sat Hans Kelsen's Vienna school. Initially it had attacked classical positivism for its inconsistencies and outdone it in terms of "purity." Now it found itself compelled to act even more forcefully against the emerging open

[9] Extensive references in Armin Mohler, *Die Konservative Revolution, 1918–1932: Ein Handbuch*, 6th edn., ed. by Karlheinz Weißmann (Graz, 2005).

politicization of state law, against natural law, and a new metaphysics. With ever greater urgency, Kelsen raised his voice in defence of democracy and of empirical–critical rationalism. Beginning in 1929 he saw that his possibilities of having any effect were dwindling in Austria, and he moved to the University of Cologne, from where the National Socialists expelled him in 1933. He initially fled to Geneva and then to the US, where he lived until his death (1973), working to the very end at the University of California, Berkeley.

How difficult it is to link this "method dispute" to political orientations can be seen from Kelsen's toughest opponent, Hermann Heller (1891–1933). As a social democrat and republican, he had at least a political affinity with Kelsen; however, he considered Kelsen's neo-Kantian separation of Is and Ought to be fundamentally wrong. He believed that it was absurd to posit the identity of the state and the legal system; indeed, he praised Kelsen "without irony" for having proven, by the consistent rigor of his thinking, the absurdity of the false path he believed the positivist theory of the state to have been on for two generations. Heller interpreted the state as a part of human culture and the theory of the state as part of the science of politics. The "reality" of the state should not be understood purely in terms of normative logic, or in purely empirical terms, or in humanistic terms, but sociologically through the comprehension of structures. This kind of theory of the state should encompass factual and normative existence, history, and the present. That posed methodological problems, but it intimates just how eager Heller was to differentiate himself from the conventional theory of the state. His state was to be grasped by the scientific study of what was real, but it should also have a normative orientation, namely as an interlinking of democracy, the state under the rule of law, and the social state.

5. THE MAIN WORKS

A. When Hans Kelsen published his *Allgemeine Staatslehre* (General Theory of the State) in 1925, he recognized in the Preface "more clearly than before" (Preface) that he was indebted to the state-law positivism of the nineteenth century, and he strongly reaffirmed his position: the identity of the state with its legal order as the coercive normative system for human behavior, the confining of scholarly work to this normative system, and the unity of the legal system. This book, differently structured than the conventional theories of state law, had a provocative effect. It began by describing what lay outside this normativity, namely the state as looked at from the perspective of sociology and political science, and then tackled the legal order of the state—the "state" in the Kelsenian sense. Even though he did posit the conventional trinity (state power, state territory, state people) as static elements, he already deviated from many traditional notions in this regard, and his deviation was all the more pronounced in the "dynamic" part of his book, which dealt with the functions of the state, the law-creating organs, and their methods. Especially provocative were the central assertion about the identity of the order of the state and the legal order, and the consistent exclusion of a moral, political, and empirical examination of the state. Disagreement was voiced particularly in Germany, where scholars had just relinquished the positivism of the pre-war period and were arguing increasingly from the perspective of sociology, power politics, or the humanities.[10] It is likely that Kelsen thus provided the most important impetus behind the writing of three important "counterbooks."

B. Rudolf Smend (1882–1975) took up the challenge on the very first pages of his tractate *Verfassung und Verfassungsrecht* (Constitution and Constitutional Law) (1928). In general he perceived a lack of positive feelings for the state (*Staatsgesinnung*) and for political ethics, even in Max Weber, Ernst Troeltsch, and Friedrich Meinecke; he criticized skepticism and an "inner alienation from the state"; and he singled out the "now consciously attained zero point with Kelsen's *Allgemeine Staatslehre* of 1925." He called it a "dead end without purpose and goal," since it offered only pure formalism and not a material theory of the state. Smend then laid out his "theory of integration" to provide the foundations for just such a theory. His intent was to create "the preconditions for a constitutional doctrine in terms of the theory of the state." Drawing on the philosophy of

[10] Axel-Johannes Korb, *Kelsens Kritiker: Ein Beitrag zur Geschichte der Rechts- und Staatstheorie, 1911–1934* (Tübingen, 2010).

Theodor Litt, he opposed all notions that were mechanistic, objectifying, or individualistic, or that legitimated and limited the state on the basis of its purpose. For him, the entire mental world was a "dialectical structure," the meaningful interweaving of mental processes. Following the sociologist Herbert Spencer, he called this interweaving "integration." Only that which integrated itself was a "state." The means of integration could be a monarch or a leader, a founding myth, or a state symbol. This could be read as a lament about a non-integrating Weimar Republic, as a reference to Italy, as the longing for "*Volk* community," but later also as the magic word of the early Federal Republic, which had so much to integrate—former National Socialists, refugees and expellees, returning emigrants, class conflicts, religious confessions, and more. The shimmering word "integration" offered itself also as a way of resolving contradictions inherent in a constitutional text. This explains its enormous success in the first two decades of the Federal Republic. Kelsen launched a sharp attack against this book (*Der Staat als Integration* (The State as Integration) (1929)), and revealed the deliberate obscurity of Smend's pronouncements, but especially his profound aversion to neo-Kantianism, liberalism, relativism, and legal positivism. For Kelsen, Smend's book had no scholarly value, but because of its suggestive language and its obvious political inferences it was also dangerous. Kelsen's verdict was no different about Erich Kaufmann's previously mentioned *Kritik der neukantischen Rechtsphilosophie* (Critique of Neo-Kantian Legal Philosophy) (1921). In this context he spoke in 1926 of a "cry for metaphysics." And a year later, the Munich Romanist Karl Vossler noted in a speech at an event marking the founding of the empire, "always in new guises the old unreason: a metaphysical, speculative, romantic, fanatical, abstract, irrationalistic, and mystical politicizing."[11] On one side, then, traditional legal positivists, who accepted the Weimar constitutional system and who sought to consolidate the institutional framework together with the *Rechtsstaat*, now linked with the politically similar "Vienna school," though its methodological rigidity was not well received. On the other side, there was the broad front of those who considered liberalism and legal positivism just as obsolete as

[11] Karl Vossler, "Rede zur Reichsgründungsfeier, Januar 1927," in Karl Vossler, *Politik und Geistesleben* (Munich, 1927), pp. 4 f.

parliamentary democracy. Some propagated a Christian corporatist state, others a "true" democracy without parliaments; that is to say, popular assemblies with acclamation, though in most cases avoiding the model of the workers' and soldiers' councils on the Russian model. All were agreed that liberalism was finished, but what form the anti-liberal future would take was still obscure.

C. Carl Schmitt's systematic treatise *Verfassungslehre* (Constitutional Theory) (1928) was also written in opposition to Hans Kelsen. It described bourgeois parliamentarianism and the *Rechtsstaat* as the "still prevailing" form, but Schmitt made clear that these forms were obsolete and unusable. He distinguished (concretely valid) constitutional law from the "constitution" as the subject of constitutional theory, and he developed the foundations of constitutions; the *Rechtsstaat* and the basic rights; the democratic, monarchical, and aristocratic elements of modern constitutions; and the associations of states. All of this was brilliantly written, but it contained a wealth of hidden reservations about the actual state in which Schmitt was moving. After 1945, also, the book was admired and republished repeatedly by the intellectual circle around Carl Schmitt, though it was interpretively defused and "democratized." Among Italian and French communists, Spanish Franquists, and German leftists around 1968, it was an often-used reference if one was looking for alternatives to the Western model of parliamentarianism.

D. As already mentioned, Hermann Heller's (1891–1933) *Staatslehre* (Theory of State Law), published in the Netherlands in 1934, can also be seen as a reaction to Kelsen's book. Heller was a committed democrat and republican like Kelsen, but methodologically he was his staunch opponent. It was unacceptable to him that the state should only be a normative order. He devised a material doctrine of the state as the blending of politological and juristic elements in order to overcome the divisions. That is why he sought contact with social reality, though he also wanted to encompass its normative predetermination. The state, as a "total context" created by acts of the human will, should be accorded autonomy vis-à-vis politics and the economy. In this sense Heller also championed a classical notion of sovereignty—once again in opposition to Kelsen. Individuals and groups should create the state by establishing a shared level of norms and values; at the same time, however, the state, as an organized decision-making entity, should, in turn, guide societal coexistence, not least through positive law. This blending was acceptable only if one dispensed with Kelsen's methodological purity. Heller was happy to pay that price, since his chief concern was the establishment of a socially just and democratic state that would save the country from the crisis it was in. His attempt to devise a theory of state law that was appropriate to the times in this sense is probably the most important such effort during the Weimar era. Hermann Heller, whom the National Socialists drove from his professorship, died in November 1933 in Madrid during a guest lecture, at the young age of forty-two. His basic idea—democracy functions only within a relative societal homogeneity achieved through a social state—cast a long influence on the Federal Republic, indeed all the way to the Maastricht decision of the Federal Constitutional Court (applied to Europe).[12]

The chief works outlined here demonstrate just how unsettled and uncertain the situation of state law was in the final years of the Weimar Republic. The Association of German Teachers of State Law (founded in 1922) was no longer speaking a common language. In the wake of Stresemann's death (1929) and the self-paralysis of the parliamentary system, the crisis was obvious. What Kurt Sontheimer called "anti-democratic thinking" was rapidly attracting a following, especially among young intellectuals.[13] They used the war vocabulary of World War I, dreamed of a *Reich* and of "Führerdom," often without having a particularly high regard for the Hitler party. Others cultivated a national Bolshevism and visions of direct democracy. Still others devised models of an authoritarian corporatist state (Othmar Spann). There was agreement that the bourgeois age was coming to an end, and with it its state order. The bourgeois–liberal "republicans of reason" (*Vernunftrepublikaner*) and champions of legal positivism were being put on the defensive. That was the state of affairs in 1932, which saw the last attempts to save the presidential dictatorship through emergency decrees and the Reich government's coup in Prussia,[14] which could no longer be undone by the

[12] Peter Häberle, *Europäische Verfassungslehre*, 7th edn. (Baden-Baden, 2011), pp. 729 ff.

[13] Kurt Sontheimer, *Antidemokratisches Denken in der Weimarer Republik: Die politischen Ideen des deutschen Nationalismus zwischen 1918 und 1933* (Munich, 1962), study edn. (Munich, 1968).

[14] Peter Blomeyer, *Der Notstand in den letzten Jahren von Weimar* (Berlin, 1999).

decision of the *Staatsgerichtshof* (Constitutional Court). "This is where state law ends," Gerhard Anschütz had written in 1919, and had been criticized for it later.[15] But he was right. The traditional doctrine of state law, not an active participant in shaping politics, but at most a supporting interpreter, was at its wit's end in 1932 with nothing more to say.

[15] Georg Meyer and Gerhard Anschütz, *Lehrbuch des Deutschen Staatsrechts*, 7th edn. (Munich, 1919), p. 906.

11

Administrative Law in the Weimar Republic

1. CONTINUATION AND ADJUSTMENT

Administrative law responded to the upheavals of the revolution and of the new Reich Constitution of 1919 with a typical time lag, as did the administration itself. The new constitutional law of the federal states receded considerably in importance; the scholarly energies were directed at interpreting the Reich Constitution. Of importance in the states were above all the reform of the communal constitution and, between 1929 and 1933, the crisis in the finances of local government. And so, following the line of Otto Mayer and Fritz Fleiner, one could maintain continuity, expand the General Part, and incorporate the new, special administrative law into the exemplary cases. The classically concise handbook by Robert Graf Hue de Grais, reissued time and again since 1881, was simply continued on the new legal foundations (26th edn. 1930),[1] as was an outline by Conrad Bornhak (1906, 8th edn. 1925). The textbooks, for the most part, combined a General Part with reference to the Reich Constitution and took examples from the respective state administrative law of Prussia, Bavaria, and Württemberg.

2. ADMINISTRATIVE LAWS OF THE FEDERAL STATES

Prussia now had a particular wealth of literature on administrative law. It discussed the administrative reform, civil service law and

[1] Gerhard Lingelbach, *Robert Graf Hue de Grais (1835–1922): Leben und Werk* (Baden-Baden, 1997).

communal law, the emerging police law that was legally enshrined in 1931, and the decisions of Prussia's Supreme Administrative Law Court (*Oberverwaltungsgericht*) pertaining to police law—one example being Julius Hatschek's *Institutionen des deutschen und preußischen Verwaltungsrechts* (Institutions of German and Prussian Administrative Law) (1919, 8th edn. 1931). By adding in the multi-volume collection of Prussian administrative laws (the so-called *Brauchitsch*), the commentaries on individual statutes, and the ongoing overviews of judicial decisions in the *Preußisches Verwaltungsblatt* (Prussian Administrative Journal), one had all the necessary tools of the trade at hand. In Bavaria one had several outlines of administrative law and the venerable *Bayerische Verwaltungsblätter* (Bavarian Journal of Administration). In Saxony, the most important contributions were found in *Fischers Zeitschrift für Praxis und Gesetzgebung der Verwaltung* (Fischer's Journal for Administrative Practice and Laws), edited by Walter Schelcher. In Württemberg and Baden the traditionally close relationship between the theory and the practice of administrative law continued, though without producing works of any greater importance. That is even more true of Hesse-Darmstadt, Mecklenburg, and the other small states, as well as the free cities of Hamburg, Bremen, and Lübeck—which were essentially content with shorter introductions or collections of texts.

3. TEXTBOOKS

The overarching accounts by Fritz Fleiner and Julius Hatschek provided students with what they needed, Fleiner's book being especially successful.[2] But it was unavoidable that a good deal of practical material had to be left out. That is why Walter Jellinek's comprehensive *Verwaltungsrecht* (Administrative Law) (1927, 3rd edn. 1931), which combined the General and Special Part, established itself as the dominant work.

[2] Julius Hatschek, *Institutionen des deutschen und preußischen Verwaltungsrechts* (Leipzig and Erlangen, 1919), 7th/8th edn. (Leipzig, 1931); Fritz Fleiner, *Institutionen des deutschen Verwaltungsrechts*, 8th edn. (Tübingen, 1928; reprint Aalen, 1995).

Jellinek's book was an encyclopedic summation of the administrative law of the Weimar Republic. Rising from the historical foundations, it contained a modernized General Part with new differentiations (non-sovereign and simple sovereign administration, administrative act upon submission, bilateral administrative act), with a doctrine of discretion, an account of legal protection in its entirety, of public liability, administrative constraints, and administrative penalties. With its thoroughly positivistic posture and the focus on the legal form that this entailed, it was a book in the tradition of Otto Mayer. The basic liberal attitude and embrace of the rule of law was in accord with the prevailing law, but no longer with the realities and the preference for collective thinking under the presidential dictatorship.

4. GROWTH OF MATERIAL IN THE INTERVENTIONIST STATE

One of the most important developments in the years between the end of World War I and the death throes of the republic (1929–32) is evident in the expansion of material and the differentiation of fields. Otto Mayer's foundational hypothesis had been that all administrative activity could be reduced to a few basic forms, which—lying dormant within the material, as it were—could be brought to light through scholarly labor that was half-intuitive, half-constructive. That was the basis of his great success. But now developments seemed to be pushing in the opposite direction. Public economic law, social law, tax law, and transportation law appeared for the first time as separate disciplines, while communal law took on entirely new dimensions. The centrifugal tendencies in civil law (labor law, economic law with corporate law, tenant law, settlement law, and land law) were interpreted—against the backdrop of the collapse of liberal bourgeois society—as the "irruption of social law into the classic private law" (Franz Wieacker) or as the "affliction of private law" (Knut W. Nörr).[3] In like manner, administrative law, which just now seemed to have been united under the roof of a General Part, was

[3] Franz Wieacker, *Privatrechtsgeschichte der Neuzeit*, 2nd edn. (Göttingen, 1967), 547; Knut W. Nörr, *Die Leiden des Privatrechts* (Tübingen, 1994).

splitting up again. The ever more numerous decisions by the administrative courts supported this trend, especially since linking decisions back to general constitutional principles, common today, was not yet practiced during the Weimar period.

In addition to the new areas of labor law and the law of workers' insurance, as social law was still called at the time,[4] the conditions of the industrial revolution gave rise to municipal sciences with their own journals and yearbooks. Scholars discussed the "social tasks of large cities" (Franz Adickes) and the legal forms of the factual emerging collective utilities. In 1938, Ernst Forsthoff captured all of this in the memorable word *Daseinsvorsorge* (provision of public utilities and services).[5] Furthermore, the state, which was now intervening ever more extensively in society, needed money. Traditionally this money was raised through taxation, and following the establishment of the empire in 1871 and in the wake of changing constitutional stipulations, it was distributed among the Reich, the states, and the local municipalities. The science of tax law that took shape in Germany, Austria, and Italy in the last two decades of the nineteenth century arose in part out of the science of public finances, in part out of administrative law. The first lecture course on tax law was probably given—almost unnoticed—in Berlin starting in 1915 by Ludwig Waldecker, an expert on public law. Several strong impulses for a scientific treatment of tax law were provided only by the financial problems following the war; by the reform of the tax system through Reich Finance Minister Matthias Erzberger, a reform that was crucial to the Reich; and by the Reich Tax Code (*Reichsabgabenordnung*), created entirely by judge Enno Becker (1869–1940).[6] The standard textbook, *Steuerrecht* (Tax Law), was written by Albert Hensel (1895–1933), the real founder of the discipline.[7]

But the core area of interventionist guidance by the state was economic law, the public-law variant of which was soon referred to

[4] Ivana Mikešić, *Sozialrecht als wissenschaftliche Disziplin: Die Anfänge 1918–1933* (Tübingen, 2002).

[5] Ernst Forsthoff, *Die Verwaltung als Leistungsträger* (Stuttgart and Berlin, 1938).

[6] Kurt Ball, *Einführung in das Steuerrecht*, 2nd edn. (Mannheim, 1922); Ludwig Waldecker, *Deutsches Steuerrecht* (Wrocław, 1924).

[7] Paul Kirchhof, "Albert Hensel (1895 bis 1933): Ein Kämpfer für ein rechtsstaatlich geordnetes Steuerrecht," in Helmut Heinrichs, Harald Franzki, Klaus Schmalz, and Michael Stolleis, eds., *Deutsche Juristen jüdischer Herkunft* (Munich, 1993), pp. 781 ff.

as law of economic administration (*Wirtschaftsverwaltungsrecht*).[8] In 1868 Lorenz von Stein had spoken of a special area of "economic administrative law."[9] A decade later, concurrent with Bismarck turning away from liberalism in domestic politics, jurists thought more and more intensively about state interventions in private law, trusts, corporations, and cartels. The relevant material was called "industrial law" for the first time in 1913, but soon "economic law," and participants discussed—in doctrinal terms—the possibilities of making contracts flexible, the interpretation according to "interests," consumer protection, and other possibilities of social protection, for example by means of general clauses with ethical content. Along the same lines, efforts were made to systematize the toolkit of control derived from administrative law, be it in the name of the "war economy," or as part of a socialist or conservative "social economy" (*Gemeinwirtschaft*) (Wichard von Moellendorff, Walther Rathenau, Rudolf Hilferding, Fritz Naphtali). Everyone imagined a strong executive state oriented toward the common good, and everyone tended to think in anti-parliamentarian and anti-liberal terms.

It was therefore no coincidence that Ernst Rudolf Huber (1903–90), operating with the ideas of the "conservative revolution" in the Hegelian style of thinking,[10] produced a first synthetic account of economic administrative law. His *Wirtschaftsverwaltungsrecht* (Law of Economic Administration) (1932) preserved its basic structure beyond National Socialism into the Federal Republic. That was possible also because it had traits similar to the "Ordoliberalism" that was emerging at the same time. The element that united all of these theoretical blueprints was the conviction that a liberalism guided only by the market was an outdated phenomenon of the nineteenth century. The only thing that was appropriate to the twentieth century, given the experiences of the world war, an economy of scarcity, and the inflation of 1923, was a tamed liberalism overseen by the state. National Socialism merely had to give this notion an authoritarian twist. And thus it was also Ernst Rudolf Huber who attempted, in

[8] Clemens Zacher, *Die Entstehung des Wirtschaftsrechts in Deutschland* (Berlin, 2002).

[9] Lorenz von Stein, *Die Verwaltungslehre, 7. Theil: Innere Verwaltungslehre, 3. Hauptgebiet* (Stuttgart, 1868), p. 15.

[10] Ralf Walkenhaus, *Konservatives Staatsdenken: Eine wissenssoziologische Studie zu Ernst Rudolf Huber* (Berlin, 1997).

1934, to sketch *Die Gestalt des deutschen Sozialismus* (The Form of German Socialism).

Administrative law did not experience, during those years, a quarrel over method and direction as in state-law theory, at least not explicitly. Most experts on administrative law were less inclined toward methodological reflections, especially since the share of practitioners who published in the field was higher than in state law. But those tensions did exist below the surface. For example, a comparison of Walter Jellinek's detailed account (1927) with Adolf Merkl's *Allgemeines Verwaltungsrecht* (General Administrative Law) (1927) offers prominent examples of traditional positivism, on the one hand, and of strict positivism (guided by theoretical reflections about the field) of the Vienna school, on the other hand. By contrast, Ernst Rudolf Huber's contributions describe an anti-positivist variant employing Hegelian vocabulary, though until 1933 it did not influence a tone that was on the whole sober and praxis-focused until 1933.

12

The National Socialist State and Its Public Law

1. THE HANDOVER OF POWER

The handover of power to the radical agitator Adolf Hitler by Reich President Hindenburg unfolded along the lines that had already become customary under chancellors Brüning, von Papen, and von Schleicher. But what was set in motion was a revolution in an atmosphere characterized by a mixture of elation and fearful reticence. The smashing of the parties was followed by the abrogation of parliamentarianism, federalism, and the duality of presidency and chancellorship, and by the dissolution of all important societal associations in favor of organizations overseen by the party—all in all, then, the transformation of parliamentary democracy into a "Führer state" without a constitution. All of this happened in about twenty-four months, without any real resistance taking shape.

The regime could take the reins so quickly because the bourgeois elites in the administration, the judicial system, and the military were willing to cooperate. They welcomed the end of the Weimar "party state" and of parliamentarianism, they cheered the end of the unions, the silencing of communists and social democrats, the expulsion of the Jews (especially Jewish lawyers and doctors), the job-creation measures, and a foreign policy focused on undoing the trauma of "Versailles." Hitler's bloody neutralizing of the SA, the party's own military wing, during the murderous action in June 1934 was registered with relief by the *Reichswehr*. Anyone who was not willing to cooperate left the country or suffered the terror of the first concentration camps. Those who were not caught up in the repressive dragnet sought to go underground and wait things out, or they fled into exile.

2. THE INTELLECTUAL DECAPITATION

In a very short period of time, German universities and intellectual life as a whole thus lost a great many internationally recognized scientists, scholars, writers, and artists. This was an "intellectual decapitation."[1] The book burnings were merely a prelude. There followed disenfranchisements and dismissals, humiliations, and the loss of personal wealth. Things were radicalized with the November pogrom of 1938, and it all ended in the Holocaust, the crime against humanity that began during the war and became increasingly systematized and bureaucratized. In spite of intensive scholarship and analysis, the Holocaust remains in the final analysis incomprehensible, the full depth of its dimensions—which have also shaped the present—unfathomable and unplumbed.[2]

Not only did public law lose its real subject under National Socialism, namely a reliable constitutional order open to scholarly interpretation. Also the field of public law itself was severely decimated. Prominent scholars were dismissed from their posts and for the most part driven from the country, largely for "racial" reasons. The experts on state law, administrative law, and international law who suffered this fate included Hans Kelsen, Erich Kaufmann, Hermann Heller, Albert Hensel, Ernst Isay, Karl Loewenstein, Franz Neumann, Otto Kirchheimer, Max Fleischmann, Ernst Fraenkel, Albrecht Mendelssohn Bartholdy and Magdalene Schoch who had habilitated under him, Karl Strupp, Gerhard Leibholz, Gerhard Lassar, Kurt Perels, Fritz Morstein Marx, Walter Jellinek, Erwin Jacobi, Hans Nawiasky, Ludwig Waldecker, Walther Schücking, and Willibalt Apelt, among others—a list that provides an inkling of what was destroyed. Because constitutional and administrative law was so

[1] Helge Pross, "Die geistige Enthauptung Deutschlands: Verluste durch Emigration," in Wolfgang Abendroth, ed., *Nationalsozialismus und die deutsche Universität* (New York and Berlin, 1966), pp. 143–55.

[2] Michael Stolleis, "Das Unverstehbare verstehen: Der Holocaust und die Rechtsgeschichte," in *Politisches Denken: Jahrbuch* (Berlin, 2011), 143–56.

specific to conditions in Germany, experts in these fields who had fled abroad had far fewer career opportunities than colleagues specializing in comparative law, international private law, or ancient legal history. Hans Kelsen, whose legal theory and works on international law were independent of national law, was an exception in this regard.

The number of students dropped in the wake of the economic crisis and under National Socialism from about 100,000 to about 37,000 (1941). In the summer semester of 1938, only forty-two women were studying law—compared to 1,175 in the summer semester of 1930, a vanishingly small number. The faculties shrank accordingly, and in some places public law came to a virtual standstill. The large faculties (Berlin, Leipzig, Munich, Vienna) changed their character and lost their profile; smaller faculties were to be given a pronounced National Socialist focus as "shock troops" (Kiel, Wrocław, Königsberg, Poznań, Strasbourg), though that goal was never really achieved because of a lack of "militant" National Socialists and because of the war. Other faculties faced the threat of closure (Halle, Frankfurt am Main) or made do with workarounds. Although a united front of opposition by the faculties did not materialize, it is certainly not the case that all yielded uniformly to the new spirit. It is not possible to accuse the faculties across the board of "failure" if one is willing to look more closely at individuals and substantive issues. Thus one can identify only four general groups: (1) those professors who emigrated between 1933 and 1938 and those who received emeritus status around 1933 or retired voluntarily; (2) the committed (mostly young) defenders of the system, closely allied, however, with a broader, middle group (3), most of whom were German-national in their thinking and initially welcomed the regime, but then gradually broke with it or fell silent; and finally a smaller group (4) that was firmly opposed to the regime (among the experts on public law, only Hans Peters and Christian-Friedrich Menger were part of the resistance or very closely associated with it).

What these university teachers published after 1933 as a whole was exceedingly heterogeneous. Some began with enthusiastic pronouncements or "fantasy pieces," but then turned to administrative law or topics that were as apolitical as possible. Between 1933 and 1936, Carl Schmitt wrote one article after another under immense pressure, lost his positions in 1936, and shifted his interests to international law. Others tried to supply the new market with textbooks (Theodor Maunz, Otto Koellreutter, Arnold Köttgen, Ernst

Rudolf Huber); still others took refuge in constitutional history or fell completely silent. Publishing activity picked up again during the war, the result of an ominous *Gemeinschaftswerk der deutschen Geisteswissenschaften* (Joint Work of the German Humanities) organized by Paul Ritterbusch (1900–45), a radical National Socialist expert on international law in Kiel. Its goal was to demonstrate the productivity of the German humanities following the hoped-for "final victory." Jurists of public law who participated included Ernst Rudolf Huber, Hermann Jahrreiß, Theodor Maunz, Ulrich Scheuner, Walter Hamel, Alexander von Freytagh-Loringhoven, Helfried Pfeifer, and Gerhard Wacke.[3]

The scholarly balance sheet of research on and the teaching of public law under National Socialism is exceedingly poor. A frenzy and extreme politicization pervaded all material. After the collapse of the regime, hardly any of it was still usable—not only because of the compromising quotes or the identification of Jewish authors in the bibliographies, but because it was almost entirely dependent on the times and the prevailing ideology. The anti-Semitic, imperialistic, or even merely turgid rants about "community" or the "Reich" simply collapsed in 1945 and heavily incriminated their authors even decades later. The destructive energies unleashed by the Nazi state also dragged this literature into the abyss.

3. JOURNALS

The legal journals, already strongly reduced during the economic crisis after 1929, now came under political pressure. While there were still 155 in 1933, by 1937 that number had dropped to only ninety-one. Many had folded or were merged with others under new names. All Jewish editors and authors disappeared. Carl Schmitt was put in charge of the venerable *Deutsche Juristenzeitung* (German Jurist's Paper) (DJZ) in 1934, but he was removed again in 1936. The DJZ—or its subscriber base—was then taken over by the *Zeitschrift der Akademie für Deutsches Recht* (Journal of the Academy of German Law) (ZAkDR), which was supposed to be the showcase of the regime

[3] Frank-Rutger Hausmann *"Deutsche Geisteswissenschaft" im Zweiten Weltkrieg: Die "Aktion Ritterbusch" (1940–1945)* (Dresden, 1998).

on legal policy. The journal *Deutsche Rechtswissenschaft* (German Legal Science), which existed from 1935 to 1942, also passed into the hands of Academy president Hans Frank. Completely controlled by the SS was the journal *Reich-Volksordnung-Lebensraum* (Reich–National Order–Living Space) (1941–3); it was a platform for advance planning for the countries to be conquered, for racial policy, and for positional infighting among SS jurists.

The *Archiv für öffentliches Recht* (Archiv for Public Law), in existence since 1885, dropped its Jewish editors and added new ones; but it slowly decayed, a seismographic reflection, as it were, of the state of the field.[4] Beginning in 1934 under Ernst Rudolf Huber, the *Zeitschrift für die gesamte Staatswissenschaft* (Journal for State Science), created by Robert von Mohl in 1844, brought together a long list of authors loyal to the regime, with the goal of renewing the old idea of a "unity of the sciences of the state," but this time under the banner of the ethnic (*völkisch*) Führer state. The equally venerable *Jahrbuch des öffentlichen Rechts* (Yearbook of Public Law) continued until 1938 under the leadership of Otto Koellreutter.

Parallel processes were evident among the journals of administrative law. The old *Reichs- und Preußisches Verwaltungsblatt* (Administrative Journal of the Reich and Prussia), which appeared weekly, remained outwardly the same until 1943, but it turned into the semi-official informational organ of the Reich government and the most important place to observe the declining judicature of the administrative courts. At the *Verwaltungsarchiv* (Administrative Archive), too, the existing editors were pushed out: Koellreutter took the helm and followed an etatistic line, which was also laid down by Reich interior minister Frick. There was also the newly created militant publication of the NS-Rechtswahrerbund (National Socialist Lawyers Association), *Deutsche Verwaltung* (German Administration). The party bigwigs published here alongside practitioners. In 1938, this journal swallowed up three others and tried to become the leading publication in the field. If we also include the journals of the administrative law of the *Länder*, which were in any case superfluous in a unitary state, which were disappearing rapidly, and which ceased publishing at the latest in 1941 due to a "paper

[4] Lothar Becker, *"Schritte auf einer abschüssigen Bahn": Das Archiv des öffentlichen Rechts (AöR) und die deutsche Staatsrechtswissenschaft im Dritten Reich* (Tübingen, 1999).

shortage," one gets the sense of a ruinous destruction of what was once a rich diversity of opinions. Not only had federalism vanished, but also a diversity of opinions was no longer "needed," and the number of decisions by administrative courts calling for commentary dropped to almost nothing during the war.

4. EMERGENCY CONSTRUCTION OF A "CONSTITUTION"

The external situation of the discipline—expulsion of Jewish and politically undesirable scholars, the decay of the universities, censorship, and a shrinking number of journals—also reflected internal conditions. The Reichstag Fire Decree of February 28, 1933 suspended the most important basic rights, parliamentarianism ceased with the Enabling Act, parties disappeared, federalism was eliminated, and after Hindenburg's death (1934) the dual leadership at the top of Reich president and chancellor also ceased to exist. Now there was only the Führer. The Weimar Constitution existed merely as an empty shell; at best the formally repeated and meaningless authorization of power by the Enabling Act (1937, 1939, 1943) was a reminder of the starting point in 1933. While there was much talk of an "emerging constitution" and "basic laws,"[5] and the advantages of the flexibility of an unwritten constitution were praised, in reality the theory of state law stood before a Nothing draped in pomposity and bombast. Hitler dreamed of a great Germanic empire and an architecture to match, of territories to be conquered, of a master race, and nations of slaves. He cared nothing for constitutional questions, legal fixation, procedures, *Rechtsstaat*, and basic rights.

In this situation, the publications of state law theory that continued mechanically no longer had a fixed core. Every statement stood under the proviso that everything could change the next day. Bold pronouncements were avoided, as they could have unanticipated consequences (also personally). That is why authors who supported the regime expressed themselves enthusiastically and vaguely in the

[5] Ernst Rudolf Huber, *Verfassungsrecht des Großdeutschen Reiches* (Hamburg, 1939), pp. 54–7.

first two years (1933–4), after which time they slowly became more cautious. To be sure, the first outlines for the needs of students were written. The new Code of Legal Training (*Justizausbildungsordnung*) of 1934, enacted by the Reichsjustiz-Prüfungsamt under the leadership of Otto Palandt (1877–1951), demanded as much.[6] The "Schönfelder" and "Sartorius" statute collection books now appeared for the first time in a loose-leaf format, because the enactment of laws without a parliament was going at full speed. But these outlines offered only the framework that was relevant for examinations. In terms of textbooks there was initially only *Deutsches Verfassungsrecht* (German Constitutional Law) (2nd edn. 1936) by Otto Koellreutter, who directed the most important journals from Munich (*Archiv des öffentlichen Rechts, Reichsverwaltungsblatt, Verwaltungs-Archiv*) and saw himself as the leading figure of German state law. He also wrote a *Allgemeine Staatslehre* (General Theory of the State) and a *Deutsches Verwaltungsrecht* (German Administrative Law). All three works were republished in the early Federal Republic,[7] in revised form, needless to say.

The only noteworthy book on National Socialist state law came from the pen of Ernst Rudolf Huber. It was published under the title *Verfassung* (Constitution) (1937) and in the second edition as *Verfassungsrecht des Großdeutschen Reiches* (Constitutional Law of the Greater German Reich) (1939). In a strongly harmonized form it offered a synthesis of what one could make of the fragments of state law if one was determined to discover the "totality" in them.

Huber described the structure of the *völkische* constitution up to the outbreak of the war, and organized the material into "*Volk*," "Führer," "The Movement," "The Structure of the Reich," and "The Legal Status of the *Volk* Comrade." All in all, the book showed the façade of the regime, written by an idealist and Hegelian who had come to National Socialism out of the youth movement and who had already demonstrated his linguistic and organizational abilities in his extensive *Wirtschaftsverwaltungsrecht* (Law of Economic Administration), and would do so again, especially in the eight-volume *Deutsche*

[6] Hans Wrobel, "Otto Palandt zum Gedächtnis 1.5.1877 bis 3.12.1951," *Kritische Justiz* (1982, no. 1), 1 ff.

[7] Otto Koellreutter, *Deutsches Staatsrecht* (Stuttgart and Cologne, 1953); Otto Koellreutter, *Staatslehre im Umriß* (Göttingen, 1955); Otto Koellreutter, *Grundfragen des Verwaltungsrechts* (Cologne and Berlin, 1955).

Verfassungsgeschichte (German Constitutional History) he wrote after the war.

5. THEMATIC FOCAL POINTS

Above the level of the basic outlines and textbooks, the debate over state law was concerned with a few thematic focal points, but these also lost importance very quickly. For example, initially there was disagreement over whether one could and should still describe the state as a "legal person" in the traditional way, or whether "community" (*Gemeinschaft*) might be the appropriate term. Behind the scences of this debate was a struggle between state and party, stable structure and dynamism, the forces resistant to change and the SS, the latter represented, for example, by Reinhard Höhn. Of course his tireless plea for a new "community" had no effect, since for all jurists who thought in practical terms the state seemed indispensable as a personal point of attribution, whether as a tax authority, as the responsible agent for administrative acts, or in international law.

Characteristic of the uncertain situation was also the debate carried on in the beginning about whether the new state was still a *Rechtsstaat* (in the manner of the nineteenth century). The activists of the NSDAP wanted to get rid of the term, because they feared its potential for criticism in the face of the emerging terror and the first concentration camps. Carl Schmitt declared that *Rechtsstaat* meant the destruction of political substance and that in the nineteenth century it had been the trailblazer for liberal democracy, Judaism, and Marxism. The formula *nationaler Rechtsstaat* (Koellreutter) or "national socialist *Rechtsstaat*" were also no real solution, which is why Schmitt proposed "the German *Rechtsstaat* of Adolf Hitler." This debate thus ended in a grotesquerie and was soon abandoned.

One relevant point of discussion was the diagnosis (certainly apt in terms of legal history) that the classic opposition of private law and public law had now been "abolished" (*aufgehoben*), whatever this mysterious Hegelian word meant. In fact, the sharpest distinction had been drawn in the nineteenth century between the law of civic society (private law, civil law) and public law (constitutional and administrative law). For the former sphere the contract was the typical legal construct, for the other the sovereign command, the administrative act. This separation arose from the political situation of the nineteenth century, when a society conscious of liberty was separating itself from the monarchical authoritarian state. But the more the state—beginning in 1878—intervened in societal processes, for example through social insurance, labor law, corporate law, and finance law; the more the state engaged in the promotion of industry; and the more lobbying groups of employers and workers, parties, churches, and big industry became involved in legislating, the more questionable the separation of private law and public law became. The outbreak of World War I gave rise to a "common law" (*Gemeinrecht*) that jumped over all existing lines of separation. And it did not disappear with the conclusion of the war, because one wished to keep the private economy, yet wanted to integrate it into the crisis management through restrictions, incentives, subsidies, or mixed businesses.

However, National Socialist jurists refashioned this situation to conclude that the boundaries between state and society had been overcome in the Führer state and in the racial community, which is why basic rights and legal protection "against" the state were superfluous, since the will of the guided community was identical with the true will of the people. Private autonomy existed only in a form that was constrained by the common good. All law was supposedly communal law, which arose from the will of the Führer and was legitimated by him. These theses were fighting words directed against the vision of the state of parliamentary democracy, against the separation of powers and the *Rechtsstaat*.

6. INTERNATIONAL LAW

Where the state had become a dictatorship in both practice and theory, foreign relations also took on a different appearance. Initially, the theory of international law at the universities, at the two institutes of international law (Berlin, Kiel), and in the Foreign Office was dominated by the "fight against Versailles," by an ending of the occupation of the Rhineland and the Saar question, by the naval agreement with Great Britain, and by the Reich Concordat with the Holy See. In this spirit, the emphasis was—following the doctrine under the Weimar Republic—on a nation's right to existence, the dignity of the state, the equality of states, the principle of non-interference, and the protection of national minorities abroad, the latter occasionally already with a menacing undertone. But this did not rise to the level of a genuine "National Socialist" theory of international law.

Only after the Nuremberg racial laws in 1935 one can observe a turning away from the "state" and toward the *Volk* in international law also. Soon thereafter, the idea of "Reich" in the sense of a hegemonic claim to leadership over other states and people also made itself felt.[8] These were essentially old ideas, but they were now given a racist twist for the first time. The creation of empires, one could read, was based on racial struggles: superior races dominated the "space" and gave the peoples they conquered "their" international law.

This amounted to a renunciation of the fundamental notion behind all international law, that of universality. Friedrich Berber, adviser to Foreign Minister Joachim von Ribbentrop, declared in 1939, in a Festschrift for Hitler, that international law should no longer be a "playground of internationalist and pacifist ideologies"; Western European and Anglo-Saxon international law should be unmasked, and German international law should "supply weapons of international law to German foreign policy in its struggle for the freedom and greatness of the German people."[9] The staunch champions of a racially interpreted international law (Höhn, Best, Lemmel) were clear opponents of the League of Nations and of universal norms—both supposedly inventions of international Judaism to weaken the Aryan race, which was capable of creating an empire. Carl Schmitt, in his growing turn toward international law after 1936, also polemicized repeatedly against liberal, universal, or pacifist lines of thinking.[10] In April 1939 he lectured in Kiel about "*Großraumordnung* under International Law with a Prohibition against Intervention for Powers outside the Sphere: A Contribution

[8] For observations made by contemporaries, see, for example, Lawrence Preuß, "National Socialist Conceptions of International Law," *American Political Science Review* 19 (1935), 504–609; Eduard Bristler (= John H. Herz), *Die Völkerrechtslehre im Nationalsozialismus* (Zurich, 1938); Victoria L. Gott, "The National Socialist Theory of International Law," *American Journal of International Law* 32 (1938), 704–18.

[9] Friedrich Berber, "Deutsche Völkerrechtswissenschaft," in *Deutsche Wissenschaft, Arbeit und Aufgabe* (Leipzig, 1939), pp. 62 f.

[10] Carl Schmitt, *Frieden oder Pazifismus? Arbeiten zum Völkerrecht und zur internationalen Politik 1924–1978*, edited with a foreword and notes by G. Maschke (Berlin, 2005).

to the Concept of the Reich in International Law."[11] Once it had been printed, the lecture attracted immediate attention abroad, where it was understood as a kind of German Monroe Doctrine of non-intervention. Domestically, there was a debate that was implicitly also a debate about war aims.[12]

Of course, not all international jurists followed the racist line of the SS. Even Carl Schmitt continued to bank on "states" in international law, as did Gustav Adolf Walz, whom he influenced.[13] Especially in the Foreign Office, at the Kaiser Wilhelm Institute for Foreign Public Law and International Law (Berlin), and within the high command of the Wehrmacht with its specialists on the international law of war, efforts were made to maintain the traditional focus, for the sake of the foreign contacts alone. But even these places certainly did not close themselves off to the new tones. Whether or not that was camouflage remains an open question.

7. ADMINISTRATIVE LAW AND ADMINISTRATIVE THEORY

In administrative law the relevant consequences were drawn from these premises. A seamless continuation and cultivation of the science of administrative law seemed hardly conceivable. In the new curriculum, the course on "administrative law" was replaced with "administration." One could interpret this (correctly) as a devaluation of the law and a negation of its intrinsic value, but also (in a more hopeful vein) as a chance to incorporate administrative reality and an invitation to revive the nearly buried tradition of administrative theory. Initially, the battle cries dominated: fight against formalism, rightfulness instead of adherence to laws, fight against subjective-public law, pre-eminence of the community over the individual ("common good

[11] Carl Schmitt, *Völkerrechtliche Großraumordnung mit Interventionsverbot für raumfremde Mächte: Ein Beitrag zum Reichsbegriff im Völkerrecht* (Berlin and Vienna, 1939), 4th edn. (Berlin and Vienna, 1941).

[12] Mathias Schmoeckel, *Die Großraumtheorie: Ein Beitrag zur Geschichte der Völkerrechtswissenschaft im Dritten Reich, insbesondere der Kriegszeit* (Berlin, 1994).

[13] Gustav Adolf Walz, *Völkerrechtsordnung und Nationalsozialismus: Untersuchung en zur Erneuerung des Völkerrechts* (Munich, 1942).

before individual good"), responsibility from the bottom up, leadership from the top down.

Unlike the disintegrating state law, however, administrative law proved tenacious and so strongly tied to practice that it could not be so readily shunted aside. The first two years (1933–4) saw a cacophony of voices, in which quickly written lectures and brochures set the tone. Ernst Forsthoff wrote *Der totale Staat* (The Total State) (1933); Ernst Rudolf Huber, *Die Gestalt des deutschen Sozialismus* (The Shape of German Socialism) (1934); Werner Sombart, *Deutscher Sozialismus* (German Socialism) (1934); Theodor Maunz, *Neue Grundlagen des Verwaltungsrechts* (New Foundations of Administrative Law) (1934); Otto Koellreutter, *Vom Sinn und Wesen der nationalen Revolution* (The Meaning and Nature of the National Revolution) (1933). The discussion then settled down in the years between 1935 and 1938, and groups began to take shape. Forsthoff repeatedly declared that the constitutional question was "finished," and he went on to say, "The most urgent tasks of the science of public law lie today in the area of the administration. The constitutional construction of the National Socialist state has been generally completed. The constitution determined by the Führerdom does not pose any problems of interpretation for science."[14] In plain language this meant: the Führer state needs no science, at least when it comes to state law.

The experts on public law who wished to be involved thus had to devote themselves to administration, they had to develop legal concepts suitable to the new authoritarian style of leadership, and they had to once again seek contact with administrative reality, which the administrative law of liberalism had supposedly lost. Picking up these catchwords and bidding farewell to the principles that were hitherto valid, or filling them with new content, offered ambitious university teachers the opportunity to occupy the new terrain. Otto Koellreutter (1883–1972) and Theodor Maunz (1901–93) presented new textbooks,[15] both with the intent of translating these slogans into administrative law suitable for teaching and for the coming generation of National Socialist *Rechtswahrer* (Preservers of the Law).

[14] Ernst Forsthoff, "Von den Aufgaben der Verwaltungsrechtswissenschaft," *Deutsches Recht* 1 (1935), 398–400, 398; see also his text "Das neue Gesicht der Verwaltung und die Verwaltungsrechtswissenschaft," ibid., 331–3.

[15] Otto Koellreutter, *Deutsches Verwaltungsrecht* (Berlin, 1936); Th. Maunz, *Verwaltung* (Hamburg, 1937).

Maunz, associate professor in 1935 and full professor in Freiburg in 1937, also wrote the programmatic article "Administrative Law of the National Socialist State" in the semi-official handbook *Deutsches Verwaltungsrecht* (German Administrative Law) published by State Minister Hans Frank, who, as an early legal adviser to Hitler and an "old fighter," was entertaining hopes of becoming minister of justice.[16] Maunz, who had habilitated under the now emigrated Hans Nawiasky, also delivered a lecture titled "The Jews and the Science of Administrative Law" in 1936 at the invitation of Carl Schmitt.[17]

In retrospect, the textbooks published under National Socialism can be organized into several groups. First there were books by older authors that retained their imprint from the imperial period and the Weimar Republic and at most incorporated a few "topical" formulas.[18] Others, by way of compromise, wanted to preserve the traditional stock and at the same time set out in search of a new line. That was the goal, for example, of the thoughtful book by Arnold Köttgen, which tried—turning away from Otto Mayer—to structure administrative law no longer according to legal forms, but according to administrative purposes.[19] But the lead was taken by books written clearly in the National Socialist spirit (Koellreutter, Maunz) and the countless refreshers and basic outlines, which were worthless in terms of scholarship, but which must not be underestimated because of their considerable influence on students.

If one surveys the publications on administrative law at that time, both the books that became increasingly rare and the articles in the *Reichsverwaltungsblatt* (Reich Journal of Administration), in the *Verwaltungsarchiv* (Administrative Archive), in the *Archiv des öffentlichen Rechts* (Archive of Public Law), and in the journals of administrative law dealing with the law of the *Länder*, one can note first of all that the bulk of what was produced was not substantially different in tone from earlier times. Administrative law was not only an ideological

[16] Hans Frank, ed., *Deutsches Verwaltungsrecht* (Munich, 1937); Maunz's article "Administrative Law in the National Socialist State," in ibid., pp. 27–48.

[17] The lecture appears to have been lost. That it was delivered is attested by the report in *DJZ* (1936), col. 1230.

[18] Ludwig von Köhler, *Grundlehren des Deutschen Verwaltungsrechts* (Stuttgart and Berlin, 1935); Wilhelm Laforet, *Deutsches Verwaltungsrecht* (Munich, 1937).

[19] Arnold Köttgen, *Deutsche Verwaltung* (Berlin, 1935), 2nd edn. (Berlin, 1937), 3rd edn. (Berlin, 1944); Bodo Dennewitz, *Verwaltung und Verwaltungsrecht* (Vienna, 1944).

battleground, but also a place of refuge for objective contributions, of the kind that was no longer possible in state law. Here one could still write in a more or less neutral fashion about issues of communal and tax law, questions of building and planning law, expropriation law or trade law. To be sure, "breach points" existed everywhere, as with the question of the freedom to build or freedom to trade, now strictly subordinated to the "common good" in the sense of the NSDAP, with the NSDAP's right to intervene in communal law, with the political questions of civil servant law, or with the evaluation of "common utility" in tax law. Yet the wealth of detail and the expertise in works on administrative law did offer some protection until 1939. All authors knew full well that they had to use a minimum of Nazi vocabulary and carefully refrain from any direct criticism of the regime.

One of the most frequently used phrases in the fight against the "liberalistic" administrative law of the past was the claim that it had been "out of touch with real life," that it had lost contact with administrative reality and had missed real human needs. Since the last third of the nineteenth century, this charge had also been leveled against the traditional doctrine of civil law. In administrative law the call was now for the incorporation of empirical knowledge, a loosening of the doctrine, the inclusion of "life," which meant, concretely, taking into account the demands of the NSDAP at all levels of the administration.

This focus on the "working administration" in the sense of Lorenz von Stein aroused great hopes of a revival of administrative theory, which had all but vanished in the last third of the nineteenth century. It had been marginalized by the definitive victory of the "juristic method" courtesy of Otto Mayer. It was hardly taught during the Weimar era. The first sign of a change was the short essay by Walter Norden, "What Is the Science of Administration and to What End Does One Study It?" (1933). Its author, forced to emigrate that same year, imagined a discipline similar to "public administration" in Britain and the US. Norden had no success, especially since his text was no longer cited after his emigration. But National Socialist authors picked up the idea.[20] They met with greater resonance, because all declared "positivism" to be the enemy, called for the incorporation of the reality of life, and wanted to implement this in the curriculum.

[20] Otto Koellreutter, "Die Bedeutung der Verwaltungslehre im neuen Staat," *Reichs- und Preußisches Verwaltungsblatt* (1933), 741–3; Theodor Maunz, "Neues Rechtsdenken in der Verwaltung," *Deutsche Verwaltung* (1935), 65 ff.; Franz W. Jerusalem, "Das

But their efforts bore no fruit, especially since the faculties had difficulties providing the basic training.

Yet the efforts by the party's offices went further. Membership was sought in the International Institute for Administrative Sciences in Brussels, a congress in Berlin was even envisaged for September 1939 (it was canceled because of the outbreak of the war), and as late as 1942 an International Academy for State and Administrative Sciences (Internationale Akademie für Staats- und Verwaltungswissenschaften) was created in Berlin.[21] Authors like Hans Peters and Gerhard Wacke (1902–76) also continued to work on books about administrative theory, though these could not be published. When another debate about a reform of the legal curriculum began in 1941, there were considerations to remove administrative training from legal training. The backdrop to these plans was the expected demand for administrative experts in the territories in Eastern Europe that would be conquered. General uncertainty thus prevailed, and the pendulum swung back. There was a lack of foundations in terms of political sciences and sociology; no canon of knowledge that could be transmitted had taken shape. Alongside the administration of the Reich, administration itself had fragmented into many rival special administrations and into the inaccessible imperium of the SS. What had emerged was a "polycracy" that was promoted in part deliberately by Hitler, in part by a general aversion to "order." In the new curriculum of 1943 one returned to the state of affairs from before 1934; the "Administration" course had disappeared once again.

8. *DASEINSVORSORGE* AND A BALANCE SHEET

A balance sheet of those years will unquestionably be negative, from whatever perspective one chooses to look at it. To be sure, the science of administrative law was not involved in the crimes of the regime as

Verwaltungsrecht und der neue Staat," in Rechts- und Wirtschaftswissenschaftliche Fakultät der Universität Jena (ed.), *Festschrift für Rudolf Hübner* (Jena, 1935), pp. 124 ff.; Edgar Tatarin-Tarnheyden, "Grundlagen des Verwaltungsrechts im neuen Staat," *AöR* 63 (1934), 345 ff.

[21] On this, see Hans-Christian Jasch, "Die Gründung der Internationalen Akademie für Verwaltungswissenschaften im Jahr 1942 in Berlin," *DÖV* (2005), 709–21.

directly as anthropology and eugenics or war studies at the universities and Kaiser Wilhelm institutes, which pursued the regime's goals in very concrete terms. But like other branches of the legal sciences, the discipline of administrative law was in a deeper sense part of the system; it supported the functioning of the administration in theory and practice, it created the semblance of the normality of an administration that operated according to the law and was controllable, and in this way it solidified the temporary pact between the Nazi state and the world of civic values.

At the same time, the constant criticism of liberalism opened the door to views about the role of administration in a state that was in fact no longer comparable to that of the nineteenth century. The Nazi state blurred all boundaries between state and society. The political goals it asserted were absolutely dominant. The individual had long ceased to be autonomous, but was dependent on the services of the state. Ernst Forsthoff, following the older line from Hegel to Lorenz von Stein, but prompted at the time by Karl Jaspers, called this *Daseinsvorsorge* (provision of the necessities of life).[22] The science of public law, he declared, should address not only administrative law, but the "working administration" in the sense of Lorenz von Stein.[23] In line with this he emphasized that modern life was characterized by the contrast between the technical possibilities of mobility and the mastery of space, as well as the simultaneous physical dependence on state services (electricity, gas, water). The administration worked in large part as an administration of public services. Citizens had to "share" in these services in order to survive: this was the Achilles heel, so to speak, of modern life. This dimension of administration related to the service-providing state became an important theme in the early Federal Republic, not least through the textbook that Forsthoff began to write already during the war.[24]

And so there was a mix of normality and terror, of deeper insights and the trite power struggles between "normal" administration,

[22] Ernst Forsthoff, *Die Verwaltung als Leistungsträger* (Stuttgart and Berlin, 1938). On this, see the fundamental work by Florian Meinel, *Der Jurist in der industriellen Gesellschaft: Ernst Forsthoff und seine Zeit* (Berlin, 2011), pp. 154 ff.

[23] Ernst Rudolf Huber, "Vorsorge für das Dasein: Ein Grundbegriff der Staatslehre Hegels und Lorenz von Steins," in Roman Schnur (ed.), *Festschrift für Ernst Forsthoff* (1972), pp. 139–63.

[24] Ernst Forsthoff, *Lehrbuch des Verwaltungsrechts, Erster Band: Allgemeiner Teil* (Munich and Berlin, 1950).

rearmament, and the "Four-Year Plan," as well as between the SS and Hitler's numerous special representatives, especially during the war. But the frequent separation between "normal" administration, the necessities of war, and the Holocaust is moot—at least if it is done with apologetic intent. Within the context of the criminality of the state, even the administrative official who behaved absolutely correctly according to the traditional rules took on a different function. His continuation in positions of responsibility created confidence and imparted a formal legitimacy to the central core of the system, which was free of any constraints. Even more problematic is the role of the administrative thinkers of the system. They were civil service criminals behind a desk, even if they had no power of command. All of the following—the dismissal of basic rights, which were now ironized as the expression of bourgeois mistrust against the state; the "struggle against subjective-public law"; the justification of oppression by the "goal"; the weakening of the bond that tied administrative actions to the law through the vague invocation of the "right of the *Volk* community"; the "overcoming" of the separation of powers; the planning for the administration of conquered territories; the intellectual preparation for the dismantling of administrative jurisdiction, for example through the exclusion of "political" cases or by solidifying the category of "sovereign acts not subject to judicial review"—all were active forms of conduct that established and disseminated these things in manifold ways in both words and text for which individuals are answerable. To that extent, the science of administrative law today has every reason to ask itself the critical question in which areas we find the soft spots of adaptation to the prevailing interests of the powers that be, and at the same time to convert these insights productively into principles of behavior: what does a free and democratic society operating in accordance with the rule of law want—and what does it not want?

13

Germany's Legal Status, Reconstruction, Two States

1. ZERO HOUR?

For all those on the Continent and in Britain affected by World War II, the situation in 1945 was catastrophic. The Germans experienced the collapse of the Nazi state, their land was under military occupation, and there was staggering material hardship. They knew or at least suspected that an enormous crime against humanity had been committed in the "Destruction of the European Jews" (Raul Hilberg) and of other groups of victims. The full dimensions became clearer only gradually in the course of subsequent decades. In retrospect one can see how deeply this "rupture of civilization" (Dan Diner) has engraved itself into the founding story of the two German states that now arose, as well as into that of the new state of Israel.

The much-quoted "zero hour" of 1945 was manifested initially in the acts of surrender, in the "Berlin Declaration," and in the documents of the Potsdam Conference (July 17–August 2, 1945).[1] They formed the starting point for the question about "Germany's legal status" that was now discussed. Incidentally, there were more continuities than ruptures in society, the administration, and the state, which means that the metaphor of the "zero hour" applies only to a very limited extent. Where it is intended to conceal continuities, it is entirely inappropriate. But it is applicable for the new beginning that was seriously undertaken by many intellectual leaders. In other words, what was liberation to some was a shock for others; what was

[1] Ingo von Münch, ed., *Dokumente des geteilten Deutschland*, vol. 1 (Stuttgart, 1968).

for many the loss of home and job was for others an occasion to blend in and keep quiet.

Following an initial phase with an emergency administration, the revival of local administrations, the emergence of *Länder* with their own constitutions,[2] and their merger in the west (Bizone, Trizone), the fundamental separation of the western zones from the Soviet Occupation Zone became clear. It seemed inevitable in the face of the geopolitical shifts. The Allied Control Council ceased to function in 1948, and both sides prepared separate constitutions, gave themselves new currencies, and broke off contact. Hopes for a reunification of east and west did survive and were also tactically employed, but given the open Stalinism in the GDR and the Federal Republic's ties to the West, they no longer had a chance of being realized.[3]

The jurists of state law and international law in east and west, likewise thrown back to an intellectual *tabula rasa* and in many cases encumbered by their own cooperation in the Nazi state, immediately and with political passion set out to interpret "Germany's legal status." Had Germany ceased to exist as a legal subject? According to the classic theory, which said that a state no longer existed if it had no territory, no state power, or no people, this view was certainly defensible. The territory controlled by the power of the German state had been reduced, and the state power itself either had been dissolved and taken over by the occupying powers, or, where present, was paralyzed and incapable of taking action. But there was also a wealth of counterarguments: the country had not been annexed, the Allies had merely assumed the "supreme authority," there was merely a capitulation and no peace treaty, and Germany had obligations under international law as well as outstanding debts and liabilities which now all threatened to become devoid of a subject to which they could be attached. Using all means of a methodology disconnected from positivism, the facts on the ground and the occupation documents were interpreted to say that Germany should be preserved not only intellectually but also legally. Politically there was also a mood opposed to the "victors," but these victors were also in agreement that it would be better, in

[2] Michael Stolleis, "Besatzungsherrschaft und Wiederaufbau 1945–1949," in Josef Isensee and Paul Kirchhof, eds., *Handbuch des Staatsrechts*, vol. 1, 3rd edn. (Heidelberg, 2003), §7.

[3] For details concerning post-war developments, see Dietmar Willoweit, *Deutsche Verfassungsgeschichte*, 7th edn. (Munich, 2013), §§41–3.

the face of the Cold War, to leave the German question open and to posit a continuing Germany. The thesis of the fall and disappearance of Germany thus did not prevail. In the early GDR, further, the continuation thesis was initially embraced, because it was more favorable for a pan-German solution under the banner of either neutrality or socialism.

This first internal debate by a theory of the state and of international law that was regaining its footing also had multifarious implications for politics, just as politics, conversely, provided the real impetus for the debates. If Germany still existed as such, even if two (provisional) states began to take shape, one also had to adhere to German nationality, recognize Germany as a subject of liability, and render it capable of acting internationally. And so a political fiction was maintained, with both sides advancing a "claim to sole representation," acting separately within the framework of the Western or Eastern Bloc, seeking to displace the other side on the international stage (the Hallstein Doctrine), and denouncing each other. The original confrontation was only slowly eased by the intra-German policy of "change through rapprochement" that began in 1969, the gradual emergence of a dissident scene in the GDR, the weakening of the Eastern Bloc, the Helsinki conferences on basic rights, and large-scale geopolitical shifts. But it still seemed that one would have to accept the parallel existence of two German states for an unforeseeable future.

2. REBUILDING THE UNIVERSITIES

Materially speaking, the universities also began from "zero" in 1945, organized makeshift operations with teachers not compromised by their past or at least approved by the occupying powers, banished Nazi literature into the "poison cabinet," duplicated the first scripts for the classroom, and sought a new intellectual beginning on a broad front. To that end, jurists fell back on "natural law" or on a "material ethics of values," though without any real success implementing this in practice. In the practical world one had to find one's way in a thicket of (still) valid old law, abrogated Nazi law, occupation law, and new *Länder* law. The invocation of the Western "value system" and the daily necessity of legal positivism thus confronted each other.

At the same time there were efforts to re-establish the faculties. Only a few of the surviving victims of the National Socialists were able or willing to return, assuming they were even invited back. Lecturers who were not compromised in some way were hard to find. Colleagues from the Soviet Occupation Zone flocked to the West. Many "followers" who were not heavily compromised had not yet been "de-Nazified." And so unacknowledged shame about the past, collegial networks, and sheer material deprivation created a pattern that was characteristic of the western zones and the early Federal Republic. Within a few years, nearly all former professors (including public-law jurists) were back in their positions, with the exception of a few who were clearly compromised, among them, above all, Carl Schmitt, Reinhard Höhn, Otto Koellreutter, and Ernst Rudolf Huber—certainly very different individuals.

The West had the nearly unchanged stock of universities (Bonn, Erlangen, Frankfurt am Main, Freiburg, Göttingen, Hamburg, Heidelberg, Kiel, Cologne, Mainz, Marburg, Munich, Münster, Tübingen, Würzburg). In Berlin, the Frederick William University, which was now located in the eastern section of the divided city, was renamed Humboldt University; in the western section the Free University was created. A German–French university was established in Saarbrücken, which shifted its orientation toward Germany again following the referendum of 1955, at least in public law. A college for administrative sciences for postgraduate training began operating in Speyer, also under French auspices; it was gradually given the rights of a university.

The challenges of reconstruction were far more severe in the east. Of the six legal faculties (Berlin, Leipzig, Halle, Jena, Rostock, Greifswald), the last two disappeared. The remaining four now became primarily educational institutions, while research and the training of functionaries shifted to the Deutsche Akademie für Staats- und Rechtswissenschaft "Walter Ulbricht" (German Academy for Political Science and Jurisprudence "Walter Ulbricht") in Potsdam Babelsberg, which had been established following the Soviet model.[4] Finally, a Juristische Hochschule des Ministeriums für Staatssicherheit (College of Law of the Ministry for State Security)

[4] With the end of the cult of personality, the name "Walter Ulbricht" was eventually dropped from its long name, and with the development of the two-state theory so also the adjective "German."

was set up in Potsdam-Golm, which over the years also received the right to confer doctoral and postdoctoral degrees. The studies produced here were in principle not intended for the public. They served the work of agents and as guidance within the secret service empire of Erich Mielke (1907–2000).[5]

At the universities, nearly all "bourgeois" professors went to the west. They were replaced with young lecturers loyal to the party line. The curricula were revised, the state examinations were replaced with a diploma and an internship, the subject of "Marxism-Leninism" was henceforth obligatory. The more the Socialist Unity Party of Germany (SED) assumed power, the narrower the space became for state and administrative law. No commentaries were permitted on the Constitution of October 7, 1949; administrative courts were abolished as of 1952; and administrative law—because of its ineradicable liberal elements that constrained the power of the state—remained an object of mistrust. With the Babelsberg Conference in 1958, which Walter Ulbricht staged to regulate legal studies,[6] "administrative law" disappeared entirely as a subject, at least verbally. Henceforth it was situated within "state law" and was given the name *Leitungsrecht* (law of guidance, or management law).[7] It was intended to express that this was a law of administrative guidance, not a law that constrained the power of the state.

3. INSTITUTIONS AND JOURNALS

With the fall of National Socialism, the "professional associations"—most of which had been abolished or co-opted by the National Socialists—also had to be rebuilt. This took place across the board in 1949—that is, simultaneously with the creation of the Federal Republic—but the groundwork had already been laid for some time. For example, the Deutsche Gesellschaft für Völkerrecht (German

[5] Michael Stolleis, "'Feindlich-negative Kräfte' in den Kirchen der DDR," *Zeitschrift für evangelisches Kirchenrecht* 56 (2011), 328–47.

[6] Jörn Eckert, ed., *Die Babelsberger Konferenz vom 2./3. April 1958* (Baden-Baden, 1993).

[7] Joachim Hoeck, *Verwaltung, Verwaltungsrecht und Verwaltungsrechtsschutz in der Deutschen Demokratischen Republik* (Berlin, 2003).

Society for International Law) (founded in 1917 and suspended in 1933) was revived in 1949. The Institut für Internationales Recht (Institute for International Law, today the Walther Schücking Institute) in Kiel began anew, and the former Kaiser-Wilhelm-Institut für ausländisches öffentliches Recht und Völkerrecht (Kaiser Wilhelm Institute for Foreign Public Law and International Law) in Berlin now continued its work in Heidelberg under the name Max Planck-Institute. The loosely organized Deutsche Rechtshistorikertag (Conference of German Legal Historians) came together in 1949, as did the Deutsche Juristentag e.V. (Conference of German Jurists), the latter a continuation of the Deutscher Juristentag of 1860. Teachers of civil law began to hold conferences, as did the teachers of criminal law.[8]

The Vereinigung der Deutschen Staatsrechtslehrer (Association of German Teachers of State Law), which had been founded in 1923 but had not met during the Nazi period, was also revived in 1949. Eighty-two professors were invited to Heidelberg, though a few members who were clearly compromised politically were not invited or stayed away. Richard Thoma (Bonn) acted as chairman by seniority and declared that the association could re-emerge "with its head held high." Of course there were plenty of internal tensions within the new association, but the members tried at least not to make them public. Lectures were delivered about "The Question of the Cabinet and the Legislative State of Emergency" and about the guarantee of legal protection of the Basic Law. Walter Jellinek (Heidelberg) explained that it was an "important task of the science of state law today" to interpret the Bonn Basic Law "in its stipulations vulnerable to crises with the utmost clarity, at a time when all political possibilities are still within the realm of the future."[9]

While representatives from the Soviet Occupation Zone still participated in the first conferences of jurists of international law, these intra-German contacts now broke down in the prevailing Cold War. Thereafter a forum for jurists from both Germanys did not exist, and

[8] The conferences organized for teachers of civil law took place (at the initiative of Rolf Dietz) every two years beginning in 1951; those for criminal lawyers were held starting in 1952. On the latter, see Thomas Rönnau and Frank Saliger, *Materialien zur Geschichte der Strafrechtslehrertagung* [1952–2009] (Privatdruck der Bucerius Law School, Hamburg, 2009).

[9] Walter Jellinek, "Kabinettsfrage und Gesetzgebungsnotstand nach dem GG," *VVDStRL* 8 (1950), 19 (Summary, point 1).

there was no Association of Teachers of State Law in the GDR. In the beginning, individual professors from universities in the east were still allowed to travel, and private contacts continued, for example, in legal history or legal philosophy. But henceforth the state and administrative laws of the western and the eastern states developed in sharp separation, especially since a binding codification of substantive law as was found in civil law (Bürgerliches Gesetzbuch) and criminal law (Strafgesetzbuch) did not exist. In the wake of the international recognition of the GDR, exchange on international law was in small dimensions revived, and there were careful rapprochements, for example through the UN. On the whole, though, a pan-German communication on jurisprudence within an open, somewhat depoliticized, context was not possible between 1947 and 1990.

Parallel to the revived or newly created institutions, the landscape of legal journals also flourished in the West, among them the *Süddeutsche Juristenzeitung* (South German Jurists' Review) and the *Deutsche Rechts-Zeitschrift* (German Law Journal) (both 1946), which merged in 1951 into the *Juristenzeitung* (Jurists' Review) (*JZ*). The British zone saw the publication of the *Monatsschrift für Deutsches Recht* (Monthly Journal for German Law), in Berlin the *Juristische Rundschau* (Legal Review), and, finally, from 1947 the *Neue Juristische Wochenschrift* (New Legal Weekly) (*NJW*). Specifically for public law, the *Archiv des öffentlichen Rechts* (Archive of Public Law) (*AöR*) resumed in 1948 with a mix of old and new editors. The *Jahrbuch des öffentlichen Rechts* (Yearbook of Public Law) (*JöR*), suspended in 1939, reappeared in 1951. The sphere of administrative law was as soon dominated by the *Deutsches Verwaltungsblatt* (German Administrative Journal) (*DVBl*), which had emerged out of the old *Reichsverwaltungsblatt*, closely connected to the revived *Verwaltungsarchiv* (Administrative Archive). Its southern German counterpart, in a sense, was *Die öffentliche Verwaltung* (Public Administration) (*DÖV*) after 1948. Just as important as these overarching organs, perhaps even more important in the first phase of reconstruction, were the journals of administrative law focused on single federal states. The oldest among them, still in existence today, was the *Bayerische Verwaltungsblätter* (Bavarian Administrative Journal).

For economic and above all political reasons, no such open marketplace of journals existed in the German Democratic Republic (GDR). Instead, a state that abolished not only federalism in 1952, but also administrative jurisdiction, and which did not allow a constitutional court, could essentially get by with two journals.[10] One was *Neue Justiz* (New Judiciary) (*NJ*) after 1947, published by the Ministry of Justice and intended largely for judges; the other, beginning in 1952, was the journal *Staat und Recht* (State and Law), which was central for public law. Until 1991, the latter reflected all the internal and often camouflaged quarrels of the legal sciences within the GDR, and those with the Federal Republic, which was denounced as the fascistoid "Bonn separatist state."

[10] The review "Vertragssystem" (1957–69), later named "Wirtschaftsrecht," and the "Sozialistische Finanzwirtschaft" (1969–89). See Michael Stolleis, *Sozialistische Gesetzlichkeit: Staats- und Verwaltungsrechtswissenschaft in der DDR* (Munich, 2009), 63 ss.

14

The New "Value System" (*Wertordnung*) and the Restoration of the *Rechtsstaat*

1. INITIAL REACTIONS TO THE BASIC LAW, COMMENTARIES AND TEXTBOOKS

Jurists of constitutional and administrative law did play a role as expert consultants in the process that gave rise to the constitutions of the *Länder* and, above all, to the Basic Law between 1945 and 1949. However, the creation of the constitution itself lay in the hands of politicians, who, in turn, had to take into account the central directives of the occupying powers. At the various stages of this process—from the London Recommendations of June 7, 1948, to the Constitutional Convention at Herrenchiemsee, to the Parliamentary Council—participants discussed the basic outlines and details of democracy, *Rechtsstaat*, basic rights, federalism, separation of powers, legislative and administrative authority, the financial regime, and other issues. The experiences with the Weimar Constitution played a role here, as did the background conditions of the Cold War. In view of the uncertain future, participants believed they were only creating something "provisional," which is also why important topics were excluded.

The final product, the Basic Law of the Federal Republic of Germany, was solemnly enacted on May 23, 1949,[1] but among the public it was seen more as a provisional arrangement. The Germans were more concerned with food supply, currency reform, the economy,

[1] Horst Bredekamp, "Politische Ikonologie des Grundgesetzes," in Michael Stolleis, ed., *Herzkammern der Republik: Die Deutschen und das Bundesverfassungsgericht* (Munich, 2011), pp. 9–35.

and the integration of refugees and expellees. Having survived was more important than a new state. And the constitution itself was seen with critical eyes. Depending on one's vantage point, to some it was not Christian enough, to others not socialist enough, and to others still too much oriented toward a judicial state. As it was, many were opposed to the creation of a partial state, because they were hoping for a pan-German solution with the consent of the USSR—incidentally, that group included not only communists, but also journalists and writers with a Nazi past. Conservative theorists of state law criticized that the executive was too weak, that there was too much federalism and too much *Rechtsstaat* and not enough provision for a "crisis."[2] But the majority accepted the Basic Law and wrote on this legal basis commentaries, essays, and textbooks.

Among the new literature on state law one should mention—apart from the "pocket commentaries," which offered little more than an annotated text—first of all the *Bonner Kommentar*. Beginning in 1950 it was published in a loose-leaf format and grew into a work encompassing fifteen binders and 100 contributors. Even though it was a treasure trove of good commentaries, including those dealing with the historical background, it was intermittently suspended, though more recently it has been re-established with a different publisher. Another commentary that began to appear in 1950 was that by Hermann von Mangoldt. Initially intended to have three volumes, it grew under Mangoldt's successor, Friedrich Klein, to fifteen volumes and then ceased. Only the fourth edition was thoroughly modernized by Christian Starck (3 vols., 1999–2001). There was also a reference work for the new judicature of the Federal Constitutional Court (Leibholz–Rinck), and an associated, practice-oriented commentary of medium size (Hamann–Lenz). But the field was dominated by the "Maunz–Dürig" loose-leaf commentary that began to appear in 1958; by now it has grown to five volumes with 10,000 printed pages. The "architecture of the basic rights," developed out of the first three articles of the Basic Law and accepted at its core also by the Federal Constitutional Court, came largely from the pen of the Tübingen theorist of state law Günter Dürig (1920–96).

[2] Thus above all Werner Weber, *Weimarer Verfassung und Bonner Grundgesetz* (Göttingen, 1949); the much more moderate Hans Peter Ipsen, *Über das Grundgesetz* (Hamburg, 1949), 3rd edn. (Hamburg, 1969); Rudolf Laun, *Das Grundgesetz Westdeutschlands* (Hamburg, 1949).

Finally, the six-volume compilation *Die Grundrechte* (The Basic Rights) by Franz L. Neumann, Hans Carl Nipperdey, and Ulrich Scheuner also played a major role in the early Federal Republic, because in the first two decades there was a particularly urgent need for monographs about the basic rights that were now immediately valid (Art. 1 (3) of the Basic Law).

The leading course book on the new state law was initially that by Theodor Maunz (1901–93), whose author had now once again put himself in service to democracy. It provided concise and reliable information about the legal situation in east and west as well as in Berlin, appeared almost annually beginning in 1952, and was part of the standard equipment for all students.[3] But the book hardly offered any historical, comparative, or legal-theoretical depth. It presupposed the state institutionally and limited its activity through the basic rights. But the latter had been activated ever since the Lüth decision of the Federal Constitutional Court (BVerfGE 7, 198), and they were to "pervade" administrative law, civil law, and criminal law in equal measure. But the domestic political scene was also changing, a new generation was announcing itself, the relationship with the GDR was changing in the wake of the building of the Berlin Wall in 1961, and a perspective opened up on the parallel public systems in Western Europe and the US. This also created a growing need for a methodologically more sophisticated textbook. Such a work appeared in 1967 under the title *Grundzüge des Verfassungsrechts der Bundesrepublik Deutschland* (Outlines of the Constitutional Law of the Federal Republic of Germany); written by Konrad Hesse (1919–2005), it went through twenty editions by 1995.[4] As the title already indicated, he understood the constitution as the generalizing framework condition for a procedural mediation between the normative cornerstones and the decisions made by the legislative process. His guiding vision was no longer the institutional state, but civil society constituted as a state; his guiding idea was the harmonizing balance of textual and societal tensions within the constitutional framework. In essence this was also the guiding principle of the Federal

[3] Theodor Maunz, *Deutsches Staatsrecht: Ein Studienbuch* (Munich and Berlin, 1951). Beginning with the 27th edn. (Munich, 1988), it was gradually taken over by Reinhold Zippelius, and subsequently by Thomas Würtenberger.

[4] Konrad Hesse, *Grundzüge des Verfassungsrechts der Bundesrepublik Deutschland* (Heidelberg, 1967), 20th edn. (Heidelberg, 1995).

Constitutional Court, of which Hesse himself was a member between 1975 and 1987.

Published not long after Hesse's book was Ekkehart Stein's textbook *Staatsrecht* (State Law), which had a clear didactic focus.[5] It began with the law that organized the state and only then moved on to the fundamental civil rights. If one had to pick one's point of orientation in legal theory, Hermann Heller is the most likely candidate. For Konrad Hesse this was Rudolf Smend and his circle of students and colleagues in Freiburg; for Maunz it was probably more or less the traditional notion of the trinity of state territory, state people, and state power.

2. THE FEDERAL CONSTITUTIONAL COURT

The strongest force in the development of all of public law in the Federal Republic was and is the Federal Constitutional Court. Certain preliminary forms had already existed for some time, such as the incidental review by the Reichsgericht (Imperial Court of Justice) of the formal—and eventually even substantive—constitutionality of a law to be applied in an individual case, and the review of administrative acts by the administrative courts since 1863 (Baden) and 1875 (Prussia, Bavaria, Austria). The Weimar Republic established a Staatsgerichtshof zum Schutze der Republik (State Court for the Protection of the Republic),[6] though individual citizens had no right to bring a constitutional complaint.

Now, in the wake of the experiences with National Socialism, a decision was made—as it already had been in the 1920s in Czechoslovakia and Austria—in favor of a constitutional jurisdiction endowed with broad authority (Article 93 Basic Law (Grundgesetz, GG)), which also adopted certain features of the Supreme Court in the US. From now on, citizens could assert that an administrative act, a court decision, indeed a law violated their fundamental rights. Judges could submit a decision-relevant law whose constitutionality

[5] Ekkehart Stein, *Staatsrecht* (Tübingen, 1968; another thirteen eds 1971–93, ed. by Götz Frank since 2000).

[6] Ingo J. Hueck, *Der Staatsgerichtshof zum Schutze der Republik* (Tübingen, 1996).

was in serious question to the Federal Constitutional Court (Art. 100 (1) GG). Likewise, a losing minority in the parliament comprising one-third (one-quarter since 2009) of the members could submit a law for review. Since 1951, nearly all questions relevant to state law have landed before the Federal Constitutional Court: "going to Karlsruhe"—the seat of the court—became a proverbial expression.[7]

To be sure, it remained a problem within democratic theory that a law enacted by the democratically elected legislature, the "final world" of the sovereign, so to speak, could now be overthrown once again.[8] But this theoretical question was pushed aside, and one followed a trend that was discernible in many countries, namely to entrust the ongoing concretization of the constitution through changing cases, in the final analysis its updating under changing conditions, to a qualified and detached court. The more this court proved itself steadfast and loyal to the basic principles, the more its reputation grew. It would appear that secularized polities whose metaphysical backdrop has faded have a special need for an institution that interprets the relevant text in a trustworthy way, reins in decision-making processes that have gotten out of hand, and thus brings about "deceleration" and calm. Where the constitutional text is more open than its surrounding society, the constitutional court can also take on the role of the driver and modernizer; the decisions by the Federal Constitutional Court during the first two decades provide ample evidence of this, especially in marriage and family law as well as in criminal law.

Of course, it remains a cause of concern that all important parliamentary decisions must also pass through the "eye of the needle" that is Karlsruhe to attain full legitimacy. Parliament no longer has the "final word"—on the one hand, on the micro level, when it comes to difficult details of social law, civil service and salary law, the

[7] Concisely: Uwe Wesel, *Die Hüter der Verfassung: Das Bundesverfassungsgericht, seine Geschichte, seine Leistungen und seine Krisen* (Frankfurt am Main, 1996); Jutta Limbach, *"Im Namen des Volkes": Macht und Verantwortung der Richter* (Stuttgart, 1999); comprehensively (including statistics): Peter Badura and Horst Dreier, eds., *Festschrift 50 Jahre Bundesverfassungsgericht*, 2 vols. (Tübingen, 2001); with largely non-juristic authors: Stolleis (Note 3); Christoph Möllers, Matthias Jestaedt, Christoph Schönberger, and Oliver Lepsius, *Das entgrenzte Gericht: Eine kritische Bilanz nach sechzig Jahren Bundesverfassungsgericht* (Frankfurt am Main, 2011).

[8] Thus Ingeborg Maus, *Zur Aufklärung der Demokratietheorie* (Frankfurt am Main, 1992), pp. 235 ff. and elsewhere.

elimination of conceivable inequities in electoral law, where the court makes regulatory suggestions, sets deadlines, or declares in a monitory way that a regulation was "still" compatible with the Basic Law. On the other hand, on the macro level, the actions of the government are reviewed for their constitutionality and tied to the participation of parliament, for example when it comes to controversial foreign or European treaties, deployments of the army (Bundeswehr), further steps toward European integration, or crises in currency policy.

During the history of the Federal Republic, the court has thus considerably altered the architecture of the Basic Law. It not only is a controller, but also has become an actor, one that classic democratic theory did not reckon with. Yet it not only checks politics, but also relieves it to a considerable degree in that the responsibility for uncomfortable decisions can be passed on to Karlsruhe. Of course, this powerful position is constrained by the fact that the court subjects itself to the criticism of the public and of scholars with its detailed explanatory statements and with the publication of dissenting votes since 1970.[9] Overall the court has proved measured and pragmatic—probably thanks chiefly to its collegiate structure in what is now its third generation of judges. Its impact as a model for other states and legal cultures is exceedingly potent. On the European level, certain formulas have become established that demarcate it from the European Court of Justice in Luxembourg and the European Court of Human Rights in Strasbourg.[10] But here, too, the court can acquire considerable influence on European policy through a line that is more strongly focused on the nation state, or one that is friendlier to integration.

3. *RECHTSSTAAT* AND FUNDAMENTAL RIGHTS

Following the defeat of the Nazi regime by the Allies and the full realization of the disenfranchisements, expulsions, and mass murders committed by this regime, the call for the traditional *Rechtsstaat*

[9] All essential information can be found in Klaus Schlaich and Stefan Korioth, *Das Bundesverfassungsgericht: Stellung, Verfahren, Entscheidungen*, 8th rev. edn. (Munich, 2010), margin numbers 48–50.

[10] Ibid., margin numbers 347 ff.

was perfectly obvious, already in the debates by those in exile and the resistance. The core of what *Rechtsstaat* meant was clear: personal and substantive independence of judges, no special or extraordinary courts, no double punishment, protection against the arbitrary deprivation of liberty, guarantees of defence, and protection against arbitrary acts by the state, especially through administrative courts. The state should respect human and civic rights, and be allowed to interfere in them only on a legal basis and to the extent that it can derive justifications for doing so from the constitution itself. This was a grand program of juridifying state power, presented with the pathos of the gesture "never again."[11]

This program was already reflected in the first constitutions of the federal states, for example in Hesse, Bavaria, and Rhineland-Palatinate. When the Basic Law was subsequently created, the restoration of the *Rechtsstaat* was a foregone conclusion. Institutionally it was embedded within the judicial system at the federal and state level, namely in five branches: ordinary justice (civil and criminal jurisdiction), labor jurisdiction, social jurisdiction (new), financial jurisdiction, and administrative jurisdiction. The judges were now declared to be independent and subject only to "law and justice." The new Federal Constitutional Court was charged not only with exercising the functions known from the earlier state jurisdiction (jurisdictional conflicts, actions between two public bodies), but also with finding a way for the immediate validity of the fundamental rights (Art. 1 (3) GG) to be implemented.

The elaboration of the *Rechtsstaat* in the Federal Republic was a process that involved a division of labor and many participants. Initially it was the ordinary courts that clarified questions of procedural and material law and provided the first directives already during the occupation period (1945–9, attainment of sovereignty 1955). Then the highest federal courts became increasingly involved. In public law, the Federal Social Court (Bundessozialgericht) and the Federal Fiscal Court (Bundesfinanzhof), but above all the Federal Administrative Court (Bundesverwaltungsgericht) were responsible for the first precedent-setting decisions. The Federal Constitutional Court (Bundesverfassungsgericht) then developed beginning in 1951 and became, in spite of many assertions to the contrary, a kind of

[11] Hasso Hofmann, "Geschichtlichkeit und Universalitätsanspruch des Rechtsstaats," *Der Staat* 34 (1995), 1–32.

"super court of appeal," especially through the extensive use of the fundamental right to a "hearing in accordance with the law" (Art. 103 (1) GG).

Alongside the courts, the legislature was working tirelessly to enshrine public law in statutes, to eliminate old material, and create new legal resources. Hardly another sphere of the prevailing law has grown as massively as public law. For the first time there were now uniform regulations governing administrative courts (1960), for the first time also a partial codification of the General Part of administrative law (Laws for Administrative Procedure of the Federal Government and the States, 1976). Although the economic system was in principle based on the free market, the state was constantly intervening, whether to gain or to keep a specific clientele (agriculture), to reduce excess capacities (mills), to support economically underdeveloped areas (border zones), to make new industries competitive, or to deal with new problems (data privacy). At the same time, the social state was expanded and even fundamentally refashioned with the pension reform of 1957. All of this gave rise to permanent balancing acts between liberal and interventionist impulses. This ambivalent policy found its most striking expression in the Law for the Promotion of the Stability and Growth of the Economy of June 8, 1967, which sought to harmoniously combine price stability, full employment, balanced foreign trade, and growth within a "magical square"—in vain, as one would soon discover beginning in 1973.

The role of the science of public law has shifted considerably as a result of these political developments. The mere fact that the courts and the legislators—from the level of local communities to the federal states, the federal government, and all the way to the European Economic Community—were constantly generating legal material that needed to be commented on and processed tied up a major share of the capacities of the field. The science of administrative law, at one time solely responsible—jointly with the courts—for creating a system and key concepts, lost its earlier function. In spite of urgent appeals, it is less and less performing its guiding function through the development of a binding doctrine.[12] This may also have to do

[12] Eberhard Schmidt-Aßmann, *Das Allgemeine Verwaltungsrecht als Ordnungsidee: Grundlagen und Aufgaben der verwaltungsrechtlichen Systembildung*, 2nd edn. (Berlin and Heidelberg, 2004).

with the fact that a widely practiced "jurisprudence of balancing and weighing" quite cavalierly ignores doctrinal commandments and prohibitions in order to deal with new problems. In state-law theory, too, the relevance of scholarly pronouncements—beyond the often misused phrase "it is unconstitutional"—has declined. It has become common that experts on state law appear on all questions that have some kind of relevance. The abundant supply of experts available to all parties has contributed to the impression of a certain arbitrariness. Each party tends to have "its" expert witness. Since the number of members of the Association of Teachers of State Law has grown about tenfold in sixty years,[13] the result is such a polyphony of statements that a comprehensive debate focused on individual questions is hardly possible any more. One scholar has therefore spoken of a "dethronement of state-law theory."[14]

Of course, such a statement would not yet have applied to the building phase of the Federal Republic, which extended to about 1960. In what was then a fairly clear tableau of state law, the statements from well-known state-law theorists played a weighty role. In Bonn they included Ernst Friesenhahn and Ulrich Scheuner, in Tübingen Günter Dürig and Otto Bachof, in Freiburg Konrad Hesse, in Hamburg Hans Peter Ipsen, in Göttingen Rudolf Smend and Werner Weber, in Munich Theodor Maunz, in Münster Friedrich Klein and Hans Julius Wolff, in Cologne Hermann Jahrreiß and Hans Peters, in Berlin Karl August Bettermann, and in Heidelberg Hermann Mosler, Ernst Forsthoff and Hans Schneider—men who set the tone and whose pronouncements were paid attention to.

What they contributed to the *Rechtsstaat* was essentially not the subject of much controversy. A consensus existed more or less about the need to complete legal protection, about the relevance of the fundamental rights, and about the institutional securing of the *Rechtsstaat*. Important innovations—in the interplay between theory and practice—were found especially in administrative law and administrative procedural law, which are by now a permanent part of the repertoire and in some cases have made their way into the legislation. Here one should mention the clarifications concerning the right

[13] The register in 2015 lists more than 700 names, including members from Switzerland and Austria. See www.staatsrechtslehrer.de.

[14] Bernhard Schlink, "Die Entthronung der Staatsrechtswissenschaft durch die Verfassungsgerichtsbarkeit," *Der Staat* 28 (1989), 161 ff.

to bring an action against a neighbor or a competitor, the questions of the legal process involving "mixed" disputes (expropriations, subsidies, contracts involving public law), the typical forms of an action in proceedings before the administrative court, the determination of whether individual planning decisions are open to challenge, a more precise differentiation of vague legal concepts and concept of discretion along with a check on discretion, and the integration of the obligatory "pretrial procedure" (§68 Verwaltungsgerichtsordnung (Code of Procedure in Administrative Cases)), or the important question of the extent of the judicial review of discretionary decisions by the administration.

Behind all of this stood basic issues of the separation of powers: should the maneuvering rooms of politics and the administration be further constrained by "juridification"? Was there a "hypertrophy of the *Rechtsstaat*" that is paralyzing the actions of the administration and the government? Above all, is it right to assign such powers to the Federal Constitutional Court that it is able, with the help of the activated fundamental rights, to cancel out ordinary statutory law, and ends up, through the constitutional complaints against decisions by the final courts of appeal, becoming the all-controlling high court? Many scholars and practitioners contributed to these debates, and in the process one could also still make out undertones from the 1930s, with the message that political decisions can be made neither in the courts nor in parliament.

A very pointed debate emerged above all over the question whether *Rechtsstaat* and social state were coequal goals of the constitution. A thesis put forth by Ernst Forsthoff in 1953 caused a stir and drew disagreement. Forsthoff maintained that "according to the system of the Basic Law," the *Rechtsstaat* was "the primary good endowed with all legal guarantees. A conjoining of *Rechtsstaat* and social state involving a curtailment of the constitutional elements pertaining to the *Rechtsstaat* is ruled out by the Basic Law."[15] The constraining and conserving *Rechtsstaat* belonged, so Forsthoff held, to the constitutional level, while the distributing social state was a matter for the flexible administration. The constitution could not provide more than a social definition of the goal of the state. The combined phrase "social *Rechtsstaat*," though found within the text of the constitution

[15] Ernst Forsthoff, "Begriff und Wesen des sozialen Rechtsstaates," *VVDStRL* 12 (1954), Leitsatz IV.

(Art. 28 (1) GG), was inherently contradictory and therefore "not a legal concept."

This thesis was rejected by most, not only because the constitution—as revealed by the history of its creation—sought precisely to conjoin these two elements, but also because displacing the social state from the constitutional level seemed to be the wrong political message. Under the banner of the economic miracle and the emerging middle-class society, the majority wanted to "unfold" the social element precisely at the constitutional level and to combine the classic *Rechtsstaat* with the social element,[16] and to do so without damaging the traditional protective function of the *Rechtsstaat*. But since the Basic Law had anchored the social state only selectively and vaguely,[17] the question arose of how the "precept of the social state" in the Basic Law could be brought into legislation, administration, and the judiciary. This was essentially accomplished by the premise that the establishment or application of all norms was bound "to the value system fixed by the Basic Law," and that system contained the commitment to the social state. That this commitment to create relative material equality also had a direct bearing on democracy, as Wolfgang Abendroth emphasized in the debate back in 1953, was barely perceived at the time.

The debate thus also touched on one of the essential points of the early interpretation of the constitution, namely the "value system" that was contained in—or undergirded—the Basic Law. This phrase experienced an unprecedented boom. The invocation of a "value system" that was extrajudicial but at the same time was grounded in (or should be grounded in) the legal system was all but inevitable, for three reasons:

1. It picked up on the value philosophy of the 1920s and in this way offered a generally accepted matrix of values. After 1945, such a matrix was even more urgently needed than after the upheavals

[16] Thus, a few years later, Hans F. Zacher, *Sozialpolitik und Verfassung im ersten Jahrzehnt der Bundesrepublik Deutschland* (1961) (Berlin, 1980).

[17] In addition to the precepts of equality of Art. 3 GG see Articles 14 (2), 15, 20 (1), 28 (1); "equivalent living conditions," Art. 72 (2) (3), old version; Art. 74 Nos. 7, 12, "public welfare," "occupational health and safety," "employment agencies, as well as social security, including unemployment insurance"; Art. 87 (2) old version, "social insurance institutions"; Art. 120 [1], "subsidies toward meeting the costs of social insurance, including unemployment insurance and public assistance to the unemployed."

of World War I, as a bulwark against either value relativism or "false" values. In the process, the Catholic camp tended to fall back on the repertoire of natural law, while the Protestant camp preferred the value philosophy following in the wake of Max Scheler and Nicolai Hartmann.

2. It offered the jurists who now had to renounce traditional obedience to the law a mental foothold that the pure text of the law could not provide. The generally accepted "anti-positivism," which, incidentally, was methodologically strikingly similar to that after 1933, only seemed acceptable if it was supported by a "value system."
3. The "system" called for promised to be scientific in the tradition of the creation of scientific systems. Jurists appreciate a "system" all the more since they have always sought to organize the law systematically; indeed, they have seen this as their true calling. This tradition was particularly strong in Germany, and it went back to the natural-law systems of the seventeenth and eighteenth centuries and to the idealistic philosophy of the nineteenth century.

Should it therefore prove possible not merely to name values, but to demonstrate that they were legally binding and even formed a system devoid of internal contradictions, their irresistibility seemed assured. The state-law theorists and constitutional judges of the early and still unstable Federal Republic reached for this "value system"; readily found it also in the Basic Law, which sprang from the same mental milieu; and operated with it as a formula that had solidified into constitutional law. The 1958 Lüth decision of the Federal Constitutional Court bundled the already older trends and decided that the entire legal system had to accord with the value system of the Basic Law.[18] Open areas in the legal system that could be used to achieve that goal were "concepts needing to be filled with values" and "general clauses," by means of whose "third-party effect" all of private law could also be connected to this value system. The court maintained that the Basic

[18] BVerfGE 7, 198 ff. For a detailed discussion, see Thomas Henne and Arne Riedlinger, eds., *Das Lüth-Urteil aus (rechts-)historischer Sicht: Die Konflikte um Veit Harlan und die Grundrechtsjudikatur des Bundesverfassungsgerichts* (Berlin, 2005). An English translation of the Lüth Decision is available at www.utexas.edu/law/academics/centers/transnational/work_new/german/case.php?id=1369.

Law was *not* a "value-neutral" system; instead, in its section on the basic rights, alongside the defensive function of the basic rights, it had also "established an objective value system." This decision thus opened the doors to a pervasion of the entire legal system with the "value system" of the Basic Law.

As a point of reference for the legal system, this was surely well intentioned, and substantively it was also in line with what was expected of a liberal democratic system under the rule of law. But it created a number of previously unknown methodological problems, as there was no unquestioned societal consensus about the values themselves. And problems arose even more so when it came to implementing them in the details of administrative law, tax law, or criminal law—not to mention the difficulty of drawing ethical boundaries to private autonomy, for example through the concept of a neutral observer.[19] If the legislative process had decided the value-oriented societal dispute, the result was now measured against the value system of the Basic Law. In an effort to provide a firmer footing to the basic rights doctrine that began to emerge in the process, observers thus set out to find a "system" in the quite abstractly formulated fundamental rights. Especially Günter Dürig developed out of the text of the constitution a trinity composed of "human dignity" as the supreme constitutional principle, and the highest fundamental rights of freedom (Art. 2 GG) and equality (Art. 3 GG).[20] This trinity was followed by the specific guarantees of the fundamental rights and by other "values" of constitutional rank, which were now related to one another through an act of weighing and balancing. This position within the "value system," which is antecedent to the application of ordinary law, tended to devalue simple statutory law. Before such law was applied, one had to examine whether it had been constitutionally enacted in accordance with the rules, but above all whether it was substantively in accordance with that value system.

[19] Elena Barnert, *Der eingebildete Dritte: Eine Argumentationsfigur im Zivilrecht* (Tübingen, 2008).

[20] Günter Dürig, "Der Grundrechtssatz von der Menschenwürde: Entwurf eines praktikablen Wertsystems der Grundrechte aus Art. 1 Abs. I in Verbindung mit Art. 19 Abs. II des Grundgesetzes," *AöR* 81 (1956), 117 ff. This article must be seen in conjunction with Dürig's commentary on Art. 1 Sect. 1, Art. 2 Sect. 1, and Art. 3 Sect. 1 of the Basic Law, in the commentary by Th. Maunz, G. Dürig, R. Herzog, R. Scholz, Munich (loose-leaf-collection) 1958 ss.

In this way, with substantial participation by the theorists of public law, modernizing interpretations of the older statutory law were carried out. Other norms were abolished as incompatible with the Basic Law. Overall this was a necessary and welcome modernizing drive for a legal system many of whose norms dated back to the imperial period, the Weimar Republic, or National Socialism. At the same time, however, the fluidity injected into the legal system attacked the foundations of the law itself. What was valid law could be deduced less and less from the texts of statutes, and increasingly from the decisions of the Federal Constitutional Court. In an aggressive tone, Ernst Forsthoff spoke of a "reshaping of the constitutional text,"[21] and picking up on this, Carl Schmitt went so far as to bemoan a "tyranny of values."[22] Both emphasized the autonomy of the legislative decisions and criticized the power of interpretation that judges had arrogated to themselves or which had come their way. Apart from methodological issues that are worth considering, their criticism also contained a good deal of resentment against the orientation of the early Federal Republic on the part of Carl Schmitt, and specifically against the Federal Constitutional Court on the part of Ernst Forsthoff.

A lot has changed since then. The Federal Constitutional Court has "taken discreet leave from the value formulas of the early decades,"[23] but it has continued its pragmatic course with a growing openness toward developments within society. *Rechtsstaat* and social state could well be conjoined at the constitutional level without greater problems. Setting these two principles starkly against each other does not reflect the real issue. The *Rechtsstaat* not only realizes itself in formal defence against illegal acts by the state. It also must contain a social component by offering protection against violations of the law that the individual cannot fend off on his own. It shows its material side where the de facto (social or technological) preconditions for the defence of "privacy" are already missing. Moreover, in the face of

[21] Ernst Forsthoff, "Die Umbildung des Verfassungsgesetzes," in H. Barion, E. Forsthoff, and W. Weber (eds.), *Festschrift für Carl Schmitt zum siebzigsten Geburtstag* (Berlin, 1959), pp. 35 ff. Arguing against Forsthoff, see Alexander Hollerbach, "Auflösung der rechtsstaatlichen Verfassung? Zu Ernst Forsthoffs Abhandlung 'Die Umbildung des Verfassungsgesetzes' in der Festschrift für Carl Schmitt," *AöR* 85 (1960), 241 ff.

[22] Carl Schmitt, *Die Tyrannei der Werte*, 3rd. rev. edn. with an afterword by Christoph Schönberger (Berlin, 2011).

[23] Schönberger (Note 22), p. 77.

rapid changes in the conditions of life, it is not possible to speak of a permanent "fulfillment" of the postulates of the *Rechtsstaat.*

Furthermore, the context of the *Rechtsstaat* has shifted since the 1950s through the emergence of new institutions on the European level. The European Court of Human Rights (ECtHR), which has been operating in Strasbourg since 1959, has developed since 1998 into a general court—uncoupled from ties to the member states of the Council of Europe—for complaints by citizens against violations of the European Convention for Human Rights adopted by the forty-seven member states. Its importance for the realization of the "European *Rechtsstaat*" continues to grow.[24]

Since 1957, the European Court of Justice in Luxembourg, created in 1952 for the European Coal and Steel Community, has been in charge of all European communities (today: the European Union and EurAtom). In two spectacular decisions it separated European law from international law and turned it into an independent legal system (*Van Gend & Loos*,1963), which can even claim precedence over national law (*Costa/ENEL*, 1964).

Since that time certain tensions have existed between these two courts and the Federal Constitutional Court with respect to precedence and the effectiveness of the protection of the Basic Rights. But, as stated, these tensions were resolved pragmatically.

Looking back, one can see how differentiated the process was by which the entire legal system was pervaded by the postulates "*Rechtsstaat*" and "protection of the fundamental rights." At first, contemporaries posited the literal, immediate validity of the fundamental rights (Article 1 (3) GG) without a transmission on the part of the legislature, though this required help from the Federal Constitutional Court to specify what this meant in concrete terms. The breakthrough of the "third-party effect" of the basic rights via general clauses and other formulas whose value-content needed to be filled in came with the aforementioned Lüth decision in 1958. In addition, gaps in the protection of the Basic Law could be closed by using the general freedom of conduct of Article 2 (1) GG as a "catch-all norm" and generally advancing the line of demarcation when "interference" in a sphere relevant to the basic rights was occurring in the first place. The strict textual link to the Basic Law was then

[24] Ed Bates, *The Evolution of the European Convention on Human Rights: From Its Inception to the Creation of a Permanent Court of Human Rights* (Oxford, 2011).

abandoned with the help of the metaphor of the "radiating effect" of basic rights not directly involved, and with the vague phrase "field of tension" (*Spannungsfeld*). By taking a "synoptic view" of various basic rights, new ones could be developed, for example concerning post-mortem protection against defamation, the right of privacy, and "informational self-determination"; in fact, a "basic right to safety" was considered. All in all, one followed the early maxim by Richard Thoma that the basic rights should unfold their "judicial effect" as "efficaciously" as possible,[25] that they should be brought into "practical concordance," and that they should be balanced against one another as gently as possible (Richard Bäumlin, Konrad Hesse, Peter Lerche). This balancing was now done through "weighing"; that is, through a weighting that was often merely intuitive and result-oriented, which led time and again to criticism in terms of legal theory.[26] The criteria for the application of the fundamental principle of "proportionality" remained equally vague. What had once been developed for the appropriate level of police action was now expanded into a fundamental principle of the *Rechtsstaat* that applied to all interventions relevant to the basic rights:[27] the greatest possible limits to interventions in the sphere of freedom that are deemed necessary. In the process of weighing and balancing that this requires, freedom—in keeping with the model of the liberal *Rechtsstaat*—should remain the guiding value, according to the maxim *in dubio pro libertate* (Peter Schneider).

The institutional guarantees in the basic-rights section of the Weimar Constitution, emphasized by Carl Schmitt already in 1932,[28] were picked up again under the validity of the Basic Law in order to endow certain institutions of private law (marriage, family, property) with an "objective" character and thus an inviolability. Likewise, one could accord institutions a certain core immunity to change (private school, universities and research, radio, social insurance, etc.). From

[25] Richard Thoma, "Die juristische Bedeutung der grundrechtlichen Sätze," in Hans Carl Nipperdey, ed., *Die Grundrechte und Grundpflichten der Reichsverfassung*, 1. Band (Berlin, 1929), p. 9.

[26] Ernst-Wolfgang Böckenförde, "Grundrechtstheorie und Grundrechtsinterpretation," *NJW* (1974), 1529.

[27] Essential: BVerfGE 7, 377 ff.—Apothecary decision.

[28] Carl Schmitt, "Die Grundrechte und Grundpflichten des deutschen Volkes," in Gerhard Anschütz and Richard Thoma, eds., *Handbuch des Deutschen Staatsrechts*, 2. Band (Tübingen, 1932), §101, III 5–7.

this one could then deduce "duties of protection" incumbent upon the state, which in turn could lead to demands for a minimum level of financial support. Of course such duties of protection could also back up classic basic rights; if the de facto space for their exercise had become too small, the state should expand it again through social services or subsidies. The duties of protection should come into play once the "prohibition of a minimum level" (difficult to define) had been breached.

All of these changes to the *Rechtsstaat* and "basic rights," brought about by the reciprocal interplay of scholarship and judicature and consolidated by judicial decisions, took place chiefly in the decades between 1950 and about 1975—during a phase, that is, of growing economic prosperity, when contemporaries believed that one could neglect the question about the "costs of the *Rechtsstaat*."[29] Only with the end of the economic miracle, which can be dated to the "small crisis" of 1967 or the end of growth after 1973, did observers begin to contemplate whether there might not have to be upper limits and appropriate gradations of legal protection after all, and whether "affordability" might not constitute an inherent limit to the realization of basic rights. This entailed, at the same time, a shift of perspective away from the doctrinal consistency of a position and more toward the functionality of an argument as well as the consequences and side effects. The latter was simultaneously an impetus to involve the empirical social sciences more actively. The emphasis on the objective "institutional" elements of the basic rights revealed that the peak phase of the individualistic view of the use of the *Rechtsstaat* and the unfolding of the basic rights since the mid-1970s had passed. The stronger objectification of the basic rights can be interpreted as an economic question about the marginal utility of the instruments employed for legal protection and the realization of the basic rights, for example when it comes to regulating access to a university education (Art. 12 (1) (1) GG).[30] But it can also be seen politically as a conservative backlash in the years of the Grand Coalition and the socio-liberal government policy after 1969. The argument of costs was employed in the process, but it was probably not the primary driving force. In other words: the "limits to growth" that were now

[29] Fritz W. Scharpf, *Die politischen Kosten des Rechtsstaats: Eine vergleichende Studie der deutschen und amerikanischen Verwaltungskontrollen* (Tübingen, 1970).

[30] BVerfGE 33, 303 (330ff.), Numerus Clausus I.

discernible, the "oil shock" (1973), and the rising national debt of those years had repercussions also for the doctrine of basic rights and were understood as a warning not to fulfill every wish asserted by the courts. Examples are state support for private schools, the expansion of universities, ordinary rates for welfare, limits on the benefits of health insurance funds, the expansion of kindergarten facilities, and many other areas where claims based on basic rights were trimmed back.

4. DEMOCRACY

Compared to the development of the *Rechtsstaat* and the elaboration of the basic rights after 1949, the Germans and their jurists had a much harder time developing a positive relationship with parliamentary democracy. The historical experiences with this form of government had not been good. The Revolution of 1848–9 had failed. During the empire, the *Reichstag* (parliament) was slow to develop an identity and was seen as an obstacle to a politics of action, or even as a "monkey house," as Emperor Wilhelm II liked to put it. The parliamentary democracy of Weimar was vilified from the left and the right and in the end paralyzed itself. The Nazi regime was utterly undemocratic; its propaganda had relentlessly hammered home the idea that true democracy was embodied in the Führer state. It is understandable that after its collapse the first concern was to re-establish the *Rechtsstaat* and "civil rights and liberties." Thus it was not the system of government that was at the pinnacle of the constitution, but the affirmation of human dignity and the basic rights. To be sure, the establishment of democracy was politically self-evident, but it was hedged about with many safeties in the Basic Law: all forms of direct democracy were excluded on the federal level,[31] central matters of the constitution were exempted from majority decision (Art. 79 (3) GG), the Federal Constitutional Court became the guardian of the constitution with its authority to declare laws enacted by parliament null and void, the role of the federal chancellor against parliament was strengthened (constructive vote of no confidence), and splinter parties were kept out of

[31] A minor exception was only a revision of the division of the federal territory (Art. 29 GG, old version).

parliament (5 percent clause). Moreover, the struggle over the elaboration of rules for the parliamentary "state of emergency" dragged on for an entire generation. There was an unfailing emphasis that democracy had to be "militant," that it must not accord any freedom to its enemies.[32] This had concrete repercussions for the definition of what constituted a party, for party financing, and for the interpretation of the special status of parliamentarians (Art. 38 (1) GG), but above all for the fight against the—variously defined—enemies of democracy, whether at the level of the parties and the parliament, with respect to access to public office, or in terms of the protection of the constitution. Two bans were subsequently issued against parties (Art. 21 (2) GG),[33] one in 1952 against the Sozialistische Reichspartei, a successor party to the NSDAP, and one in 1956 against the KPD, which was followed by a series of criminal proceedings.[34]

If one puts all of this together, one can recognize a profound traumatization that can only be explained historically, an aversion against "party bickering" and parliamentarianism generally, but in addition also direct effects from the situation of the Federal Republic within the Cold War. The front lines of that conflict cut right through Germany. Since the Berlin blockade of 1948, the popular uprising on June 17, 1953, and the building of the Wall in 1961, nerves were badly frayed. If too much liberalism threatened stability, liberalism had to yield. "Militant defensiveness" (*Wehrhaftigkeit*), "loyalty to the constitution" (*Verfassungstreue*), "enemy of the constitution" (*Verfassungsfeind*), "forfeiture of basic rights" (*Grundrechtsverwirkung*), "professional disqualification" (*Berufsverbot*), and "party bans" (*Parteiverbote*) became common words and phrases. No such things existed in Austria or Switzerland on a legal level, nor were comparable scholarly energies expended on them.[35]

However, the starting points of the reaction to National Socialism, on the one hand, and to the Cold War, on the other, were gradually

[32] Erhard Denninger, ed., *Freiheitlich demokratische Grundordnung: Materialien zum Staatsverständnis und zur Verfassungswirklichkeit in der Bundesrepublik*, 2 vols. (Frankfurt am Main, 1977). Summary in Jürgen Becker, "Die wehrhafte Demokratie des Grundgesetzes," in J. Isensee and P. Kirchhof, eds., *Handbuch des Staatsrechts*, vol. VII (Heidelberg, 1992), §167.

[33] BVerfGE 2, 111 (SRP); 5, 85 ff. (KPD).

[34] Alexander von Brünneck, *Politische Justiz gegen Kommunisten in der Bundesrepublik Deutschland 1949–1968* (Frankfurt am Main, 1978).

[35] See the discussion contributions by Walter Haller and Siegbert Morscher in *VVDStRL* 37 (1979).

left behind beginning in the 1960s. West Germany integrated itself into Europe, a new generation of sociologists, political scientists, and jurists returned with the experience of having studied in the US, and the weights within domestic politics were shifting. With the Godesberg Program (1959), the Social Democratic Party became an electable alternative for the bourgeois middle class. At the same time a new phase in the processing of the Nazi crimes began: in 1961 the Eichmann trial in Jerusalem drew the rapt attention of the entire world; 1962 saw the Spiegel affair, a spectacular interference of the Bonn government in freedom of the press, which also led to the departure of four ministers of the Free Democratic Party from the government. Adenauer resigned in 1963, and the first lecture series about the role of the universities under National Socialism was held in 1965.[36]

As heterogeneous as these events might seem, they did signal an end to the post-war period and the growing sense in civil society that the country was embarking on the path to something new. Civil society wanted to have a voice, sought new forms of democratic participation, organized itself into more and more citizen initiatives, raised questions about the Nazi past, and because of the war in Vietnam dared to voice the first criticism of the US, the protective power hitherto revered with gratitude. The word "democracy," in particular, now turned into a rallying point. Newly elected president Heinemann called for "more democracy" in July 1969, and the new chancellor Brandt followed up in September 1969: "Let's take a chance on more democracy." And so, in the wake of a general reorientation of the Federal Republic, "democracy" became a universally used slogan. It accompanied the disappearance of the patriarchal model of the family along with new role models from the women's movement and the ideal of an "anti-authoritarian upbringing," the implementation of co-determination in the workplace,[37] debates within the churches over "committees representing employees," participation of pupils

[36] Munich: Die deutsche Universität im Dritten Reich (The German university in the Third Reich), 1966; Tübingen: A. Flitner, ed., *Deutsches Geistesleben und Nationalsozialismus* (Tübingen, 1965); Berlin: Nationalsozialismus und Deutsche Universität (National Socialism and the German university); Giessen: *Kritische Justiz*, 1968–9. Additional events in Münster, Frankfurt a.M., Göttingen, and Kiel followed. See Michael Stolleis, *Recht im Unrecht: Studien zur Rechtsgeschichte des Nationalsozialismus* (Frankfurt am Main, 1994; with a new afterword 2005); English translation: *The Law under the Swastika*, translated by Thomas Dunlap (Chicago, 1998).

[37] Co-determination law of May 4, 1976, BGBl. I, 1153. On this see BVerfGE 50, 290–381.

in school, the reorganization of university leadership ("one-third parity"), and the selection of candidates in the political parties. In other words: the demand for more democracy was employed wherever hierarchies and established power structures existed. On the one hand, this was a necessary modernizing push in the direction of more transparency; on the other hand, there were also considerable negative side effects when it came to technical questions that could not be decided by a majority, or where de facto inequalities were obscured by the demand for the participation "of all in everything." But the phrase "grassroots democracy," which tends toward an identitarian democracy, was soon worn out through its tactical deployment to push through egotistic goals. Likewise, the demand for "openness" was depleted as it became evident that limitless openness led to the violation of rights of privacy or to "grandiose speechifying" while the real decisions shifted back into arcane realms.

This development was a challenge to state-law theory, for previously the issue had been chiefly the *Rechtsstaat* and the pervasion of the legal system with the basic rights and with the "value system" they contained. To be sure, it had certainly not neglected the topics of electoral law, parliamentary law, party bans, or "militant democracy." But what dominated was the defensive posture: Bonn was not to become "Weimar"; that is, a failed democracy. Consequently, scholars were more concerned with hedging democracy than with its actual content. Only a minority of teachers of state law were willing to release the principle of democracy from its restriction to the electoral process for the *Bundestag*, the *Länder* parliaments, and the representative municipal bodies, and to acknowledge it as the universal organizing principle of society.

But now a new perspective was gaining ground. The separation of state and society, handed down from the nineteenth century but de facto already obsolete since World War I, was now questioned also theoretically. The state no longer appeared as the neutral power superimposed upon society and committed to the common good, but as a subsystem formed by society itself with special tasks and financing. Legislating was nothing other than the majority will condensed into legal norms. "Common good" was no longer a fixed "value" defined by moral or political elites, but the result of a pluralistic decision-making process within society and the state. The common good was what emerged within the constellation of forces as "public interest" through the procedural process. With that, the previous aversion of state-law doctrine to societal forces also lost its theoretical backing. They were part of the decision-making process, in which the parties also played an essential role, a process that intended to guarantee that the state, democratically occupied on a temporary basis, continuously renews itself both institutionally and intellectually. The state, so the message goes, is society itself seen from a particular perspective.

This development was strongly and consistently supported by the Federal Constitutional Court when it repeatedly pointed to the process of free and public decision-making that was vital to democracy. Numerous decisions were issued concerning freedom of the press and radio, freedom of artistic expression, and eventually also freedom of association and demonstration (Art. 8 GG).[38] This was preceded or followed by countless judicial decisions on demonstrations and counterdemonstrations, sit-ins, and other means of attracting public attention. They were based on the notion described above that basic rights should be interpreted in such a way that they could unfold their effects as broadly and efficaciously as possible. This was in line with the carefully constructed protection of individual rights. At the same time, this notion was linked to that of an open civic society, one that was not dominated by an authority, but formed its "state" by itself in a democratic process—in short, a pluralistic "civil society." The fact that the number of individuals organized into citizen initiatives soon surpassed membership in political parties was significant for this trend.

A certain institutional inertia of the theory of state law was evident in the fact that only one of the many annual meetings after 1949 was explicitly devoted to the topic of "The Democratic Principle in the Basic Law." That happened in 1970 in Speyer, in the immediate aftermath of the upheavals at the universities and within society triggered by the year 1968. The invited speakers were Werner von Simson, a former diplomat and expert on European law, and Martin Kriele, an expert on state law from Cologne.[39] Soon after, there was a second meeting (1974) that dealt with the "Parliamentary System of Government."[40] At both meetings there was a consensus that while

[38] BVerfGE 69, 315 (342 ff.)—Brokdorf.

[39] Werner von Simson and Martin Kriele, "Das demokratische Prinzip im Grundgesetz," *VVDStRL* 29 (1971), 3 ff., 46 ff.

[40] Thomas Oppermann and Hans Meyer, "Das parlamentarische Regierungssystem," *VVDStRL* 33 (1975), 7 ff.

the principle of democracy was subject to different requirements in state and society, it certainly had to be regarded as the basic unifying idea of these two closely intertwined spheres. It was made equally clear that no real alternative to the representative parliamentary system existed, but that greater flexibility should be possible with regard to the barriers to direct democracy that were too rigidly conceived in the post-war period, for example on the level of the *Länder* or the municipalities.

Thus, on a purely descriptive—but also affirmative—level, one can speak of a successful learning process on the road to democracy within society, politics, and state-law theory. The anti-democratic and anti-parliamentary biases handed down from the Weimar period and National Socialism were gradually dismantled the more the practice of democracy was consolidated and survived the test of changes in coalitions and governments. The political anchoring of the "Bonn democracy" within Western Europe caused the old prejudices against Britain and France to fade away, just as, conversely, Germany was perceived as a successful democracy. The US was in any case admired at the time as a helpful and generous nation. There was a confluence of positive experiences in the political realm, a series of "pro-democratic" decisions by the Federal Constitutional Court, and a change of sentiment within legal studies.

Behind the latter were probably also generational reasons. The university teachers appointed after 1933 retired in the decade between 1960 and 1970. Their students had grown up academically in the early Federal Republic and identified not only with the *Rechtsstaat* and the social state, but also with democracy. However different the thinking of the university teachers at the time may have been, they were all committed democrats—that was the crucial difference to the Weimar Republic.

5. FROM THE GENERAL THEORY OF THE STATE TO CONSTITUTIONAL THEORY

The gradual transformation of a country that was rising from a dictatorship and a devastating military defeat into a *Rechsstaat*, a social state, and a democracy can be traced from the development of state theory to the general theory of the state or constitutional theory. During the first two decades, the classic "general theory of the state" had fallen almost entirely silent. Except for smaller recapitulations from the Weimar era (Rudolf Laun, Friedrich Giese, Hans Helfritz, Richard Thoma, Otto Koellreutter, Ernst von Hippel), there was only one larger *Allgemeine Staatslehre* (General Theory of the State) by Hans Nawiasky, published between 1952 and 1958. The reprints of Rudolf Smend's *Verfassung und Verfassungsrecht* (Constitution and Constitutional Law) and Carl Schmitt's *Verfassungslehre* (Constitutional Theory) of 1928 presented the texts that had been so passionately discussed in their day. A virtual new discovery of the late 1960s was Hermann Heller's *Staatslehre* (Theory of the State), which had appeared in 1934 in the Netherlands, and was all but ignored in Germany. Thus the tableau of the 1930s was completely available again, though revealingly enough without Hans Kelsen's *Allgemeine Staatslehre* (General State Theory) (1925), which was considered decidedly "passé" in the Federal Republic, while it attained almost canonical status in Austria.

The times were not favorable to a general theory of the state or a democratic constitutional theory. The Federal Republic still considered itself a "provisional entity," a German state from which a part had been amputated and which, since 1961, had been also officially divided by reinforced border installations. Germany was not capable of acting as a whole. The western and the eastern states denied each other's right to exist. While Herbert Krüger's major work *Allgemeine Staatslehre* (1964) was respected as a learned treatise, its basic position was considered antiquated. At least it was not hostile to the associations, but remodeled them into veritable public organs. Yet Herbert Krüger did not reach the intellectual mainstream, and the same was true of the slightly later *Allgemeine Staatslehre* by the Austrian Felix Ermacora (1970).

In the meantime, though, political science began to regain its footing and to form various "schools"—in Freiburg (Arnold Bergstraesser, Wilhelm Hennis), Berlin (Otto Heinrich von der Gablentz, Ernst Fraenkel, Ossip Flechtheim, Otto Suhr), Hamburg (Siegfried Landshut), Heidelberg (Carl Joachim Friedrich, Alexander Rüstow, Dolf Sternberger), Cologne (Ferdinand A. Hermens), Frankfurt am Main (Max Horkheimer, Theodor W. Adorno, Carlo Schmid, Iring Fetscher), and Munich (Karl Loewenstein, Eric Voegelin, Kurt

Sontheimer, Hans Maier).[41] In 1965, the sociologist Ralf Dahrendorf (1929–2009) published his famous book *Gesellschaft und Demokratie in Deutschland* (Society and Democracy in Germany). All representatives of the field were shaped more or less by experiences in the US or Britain, by a scene that had no "state theory" but rather the complex concept of "government," the plural formation of the political will, which accentuated "decision-making" and questions of electoral law. The place of the "common good," compromised by Nazi rhetoric and seemingly occupied religiously in Catholic social theory, was now taken by the more sober "public interests," which had to assert themselves against other "interests." Research on parties and elections also got under way, opinion research became an important factor, and television turned into the "fourth power."

Accordingly, new interests came to the fore also in state-law theory. In 1971, Ernst Forsthoff wrote a widely read, resigned book with the title *Der Staat der Industriegesellschaft* (The State of Industrial Society), a farewell to the classic state.[42] At the same time, however, a new generation announced itself. *Allgemeine Staatslehre* (General State Theory) by Roman Herzog was published in 1971, and *Einführung in die Staatslehre* (Introduction to State Theory) by Martin Kriele in 1975. These were measured, reformist-conservative books with a basic liberal structure, but at their core they proceeded from the state, not from the constitution.[43] If one opted for the establishment and not merely the limitation of the state through its constitution, one logically had to write a "constitutional theory." In that case the state shrank to the potential state of emergency; but it, too, was fenced in by constitutional law in 1968. The citizen was granted a right of resistance, also on the constitutional level (Art. 20 (4) GG). States of emergency and resistance intruded from the realm outside the constitution and were translated into constitutional law. To date, neither form of dealing with a crisis has been subjected to a serious test—fortunately.

[41] Wilhelm Bleek and Hans J. Lietzmann, eds., *Schulen in der deutschen Politikwissenschaft* (Opladen, 1999); Wilhelm Bleek, *Geschichte der Politikwissenschaft in Deutschland* (Munich, 2001).

[42] Critical review by Peter Häberle, "Retrospektive Staats-(rechts-)lehre oder realistische Gesellschaftslehre?," *Zeitschrift für Handelsrecht* 136 (1972), 425 ff.

[43] Peter Häberle, "Allgemeine Staatslehre, demokratische Verfassungslehre oder Staatsrechtslehre?," *AöR* 98 (1973), 119–34 (and in Peter Häberle, *Verfassung als öffentlicher Prozess*, 2nd edn. (Berlin, 1996), pp. 271 ff., with postscript at p. 289).

Between 1965 and 1975, the "student movement" also awakened a theoretical interest in older revolutionary literature, in literature dealing with democratic theory, or in general with legal theory. Much was "excavated," newly translated, and printed in pirated editions. Marx and Lenin as well as the Soviet theoreticians who had been swamped by Stalinism were read again. A "Trotskyism" was also revived, especially by the Belgian theorist Ernest Mandel (1923–95). Under the surface, anti-liberal currents from the right and the left converged. The so-called "extra-parliamentary opposition" (*außerparlamentarische Opposition*) picked up anti-parliamentarian ideas of the 1920s, placed hopes in "soviets" with rotating membership, in contact with the grass roots and the democratization of all decisions. "Resistance" was articulated in many different ways, not least in the differentiation—untenable in a *Rechtsstaat*—between violence against things and violence against people. The legal contributions to this debate were collected above all in the journal *Kritische Justiz* (Critical Legal Studies) (founded in 1968). But there, too, the contributions to state theory dried up after about 1972. Other themes seemed more important in the politics of the day; a noteworthy and lasting state theory did not come about. At times, even the left-liberal forces fell behind the orthodox Marxist forces, at least until the first cracks in the edifice of the Soviet Union became visible from about 1985.

Of greater importance over the long term was the rediscovery of the modern theory of science and of analytical philosophy, to the extent that they devoted themselves to linguistic–normative problems. In this field a great deal that had perished in Austria and Germany needed to be brought to light again—such as the Vienna school of science theory (Moritz Schlick, Rudolf Carnap, Otto Neurath, Hans Hahn); the solitary genius of Ludwig Wittgenstein; the works of Alf Ross, Herbert L. A. Hart, and above all of Hans Kelsen. While the last of these had remained present in Austria, it had also been dogmatized in a normative positivism. All of this taken together amounted to a renunciation of the philosophical premises of the immediate postwar period. Contemporaries recognized and appreciated the gain in linguistic precision and the rule of law, compared to the ontological preconditions, essentialist arguments, and conventions of value hierarchies that were often foisted onto the interpretation of laws. Kelsen's old insight—that parliamentary democracy, legal positivism, and an epistemological relativism were mutually supportive and that adherence to the text, rationality in interpretation, and the disclosure of evaluation criteria belonged together in the process—came alive again. It was no coincidence that a new journal, *Rechtstheorie* (Legal Theory), began publishing in 1970, thus establishing a new field alongside legal philosophy. Juristic logic and methods theory also came back out of the shadows.

The new interest in philosophy and theory also benefited the basic problems of state and constitution. Already the question of the "constitutionality" or "unconstitutionality" of sovereign acts that was permanently associated with the judicature of the Federal Constitutional Court transitioned semantically from the state to the constitution. Constitutional thinking became superimposed on state thinking. Even if the majority of state-law theory did not want to follow Kelsen's identification of state and legal system, there was no doubt about the general dominance of constitutional thinking. Cautionary voices therefore already spoke about a "forgetting of the state" and warned against seeing the state merely as a reserve in case the constitutional order collapsed; that is, for a state of emergency.[44] The transition from "state law" to "constitutional law" was thus in the air, especially among authors who came from outside Germany. Former Germans with experiences in the US published "constitutional theories" early on (Carl Joachim Friedrich, *Der Verfassungsstaat der Neuzeit* (The Constitutional State of the Modern Period) (1953); Karl Loewenstein, *Verfassungslehre* (Constitutional Theory) (1959); Ferdinand A. Hermens, *Verfassungslehre* (Constitutional Theory) (1965)), while authors in the German tradition continued unchanged to pen "general state theories" (Herbert Krüger, 1964; Felix Ermacora, 1970; Thomas Fleiner, 1980; Reinhold Zippelius, 1969; Roman Herzog, 1971; Martin Kriele, 1975; Hans Herbert von Arnim, 1984; Karl Doehring, 1991; Burkhard Schöbener and Matthias Knauff, 2009).

Only a few ventured into a terrain that had been ambivalently occupied by Carl Schmitt in 1928, and to title their books also *Verfassungslehre* (Constitutional Theory) (Peter Häberle, *Verfassungslehre als Kulturwissenschaft*, 1982; Görg Haverkate, *Verfassungslehre*, 1992; Peter Häberle, *Europäische Verfassungslehre*, 2006; Philippe Mastronardi, *Verfassungslehre: Allgemeines Staatsrecht als Lehre vom guten und gerechten Staat*, 2007). This hesitant switch did not only reflect semantic problems. Rather, the issue was the

[44] References in Christoph Möllers, *Der vermisste Leviathan: Staatstheorie in der Bundesrepublik* (Frankfurt am Main, 2008).

very existence of the classic state as a life form. Anyone who today insists on the state, state law, and state theory tends to find himself in a defensive position vis-à-vis tendencies of the old European model of the state to become transformed or dissolved within a European federation of states or a unique kind of entity which, as the "European Union," has assumed some functions of the state but is itself not (yet) a state. Anyone who prefers the semantic field "constitution" can—with far fewer theoretical qualms—move beyond the traditional state to a new form of "open statehood" and a state-like European federation; indeed, he can contemplate a constitutionalization of the world order that is shaped above all by human rights. Both actual political developments and their theoretical reflection are still open when it comes to this crucial question.

15

The Social and Interventionist State of the Federal Republic

1. SOCIAL STATE AND "SOCIAL LAW"

Following the military and material collapse of the Nazi regime, those parts of social insurance, communal welfare, and the welfare organizations that were still more or less viable were revived with the greatest difficulty at the level of the *Länder*. After the currency reform of 1948 and the founding of the Federal Republic in 1949, and with the economic upswing, social safety systems also began to recover again. Thereafter they were continuously expanded (initially above all benefits for war victims, the system of burden sharing, housing market regulation, welfare, social jurisdiction). Beginning in 1975, pensioners also shared in the general prosperity, thanks to the fundamental conversion of old-age pensions to the pay-as-you-go-system and their indexing.[1] In 1961, the old welfare (*Fürsorge*) was replaced by the modern and more effective "social assistance" (*Sozialhilfe*), and youth welfare law took the place of the Reich Youth Welfare Law of 1923.[2] This movement of expansion was materially possible on the basis of the "economic miracle," but it was also supported by a consensus-based policy in the shadow of the division of Germany. The phase of expansion extended to about 1973. Since then, the hulking tanker that is the social state, whose budget in 2010 was more

[1] Hans G. Hockerts, *Sozialpolitische Entscheidungen im Nachkriegsdeutschland: Alliierte und deutsche Sozialversicherungspolitik 1945 bis 1957* (Stuttgart, 1980); Michael Stolleis, *History of Social Law in Germany*, translated by Thomas Dunlap (Springer, 2014), pp. 191 ff.

[2] Christa Hasenclever, *Jugendhilfe und Jugendgesetzgebung seit 1900* (Göttingen, 1978).

than €760 billion, is being steered with the help of adjustment laws and—it is hoped—enabled to deal with the emerging demographic crisis of an aging population. Retirement benefits and pensions as well as the rising costs of health insurance will have to be imposed on younger workers. Beginning in 1994, private nursing care insurance was added as the "fifth pillar," but it, too, will be able to bear only part of the future burden of old age.

The elaboration of the social state, which is fundamentally but still only selectively enshrined in the Basic Law (Art. 20 (1); Art. 28 (1); Art. 14 (2); Art. 74 Nos. 7, 12, 15, 16, 19, 19a; Art. 87 (2); Art. 91e; Art. 95; Art. 120 (1.4)) has by now taken place with accompanying social legislation during all legislative periods. The system of social benefits was steadily expanded or revamped, circumscribed or tied to narrower criteria in order to improve it overall or preserve it as one of the most effective, but also one of the most expensive, systems in the world.[3] This legislation was accompanied by the three-tiered social courts, with the Federal Social Court at the top, which added greater specificity to laws. Their judges, who frequently also cooperate with the practitioners of the social administrations on the federal level and in the *Länder*, have often made a name for themselves also as authors writing about and commenting on social law.

For a long time social law was therefore a domain of legal praxis and to a large extent it still is so today. The heterogeneous sections of public and private "welfare" (social assistance), aid for children and young people, provision for war victims, and the large, contributions-based block of social insurance first come together quite late into a more or less coherent "social law." If the focus was on the employment relationship, then social insurance appeared as its annex, which meant that labor law seemed in charge as part of civil law. If one emphasized the compulsory character of social insurance, it seemed a better fit with public law, but because of the insurance character it was fundamentally different from all benefits financed by taxes. At the universities, social law existed as a typical secondary field. Only in the 1960s did it become customary to speak of social law in a comprehensive sense. It was now seen as being held together by basic purposes. Those purposes were provision for the future, the balancing of different living situations in a spirit of solidarity, and the guarantee of a

[3] Manfred G. Schmidt, *Der Deutsche Sozialstaat: Geschichte und Gegenwart* (Munich, 2012), pp. 62 ff.

subsistence level in the name of "human dignity." The various social benefits slowly grew together into a coherent whole, demanded by the constitution, spelled out by legislation, and promoted by the political realm, which now also began to set up separate social budgets. This new perspective created pressure for codification, for the "Code of Social Law" (*Sozialgesetzbuch*) that was begun in 1976 and completed a generation later. It was obvious now—also in public opinion—that the social benefits system was part of the core of society; it was a twin of the productive national economy, a guarantor of domestic peace and stability. But since it is also very expensive, it is accompanied by the constant worry whether it can sustain its standards also in times of demographic shifts.

Jurisprudence participated in this process since the 1970s, whether it came from private law (Gitter, von Maydell, Eichenhofer), or predominantly from public law (Zacher, Rüfner, Ruland, Becker, Schnapp, and others). Professorships for social law were created, textbooks were published, the examination regulations responded. Parallel to European integration, a "European social law" also took shape.[4] Yet this development was not linear, but rather tracked the ups and downs of real or asserted societal needs. In the end, the intellectual climate decided whether social law or international banking law would be given preference when a new chair was about to be established. Under the banner of economic neo-liberalism, social law fell out of favor again. But that changed yet again under the impact of the financial crisis and rampant youth unemployment in several countries of the European Union. Although social benefits are not primarily suited to supporting the economy, they do bridge times of crisis, and with their redistributory effect they pre-empt dangerous social escalation. Above all, they secure a decent life for the generation of pensioners.

2. SUSTAINED INTERVENTION

The social state is only one example of a much more comprehensive process that we describe with the rather imprecise phrase

[4] Eberhard Eichenhofer, *Geschichte des Sozialstaats in Europa: Von der "sozialen Frage" bis zur Globalisierung* (Munich, 2007).

"interventionist state." What it refers to is the application of the maxims of economic liberalism that is evident in the late nineteenth century. These maxims (free development of individual, political, and economic powers, free trade) never came into play fully in Germany. Ever since the solicitous–authoritarian welfare state of the eighteenth century, the position of the interventionist state was traditionally a strong one, and it remained that way also in the first half of the nineteenth century. Following an economic crisis around 1873, the so-called *Gründerkrach* (Panic of 1873), another turn toward state guidance of societal processes had begun, especially by way of laws passed by the Reichstag. It began with the creation of social insurances for workers against illness (1883), accident (1884), disability, and old age (1889). But it was then extended into general economic life, for example through broad legislating on corporate law and social law, on the right to intellectual property, on banking oversight, on the supervision of trades and commercial activity, on the dangers emanating from industry (technical inspection boards), and on the protection of the new target group of "consumers" (e.g., food safety). But the state's promotion of science and scholarship through large research institutions (Kaiser Wilhelm Society, 1911) now also intervened in a targeted way in previously self-governing university research. In like manner, the academies of science also set up more and more generation-spanning long-term projects, through which scientific talent was both fostered and retained.

This initially still manageable "interventionism" received a massive boost from World War I. There was an instant emergence of previously unknown mixed forms of private and public law, directed at promoting and overseeing all goods of any significance to the war. After the war, millions of people had to be cared for and returned to gainful employment. The crisis management of the Weimar Republic did not permit a return to "non-intervention." That was all the more true for National Socialism, with its focus on authoritarian control: it immediately imposed the regulatory web of the "Reich Food Estate" on the agrarian market, and gradually and without hesitation curtailed whatever spheres of freedom still existed in the interest of creating jobs, rearming the country, and meeting the needs of war. As in the Soviet state, the "plan" now reigned, with targets for investment, research, and the output of goods of every kind, though in a way in which private property and entrepreneurship were preserved.

After 1945, all four occupation zones were confronted once again with the problems of war damage, providing work and housing, caring for victims of the war, and rebuilding institutions. Nothing seemed possible without help "from above," whether from the Marshall Plan or the public sector of the *Länder* that was slowly recovering its ability to act. In the beginning, all vital goods were directly allocated, and the market functioned only under externally imposed restrictive conditions. Only when the economic situation improved was the rationing of most goods lifted, though very late in the case of the housing market. Conversely, the agrarian market soon returned to dual control by means of subsidies and (likewise subsidized) restrictions—now at a European level. The production of coal and steel was "Europeanized" within the European Coal and Steel Community, and European external tariffs protected against cheap imports from developing countries. The national and European institutions that had always professed their commitment to "freedom" and "liberties" de facto regulated wide segments of social life, and indirectly they also guided the behavior of society through social law, tax law, health care law, consumer law (including copyright law), factory inspection, and environmental law. Crucial indicators were European export and import interests, and concern for agriculture, but also near-term goals that could attract a consensus (e.g., seat belt and helmet laws, smoking bans, new kinds of light bulbs). What is capable of generating a consensus in the complex decision-making process between the national governments and "Brussels" is promoted, restricted, or prohibited. Nearly all marketable products and services are today subject to sovereign permission and oversight.

With respect to the law and jurisprudence, these processes were of central importance in so far as they forced constitutional law and administrative law to thoroughly review their foundations and compare them with those of European neighbors. The basic model of the democratically constituted *Rechtsstaat* was based on the separation of the spheres of state and society, as enshrined in the constitution. The distance between the two is determined by the basic rights; every intervention by the executive in the basic rights requires a parliamentary law that defines precisely the occasion for and the degree of the intervention. If such an intervention is controversial, independent courts, which are also bound by law and justice, decide whether a valid legal basis exists, and whether the administration has applied it in accordance with written and unwritten higher law—in other words, in a way that accords with the *Rechtsstaat*. Above all, it must be determined whether the interference was necessary, suitable, and not "disproportional" to the desired goal.

This basic model has by no means vanished: it is applied as it always has been in the everyday cases of police law, commercial law, building law, or expropriation law. The classic "defence against danger" is indispensable in the core area of the state's activity. But the environment of administrative practice and that practice itself have changed in many respects.

Since the second half of the twentieth century, at the latest, the state has grown beyond the "defence against danger" and in the process has made use of societal forces in almost every respect. In the area of social benefits, the systems consist of not only the large public-law based social insurance schemes and the state and municipal social administration, but crucially also the institutions of the church and associations, of free organizations and private businesses. Social assistance, aid for children and young people, the hospital system, facilities for the disabled, nursing care, and much more could not function at all without the cooperation of such non-state institutions.

Moreover, already in the nineteenth century it was recognized that large-scale facilities and infrastructure for essential services (energy, water and sewage, mail services, transportation, fire protection, and disaster protection) could not be built and maintained without the cooperation of state and society. As we have seen, Ernst Forsthoff's *Daseinsvorsorge* of 1938 described the phenomenon of the dependence of the individual on essential services, a dependence which—in a decidedly anti-democratic context—was to be mitigated through a right of participation. In the debates that followed, the spectrum of such essential provisions expanded to include all services belonging to "infrastructure,"[5] but it also encompassed a sufficient provision for

[5] Georg Hermes, *Staatliche Infrastrukturverantwortung* (Tübingen, 1998). That the Federal Court (*Bundesgerichtshof*), in a landmark decision of January 25, 2013 (Aza III ZR 98/12), awarded damages for an outage of the Internet, assuming it was the fault of the provider, signals that in the future all institutions used by society as a whole will be liable under civil law. However, if that is the case, then they are also subject to basic rights, regardless of their legal form.

kindergartens, schools, and educational and cultural facilities of every kind, indeed, the creation of a living and working environment free from harm "for all." Even if the latter may be a goal that can never be fully achieved, the very idea meant that the state had to be constantly active in an interventionist manner, and that it had to cooperate with social actors at all levels. The latter is for the most part only possible on the basis of the private-law or public-law contract, but also through informal cooperation and de facto supplementation. In addition, on the basis of laws, citizens are given a multitude of "benefits"—not only those of social law, but also those that promote the economy, that compensate for reductions in land under cultivation or in taking care of alpine pastures, that reduce capacities, and that promote innovations in alternative energy or other technologies of the future—all in all, a vast and unmanageable number of incentives and compensatory benefits. This has given rise to a new "benefits administration law" (*Leistungsverwaltungsrecht*), which is interconnected in multifarious ways with the traditional "administrative law of intervention" (*Eingriffsverwaltungsrecht*). The one is no longer conceivable without the other.

3. CHANGES IN ADMINISTRATIVE LAW

The doctrine of administrative law had to respond to this in a multitude of ways. In addition to the archetypical interventionist or burdensome administrative act, it initially devoted itself to the promotive administrative act, which could, of course, have negative repercussions for third parties. Moreover, the single act was joined by the permanent "relationship of administrative law," roughly comparable to the "continuous obligation" in civil law, from which rules about impairment of benefits were now also taken over into public law. To capture subsidies, one had to differentiate the promotive administrative act as the basis of the benefit from the civil-law transaction to fulfill a contract, for example when a bank grants a credit (two-stage theory); but one could also have recourse to pure public-law constructs that guaranteed uniform legal protection. Furthermore, every action aimed at individuals raised questions of equality when others came away empty in similar cases or, for example, civil servants with equal qualifications were not promoted (legal action by a competitor). A separate national and European contracting law developed in the competition over public contracts in order to distribute such contracts equitably and to avoid corruption.

Substantial changes in practice and theory also occurred in lengthy approval procedures with many involved parties—e.g., in the construction of airports or highways, the laying of railroad tracks, and other encroachments in densely settled areas or in nature. The forms of participation developed by the legislature when it came to planning made the originally internal administrative procedures into public issues with numerous participants; indeed, they offered the possibilities for direct democracy at the local level. Well beyond the old "plans" (budget plan, development plan), now transportation plans, landscape and environmental plans, social plans, youth plans, and school and university plans were part of the day-to-day activities of the administration. Until the 1960s this was not emphasized very much within the framework of the free market, especially since one did not like to see parallels with the Four-Year Plans of National Socialism or above all the planned economy of the Eastern Bloc. But the reality was undeniable and was gradually reflected in scholarship.[6] Planning became the "key concept of our future."[7] During the communal reorganization (1967–78), planning was done with enthusiasm and often by ignoring reality. In the first economic crisis in 1966–7, global forward-looking planning seemed like the sensible approach to take. A central planning office was set up in the Chancellery under Horst Ehmke. Planning law became an examination subject in law studies. But once the euphoria had waned and numerous examples of poor planning came to light, the efforts subsided again after 1976. Permanent "planning" and "reforming" continued only in the classic experimental field of social policy and the school and university system.

The science of public law responded to all of these changes by dividing into specialized areas. It created new courses, chairs, journals, series, and professional congresses. Public economic law,[8] already

[6] Max Imboden and Klaus Obermayer, "Der Plan als verwaltungsrechtliches Institut," *VVDStRL* 18 (1960), 113–215.

[7] Joseph H. Kaiser (ed.), *Planung*, vol. 1 (Baden-Baden, 1965), 7.

[8] Reiner Schmidt, *Öffentliches Wirtschaftsrecht: Allgemeiner Teil* (Berlin and Heidelberg, 1990); Reiner Schmidt, *Öffentliches Wirtschaftsrecht: Besonderer Teil,*

created during the Weimar period, was now joined by social law,[9] environmental law,[10] regional planning and special planning law,[11] science law,[12] media and telecommunications law,[13] energy law,[14] data privacy law,[15] and technology law.[16] An effort was made to pragmatically differentiate these fields—which were more like conglomerations of the most diverse norms rather than systematically organized new creations—and to develop separate guiding principles for each. The bewildering complexity of modern administrative law that is created in this way, and which is reflected also in the specialization of scholars and professional journals, as well as in the courts and their jurisdictions, is growing into a problem of modern legal systems, that of "multinormativity."

On the one hand, one could be content for a long time that there was little to add to the basic building blocks developed in the theory of legal forms by Otto Mayer in 1895. Burdensome and promotive administrative acts continue to be taken, today increasingly in electronic form; public-law contracts are entered into; plans are developed and local statutes are enacted; distinctions are made between corporations, institutions, and foundations. The permanent relationship of administrative law has been added, though of course without acquiring any distinct doctrinal contours. On the other hand, looking at the legal forms in the core area is deceptive. Not

2 vols. (Berlin and Heidelberg, 1995–6); Reiner Schmidt and Thomas Vollmöller, *Kompendium Öffentliches Wirtschaftsrecht* (Berlin and Heidelberg, 1998–2004).

[9] Ivana Mikešić, *Sozialrecht als wissenschaftliche Disziplin* (Tübingen, 2002).

[10] Michael Kloepfer, *Umweltrecht*, 3rd edn. (Munich, 2004); Reiner Schmidt and Wolfgang Kahl, *Umweltrecht*, 8th edn. (Munich, 2010); Rudolf Steinberg, *Der ökologische Verfassungsstaat* (Frankfurt am Main, 1998); Reinhard Sparwasser, Rüdiger Engel, and Andreas Voßkuhle, *Umweltrecht*, 5th edn. (Heidelberg, 2003).

[11] Rudolf Steinberg, Martin Wickel, and Henrik Müller, *Fachplanung*, 4th edn. (Baden-Baden, 2012).

[12] Eberhard Schmidt-Aßmann, "Wissenschaftsrecht im Ordnungsrahmen des öffentlichen Rechts," *JZ* (1989), 205 ff.

[13] Joachim Scherer, *Telekommunikationsrecht und Telekommunikationspolitik* (Baden-Baden, 1985).

[14] Hans-Peter Schneider and Christian Theobald, *Recht der Energiewirtschaft: Praxishandbuch*, 3rd edn. (Munich, 2011).

[15] Spiros Simitis, ed., *Bundesdatenschutzgesetz*, 7th edn. (Baden-Baden, 2011).

[16] Udo Di Fabio, "Instrumente des Technikrechts," in Klaus Vieweg, ed., *Techniksteuerung und Recht* (Cologne, 2000), pp. 9–21; Miloš Vec, "Kurze Geschichte des Technikrechts," in Martin Schulte and Rainer Schröder, eds., *Handbuch des Technikrechts*, 2nd edn. (Heidelberg, 2011), pp. 455 f.

only do legal forms that seem to have stayed the same change their meaning under changed circumstances—no different from acts of speech within varying contexts—but also administration and administrative law have changed fundamentally in recent decades, parallel to the shifts between state and society. Socially and technologically we are living in a phase of great acceleration. Problems of natural sciences are being researched worldwide and with intense competitiveness, and involving the deployment of major governmental and industrial resources. The intervals in which knowledge becomes obsolete are becoming ever shorter, especially since every innovation or new discovery is instantly available electronically.

So where do we stand today? Fixing a position is famously difficult if one is moving at great speed. One may well debate whether, following the era of agriculture (the primary sector) and subsequent industrialization (the secondary sector), we have entered a post-industrial age of services (the tertiary sector).[17] Be that as it may, there is no doubt that the law of administration has, on the one hand, enormously expanded the sphere of its application, while, on the other hand, having lost its conventional contours and the reliability of its doctrine.

Initially, the development of the administration within the context of the post-war *Rechtsstaat* and social state, with their emphasis on basic rights, entailed that the new administrative law had to regroup. Now administrative law was indeed "concretizing constitutional law" (Fritz Werner). At first this meant the refinement and completion of the protection of basic rights within administrative law, including the ubiquitous principle of the "proportionality" of encroachments, the development of new protective goods and obligations of protection on the part of the state,[18] the interpretation of traditional administrative law in line with the constitution, and the shift from an administration acting authoritatively to a cooperating

[17] Persuasive counterarguments are in Jürgen von Kruedener, "Von der Dienstleistungsgesellschaft zur Industrial Society," in Karl Hardach, ed., *Internationale Studien zur Geschichte von Wirtschaft und Gesellschaft* (Frankfurt am Main, 2012), pp. 533–50. For a general overview on the acceleration, see Hartmut Rosa, *Soziale Beschleunigung: Die Veränderung der Zeitstrukturen in der Moderne* (Frankfurt am Main, 2005).

[18] Developed above all in BVerfGE 39 (1975), 1–95 (obligation of protection on the part of the state toward developing life).

administration with new behaviors and involving the adoption of contractual forms from civil law.

At the congress of state-law teachers in Regensburg in 1972, Otto Bachof (1914–2006) took stock of these changes. He pointed to the pervasion of administrative law with the constitutional guidelines relating to the *Rechtsstaat* and the social state, to the refinement of the control of administrative actions by the *Rechtsstaat*, and to the expansion of legal forms by the law governing the administration of benefits. A fundamental renewal of the doctrine of administrative law was not something he considered necessary. The much younger Winfried Brohm (1932–2012) emphasized modernizing features much more strongly, such as the new forms of participation in planning, more careful parliamentary oversight of the executive, the elaboration of "relationships of administrative law," and corresponding public law on "disruption of benefits."

A mere four years later (1976), there was the first comprehensive legal regulation of administrative procedure, simultaneous in various statues at the federal level and for the *Länder*, combined with a statutory codification of the uncontested parts of the material general administrative law.[19] This was the legislative conclusion to efforts that reached back to the 1930s. Henceforth one could draw directly on the law and accompanying commentaries. Textbooks, which had previously been the decisive authorities, receded into the background. Changes to procedural law were a matter for legislation. It responded to the needs of praxis but also to the growing permeability of the boundaries between public law and private law, as well as to the postulate of "democratization." Now there were rights of information and consultation, mass actions were regulated (§§17–19 VwVfG (Verwaltungsverfahrensgesetz—Law of procedure in administration)), electronic communication was introduced into the law (§§3a VwVfG),[20] the public-law contract—long since practiced—was incorporated (§§54–62 VwVfG). Complicated administrative

[19] Verwaltungsverfahrensgesetz i. d. F. v. 23.1.2003 (BGBl. I, 102), most recently amended by a law of May 5, 2004 (BGBl. I, 718), as well as correspondingly for the federal states.

[20] On this see, Martin Schulte, "Wandel der Handlungsformen der Verwaltung und der Handlungsformenlehre in der Informationsgesellschaft," in Wolfgang Hoffmann-Riem and Eberhard Schmidt-Aßmann, eds., *Verwaltungsrecht in der Informationsgesellschaft* (Baden-Baden, 2000), pp. 333–48.

procedures were broken down into smaller segments to make them procedurally manageable, and at the same time efforts were made to counteract the slowing down of all procedures (§§71a–e VwVfG).

In principle, the changes that have been mentioned can still be managed today with the accustomed legal forms and the relevant procedures. But what is becoming evident is new changes in the overall state of affairs. To begin with, there is an increase in regulatory density, namely at the level of the communities, the *Länder*, the federal government, Europe, and in part also in international law, to the extent that the latter codifies standards by way of international treaties (environmental protection). Depending on the concrete goals or extant danger, the conventional instruments of public law are put to use (oversight, reservation of approval, prohibitions), but guidance is also exerted indirectly through levies of financial incentives. The more extensive the projects, the more regulations apply, and the greater therefore the chances for opponents to slow things down by either regular or irregular means. There is a growing sense that modern industrial societies, which have pursued ever more sophisticated and also successful prevention, are reaching limits with their "juridification." Marginal utility declines as safety provisions increase, and the costs of processes rise.

What is referred to as "multinormativity" creates problems also in that it is becoming more and more difficult to map the complex regulatory structures onto a single decision-making level, that of the decision in a legal dispute. Legal proceedings involving larger construction projects in the public sector can easily take a decade today, and the same is true of lawsuits for damages between corporations and banks or insurance companies, or of coming to terms with human "mistakes" in criminal law.

Added to all of this is a blurring of the boundaries between public law and private law. The kind of categorical dichotomy of the legal system that was the intent and idea in the nineteenth century hardly still exists today. Its only refuge is in the assignation of judicial processes. The interventionist state, which has to share its monopoly of sovereign guidance today with institutions organized under private law (of the public and the private sectors), makes use of the legal forms of public law as well as those of corporate law (which, in turn, depends on tax law) to achieve "effects." The pervasion of the entire legal system with "purposes" renders the question about legal forms secondary. Of course, what remains open is the question of how actors operating under civil law can be bound to the protection of freedom by basic rights.

The result is the emergence of regulatory "mixed areas" that are guided by "protective purpose" usually justified in terms of constitutional law (investor protection, environmental protection, consumer protection, the protection of children and families, gender equality, protection of minorities, and so on). This protective purpose then acquires bodies of norms, though they do not form an inner unity or a "system." In many areas regulation is done in sovereign fashion, in others one opts for "self-regulation," which in turn has to be protectively "regulated," with the result that here, too, a mix of laissez-faire and oversight emerges. Correspondingly weak in all areas is therefore the creation of "General Parts" that could be situated—in a way that relieves stresses and provides structures—between the constitutional norms and the concrete regulations. The crucial achievements of guidance emanate today from references to constitutional norms, from emerging "principles," and from chains of "consolidated" judicature. On the one hand, we therefore find the justified appeal to preserve the systematically evolved core of administrative law in order to prevent the development of a jungle of special doctrines on various regulatory levels and in various regulatory fields.[21] On the other hand, modern administrative law is actually seeking to *distance* itself from older administrative law, which, in the tradition of Otto Mayer, set great store by the unifying function of the legal forms in the *Rechtsstaat*. Administrative law is now perceived much more strongly and classified from the perspective of its function of "guidance."[22] The most important trends mentioned today are "privatization, economization, digitalization, Europeanization, and internationalization." Alongside the traditional demand of the *Rechtsstaat* that all areas be bound by the laws, these trends are now supposed to accord also with the new goals of "efficiency, acceptability, willingness to cooperate, flexibility, and feasibility."[23]

[21] Eberhard Schmidt-Aßmann, *Das allgemeine Verwaltungsrecht als Ordnungsidee: Grundlagen und Aufgaben der verwaltungsrechtlichen Systembildung*, 2nd edn. (Heidelberg, 2004); Eberhard Schmidt-Aßmann, *Verwaltungsrechtliche Dogmatik: Eine Zwischenbilanz zu Entwicklung, Reform und künftigen Aufgaben* (Tübingen, 2013).

[22] Wolfgang Hoffmann-Riem, Eberhard Schmidt-Aßmann, and Andreas Voßkuhle, eds., *Grundlagen des Verwaltungsrechts*, vols. 1–3 (Munich, 2006–9), vol. 1, 2nd edn. (Munich, 2012).

[23] Ibid., foreword to the 1st edn. of vol. 1.

Indeed, the tasks of the administration and its position vis-à-vis the law are changed under these keywords. The more this "law" is seen in functional terms, the more it will lose its intrinsic value and become capable of being replaced by other "expedient" means. This interchangeability of legal forms and the move of dispensing with them in the name of "self-regulation" make it increasingly difficult to believe in the guiding effect of a doctrine condensed into a "General Part." What happens today often (and increasingly) is that the special regulations—bypassing a General Part—are tied directly to the justifying foundation in constitutional law. Such a foundation seems to offer greater security than a consensus-based doctrine, also because of possible reviews by the constitutional court.

A historical consideration might make this plausible (though, of course, it does not "prove" anything).

When the legislative process created the "General Parts" of criminal law (1871), the Civil Code (1896), the Reich Insurance Code (1911), and the Reich Tax Code (1919), these subsystems of the law depended for guidance on a part that preceded them. The constitutional law at the time (Reich Constitution, constitutions of the *Länder*) was not a candidate for this role, in part because it offered no substantive orientation through basic rights (Reich Constitution), in part because the basic rights lacked immediate validity. This situation also gave rise to the creation of the General Part of administrative law, chiefly at the hands of Otto Mayer (1895). He carved out the legal constructs that underpinned all administrative action. That made it possible for courts or scholarship to recognize them in concrete cases and to subject them to the ordering principles of the *Rechtsstaat*. In this sense one could say that "constitutional law passes, administrative law endures," because he was referring not to the details of administrative law, but to the fundamental legal constructs. However, if the central guidance of an administrative law that has become diversified shifts from the General Part to the constitution and constitutional judicature, the guiding function of a General Part is devalued. In other words: the General Parts of criminal law, civil law, and public law around the year 1900 fulfilled a function that has been increasingly taken over, in the decades of the Federal Republic, by the "value system of the Basic Law." Anyone who wants to affirm a legal position today usually does so not by invoking a proposition of doctrine, but by pointing out that his conclusion accords with the constitution, especially the basic rights.

This has the advantage of greater plausibility and public impact, but the clear disadvantage that propositions of constitutional law are nebulous and open to interpretation—or, to put it in institutional terms, it strengthens the position of the institutional guardians of the constitutional text, the judges of the Federal Constitutional Court. Accordingly, the role of jurisprudence, in the orbit of which the General Parts were created and cultivated, has lost weight.

4. THE EXPANSION OF UNIVERSITIES

An industrialized country that depends crucially on a skilled workforce must continue to invest in and to guide the educational sector. It must eliminate social barriers to access, promote the education of women, calibrate educational institutions to reflect societal needs, and balance out fluctuations in demographic cohorts. The university system of the 1960s was no longer able to do justice to these demands. The "German educational catastrophe" was proclaimed in 1964,[24] and thereafter many things began to shift.

Between 1965 and 1975, public awareness was dominated above all by the "student movement." That movement was prepared by the lecture courses on the Nazi past of the universities; it absorbed the criticism of the US due to the war in Vietnam, as well as the general upheaval in lifestyle, gender relations, and the "felt" end of the postwar period that was evident from a multitude of indicators. A radicalized side branch of this movement mutated into a terrorist group (the RAF), while the majority of this politicized generation carried on reformist impulses. That it itself gave rise not only to more relaxed social behaviors, but also to the hardening effects of a subsequent generation that was once again more conservative, is no doubt part of the generally visible dialectic of social developments.

Between 1960 and 1980, the number of students—especially female students—rose sharply, the universities were enlarged, and the system was expanded in singular fashion through the establishment of twenty-four new institutions of higher learning between 1963 and

[24] Georg Picht, *Die deutsche Bildungskatastrophe: Analyse und Dokumentation* (Freiburg, 1964), 2nd edn. (Munich, 1965).

1978. Legal faculties or departments arose in Bochum, Mannheim, Giessen, Konstanz, Regensburg, Bielefeld, Trier-Kaiserslautern, Augsburg, Bremen, Hanover, Osnabrück, Hamburg, Bayreuth, and Passau. A decade of particularly intense reforms and attempted reforms followed. A "single-tier training of jurists" was tested at a few universities between 1971 and 1984 but then discontinued, even though it proved successful. The curriculum taught "basic courses" and "electives," and this fundamental approach has persisted to this day. But many approaches to reform foundered in the conditions of the mass universities. The relief that was expected to come from the offerings of legal training at the technical colleges (*Fachhochschulen*) barely materialized. Above all, the integration—invested with such high hopes—of theory and practice, on the one hand, and of the social sciences into legal training, on the other, did not attain permanent canonization in the curricula, was left to the personal interests of teachers, and therefore petered out from around 1974.

As a result, "academic reform" has remained a constant topic under more difficult external conditions, especially with respect to financing. In the most recent past, the political and economic spheres have driven a clear focus on economic utility. The quality of research is being increasingly judged by the amount of "third-party funding" it is able to attract. A national "ranking" (often done in an amateurish manner and driven by special interests) is forcing the administration of the universities into a national competition over "excellence." In some sectors the conditions of research may have been improved in this way. Overall, however, the virtually unanimous view of those involved is that the level of research and teaching has not improved, rather the contrary. The basic subjects (philosophy of law, legal theory, legal history, comparative law) are suffering, and the pressure to accelerate the course of studies and the school-like instruction this entails are creating a legal training that seems more like something one would find in technical colleges. The great attractiveness that the German model of higher education had for foreign jurists is waning.[25]

[25] The previously mentioned recommendations of the "Perspectives of Jurisprudence" scientific council of November 9, 2012, recommend a robust strengthening of the basic subjects, with a view to the international attractiveness of the German training of jurists, but also out of concern over maintaining the scholarly character of a university education.

For public law, the expansion of the universities meant a multiplication of teaching personnel, which can be read from the membership numbers of the Association of German Teachers of State Law, and a similar multiplication of printed material, especially commentaries and textbooks. The various directions of public law within the universities were never really able to develop clear profiles, or these were ground down again, after a good start, by mass education.

16

The State Law, International Law, and Administrative Law of the GDR

1. BASIC POLITICAL STRUCTURE

The state law and administrative law, as well as the international law, of the GDR were from the very beginning closely tied to the guidelines laid down by the SED, the state party. Adherence to the party line was controlled at all levels: through the politically guided pre-selection of the students, to the teachers appointed to faculty positions, the curricula, the textbooks, and the examinations. An administrative jurisdiction no longer existed; a constitutional jurisdiction was already ruled out ideologically by the—fictive—identity of the people's will and lawmaking process. A free commentary on the constitution, which could have led to divergent views, was unknown. As a result, nuances in the formation of scholarly opinion, which certainly existed, must be reconstructed from a careful reading of the two journals *Staat und Recht* (State and Law) and *Neue Justiz* (New Judiciary).

As was already mentioned, especially grievous for praxis was the de facto disappearance of administrative law as a result of attacks by the party leadership at the Babelsberg Conference in 1958. In a sense, this was the end point of the era of Walter Ulbricht, which was shaped by the opposition between East and West, and by the fear of popular uprisings (June 17, 1953; but also in Poland and Hungary). In 1961, the building of the Wall and of the border fortifications, which were intended to prevent the flight of East Germans to the west, brought a certain easing of tensions internally. A new, sovereign GDR constitution went into effect in the spring of 1968; its section on basic rights created some hopeful signs, but those disappeared again in August 1968 with the crushing of the "Prague Spring."

The change from Walter Ulbricht to Erich Honecker in May 1971 initially brought some minor relaxations and improvements, which were aimed at inner stabilization. In foreign policy, the GDR agreed to participate in the CSCA conferences, probably in the hope that it might be able to control a dissident scene that could emerge from them. The final document of Helsinki (1975), the government's decision to strip Wolf Biermann of his citizenship (1976), Rudolf Bahro's book *Die Alternative* (The Alternative) (1977), and the Polish Solidarity movement from 1980 on showed that the system could not sustain the pressure from below in the long run. The economic difficulties, which were only temporarily ameliorated but not resolved by a West German loan of 3 billion marks in 1983, were added to the mix. When the Soviet Union eventually adopted its policy of glasnost and perestroika beginning in 1985, and thus initiated the process that led to its own demise, the most important pillar of the SED's rule was gone.

In the field of state law, a two-volume publication of documents and commentary had existed since 1969. The first textbook on the state law of the GDR appeared in 1977, a second edition was issued in 1984. Needless to say, both works were collective efforts controlled by the party. They also carried out the transition from the pan-German politics of the early years to the two-state theory. All reminders of the German nation had been erased. The tone of the whole thing reflected the state of an aging dictatorship: militant passages as introduction, descriptive positivism for the actual textbook, and no criticism of one's own system.

In contrast to this, the "state law of bourgeois states" was also taught at the universities in East Germany. This field had to be sensitive to changes in foreign policy, but at its core it was supposed to show why and how the world of capitalism was doomed to fail. But clever authors could also use their writings on this subject to describe institutions they would have liked to see realized in their own country. Moreover, they enjoyed the privilege of being able to study the books of the "enemy," which were otherwise difficult to procure.

Similarly, international law offered a window onto a world the East German population was not allowed to see. Initially it accompanied the policy of the SED in the Cold War. At first the translation of a Russian textbook—*Völkerrecht* (International Law) (1967)—was good enough for the classroom. But when the Basic Treaty with West Germany (1972) offered a new basis, and the international recognition of East Germany was achieved with admission to the United Nations (1973), international law was also invigorated and was able to connect with the debate in the West. A separate textbook on international law was published in 1973; a second edition followed in 1981. Unchanged in its fundamentals, but flexible in its reaction to the political changes, it is now a unique historical document.

A field that suffered most heavily was administrative law, which was indispensable to everyday life. Having seemingly vanished in the wake of the Babelsberg Conference of 1958, it reappeared—now integrated into state law—under the designation *Leitungsrecht* (guidance law). In substance, such an area of the law was essential to the planning and the sovereign guidance of the GDR economy, with its agricultural and handicrafts cooperatives and the law of the state-owned enterprises and combines. In order to make this legal field of the "socialist planned economy" (Art. 3 of the GDR Constitution of 1968) teachable again, the powers that be listened to the voices of the practitioners in 1972 and commissioned a new textbook. The "administrative law" course was approved in 1977, and the textbook *Verwaltungsrecht* (Administrative Law) was published in 1979 by the state publishing house, under the aegis of the Academy for Political and Legal Sciences of the GDR. Its material was now entirely tailored to the needs of the administrations in East Germany. The side of individual rights was excluded, and the authors continued to emphasize that there was still no need for an administrative jurisdiction.[1] The "petition system"—that is, the right of every East German citizen to approach the authorities and party offices with requests and complaints—was sufficient, it was argued.[2] Nevertheless, a few authors clung to the idea of judicial oversight of the administration (Karl Bönninger, Wolfgang Bernet).[3]

[1] Things were different in the second edition of the book in 1988, which underscored the importance of legal protection for citizens and indirectly called for an administrative jurisdiction.

[2] Gesetz über die Bearbeitung der Eingaben der Bürger vom 19. Juni 1975 (Law on the Handling of Petitions by the Citizens of June 19, 1975).

[3] Joachim Hoeck, *Verwaltung, Verwaltungsrecht und Verwaltungsrechtsschutz in der Deutschen Demokratischen Republik* (Berlin, 2003), pp. 217 ff.

2. INSTITUTIONS AND JOURNALS

In the west, a coexistence gradually emerged again between university education and institutionalized basic legal research, especially through the Max Planck institutes for foreign public law and international law (Heidelberg), for foreign and international private law (Hamburg), for European legal history (Frankfurt am Main), and for foreign and international criminal law (Freiburg). By contrast, in East Germany the dualism between the Academy for State and Law (Babelsberg) and the law faculties in Berlin, Halle, Jena, and Leipzig was much more pronounced. The universities were primarily engaged in legal training—in public law, for example, through one instructor each for the fields of state law, administrative law, international law, and the state law of bourgeois states. The instructors usually grew up within their home universities; the kind of competition between universities that was found in the West, with instructors applying for appointments elsewhere or being recruited, generally did not exist, though there certainly was movement between the Academy, the universities, and the Ministry of Foreign Affairs, in the latter case in the field of international law, for example. Those engaged in teaching were mostly members of the SED, though membership in the other "block parties" was apparently also acceptable.

In 1971, the Deutsche Akademie für Staats- und Rechtswissenschaft *Walter Ulbricht* (Walter Ulbricht German Academy for State and Legal Science) shortened its name to Akademie für Staats- und Rechtswissenschaft der DDR (Academy for State and Legal Science of the GDR). Neither the name Ulbricht nor the word "German" was tolerated any longer. The Academy was a "university for state functionaries," who were offered continuous courses, but above all a research institution that served the purposes of the Central Committee of the SED; in fact, the Academy was under the authority of the SED.

As already mentioned, the debates over legal questions within the framework permitted by the SED took place chiefly in two journals. *Staat und Recht* (State and Law) was published between 1952 and 1991, and it provided the forum for fundamental debates. Here is where the battles were fought over the "party line," the position toward other countries and the Federal Republic, or the delicate question of the historical "legacy," though it also published reviews of new books, always hedged about by official words of greeting and carefully filtered by the editors. By contrast, the journal *Neue Justiz* (1946/

47–1990) was more strongly oriented toward praxis of the judiciary. It largely served the courts, state prosecutors, and lawyers. As a mirror of public law it is less fruitful than *Staat und Recht*.

The foundations of legal science in the GDR collapsed with reunification in 1989–90. In particular, the totality of state and administrative law of this state became entirely redundant. With very few exceptions, there was no reason any longer to consider it valid law. The specific elements of an international law related to the GDR also became historical artifacts. Nothing seemed usable any longer, except for solid works on legal history or the history of philosophy. Empirical studies of legal sociology will also remain of interest for historical retrospective of social conditions—or they may sink into oblivion as mere products "of their time." Accordingly, most of the reference books turned into waste paper. The faculty was evaluated, and most were sent into retirement or dismissed.[4] The legal faculties, now founded once again, or for the first time, in Rostock and Greifswald, Potsdam, Frankfurt and der Oder, the Humboldt University of Berlin, Jena, Erfurt, and Dresden took over very few teachers from the time of the GDR and filled their ranks overwhelmingly with younger academics from the west.

[4] Inga Markovits, *Die Abwicklung: Ein Tagebuch zum Ende der DDR-Justiz* (Munich, 1993); Inga Markovits, *Gerechtigkeit in Lüritz: Eine ostdeutsche Rechtsgeschichte* (Munich, 2006).

17

European Law and International Law

European law is the supranational law—born after 1945 out of diverse political impulses—of the institutions with "European" tasks that are emerging in Western Europe (Brussels, Strasbourg, Luxembourg).[1] It does not follow a pre-existing blueprint, but is shaped by a consistently compromise-driven politics. In the wake of two disastrous world wars, with Germany at their center, the ideas of European integration, which had been in the air for centuries, entered a phase of realization. The reconstruction of Western Europe with substantial US support (the Marshall Plan) spurred common action. The young Federal Republic, initially preoccupied entirely with repairing the damages of war, with the occupation statute, and with the conflict over the division of Germany, participated progressively in the moves toward European integration and became one of the important founding members of the European Economic Community with the "Treaties of Rome" in 1957.

The legal concepts used until then, which led to a "Europe as legal community,"[2] came from traditional state law and especially international law, but also from international economic law, antitrust law, and competition law. The major treaties, at any rate, were international treaties between sovereign states, which were transformed

[1] Initially we are talking about the Organization for European Economic Co-operation (OEEC, 1948), the International Ruhr Authority (1949), the Council of Europe (1949), the European Payments Union (1950), the European Coal and Steel Community (1951–2002) and the General Agreement on Tariffs and Trade (GATT, 1951), the Western European Union (WEU), the European Defense Community (1952–4), and the European Economic Community (EEC, 1957).

[2] Walter Hallstein, *Der unvollendete Bundesstaat: Europäische Erfahrungen und Erkenntnisse* (Düsseldorf, 1969).

into the law of the state in Germany by way of Article 59 (2) of the Basic Law. But the more time passed, the more it became apparent that European law constituted a normative type of its own.[3] The Association of Teachers of State Law addressed the topic in 1959 and 1964, and there was a growing chorus of voices that recommended European law as a separate discipline in the training of lawyers.

Hans Peter Ipsen led the way with a major exposition; others followed.[4] In the laws of the *Länder* dealing with the training of jurists, European law was placed into a group of electives together with general state doctrine and international law. Dissertations and habilitation theses followed, and a large number of journals on European law appeared. Within a decade a new field had emerged. Today it is divided into sub-disciplines that discuss questions of state theory, state law, subsidy law, police law, data privacy, and communications law. Every imaginable topic of state law—e.g., consumer protection, social and health care policy, crime policy and criminal procedures, transportation, the energy economy, all the way to law dealing with religion—has "European" implications and can no longer be adequately dealt with without a knowledge of European law. Institutions and a normative network continue to consolidate themselves through lawmaking in Brussels and Strasbourg and above all through the decisions of the European Court of Justice in Luxembourg. One can observe an inherent momentum of homogenizing processes, which work fairly continuously within the context of the broader political climate. Homogenization lowers transaction costs and opens up new markets for those whose standards prevail.

The European Union is not a state in the conventional sense, but rather a multifarious community of nations with very different languages and cultures, a community, though, which—all contrary currents notwithstanding—seems to be becoming more and more state-like. With a parliament, an executive, and a judicial system, it possesses the basic institutional structure; and since the Treaty of Lisbon that went into effect in 2009,[5] it also has a constitution, which,

[3] Comprehensively Anna Katharina Mangold, *Gemeinschaftsrecht und deutsches Recht: Die Europäisierung der deutschen Rechtsordnung in historisch-empirischer Sicht* (Tübingen, 2011).

[4] Hans Peter Ipsen, *Europäisches Gemeinschaftsrecht* (Tübingen, 1972); Albert Bleckmann, *Europarecht* (Cologne, 1976); Leontin-Jean Constantinesco, *Das Recht der Europäischen Gemeinschaften* (Baden-Baden, 1977).

[5] On this in detail BVerfGE 123, 267.

jointly with the Charter of Basic Rights (2000), is fulfilling classic expectations about a process of "constitutionalization." The European Union has its own legal personality, and pursues its own foreign, defence, economic, and social policy. Much is unfulfilled or unrealizable, much is in the process of evolving, and must be made concrete in lengthy negotiations. The economic and social problems of new member states are obvious and can be resolved only by decades of exertion. The entire system is cumbersome and requires considerable financial resources. And the fact that some member states, chief among them Greece, have triggered a financial crisis that has shaken confidence in the common currency merely reveals that a currency union without a corresponding institutional foundation, which can be achieved only by giving up certain aspects of sovereignty, does not function, which means that there is a great need for remedial improvements.

In all European countries the science of public law has dealt at length with the processes I have described. With a wealth of memorable formulas, it tries to make clear that the Europe of today is neither an "association under international law" (federation of states), nor a classic federal state, as it was sketched early on after the model of the "United States of America." Instead, we are dealing mostly with hybrid forms with new content, for example when we hear of "integration association," "federal association," "confederation of states" (*Staatsverbund*), or "constitutional confederation" (*Verfassungsverbund*). The more broadly conceived formulas, too, such as "integration community," "supranational federalism," "open constitutional state," or "emerging constitutionalism" merely reveal the strenuous search for appropriate words to grasp something that is without precedent in the long history of Europe.

In view of the fundamental questions concerning the path that the European states should take in the future, it is no surprise that contrary positions are emerging within the scholarly debate. One position is essentially pro-Europe, emphasizing the need for further integration and a corresponding renunciation of elements of national sovereignty. The other places greater emphasis on the reservations attached to the nation state, on the contractual nature of the European Union, and on the traditions of the constitutional state. To date the Federal Constitutional Court has tended to be favorable toward integration in its decisions, though it has also been consistently concerned to preserve the rights of the German national parliament. The position that in the final analysis it must be the parliament elected by the people that approves essential changes in the political form is consistent with democratic theory. But it is also beyond question that changes in legal form can take place when the political majorities so decide. Such changes cannot be blocked by invoking the immutable "sovereignty" of an individual state. After all, beginning in the sixteenth century, "sovereignty" was a key concept in the emergence of the modern state that could be used to illustrate in a catchy way the competences under international law, the status as public employer, currency sovereignty, and other core elements of princely rule.[6] This concept is subject to historical change, and in the age of supranational unions and of globalization, it has almost completely lost its conventional functions. Especially in Europe, which has already created supranational "state powers," and which has external borders, a domestic market, and a currency of its own, one cannot close one's eyes to what is a fundamental change.

The genesis of a "European law" and of European institutions that I have sketched here originally came out of the context of international law, but it has been moving away from it since the 1970s. International law itself, a discipline that after 1945 had to be slowly freed from its ties to Nazi foreign policy and the international law of war, found itself immediately confronted, at the Potsdam Conference of 1945, with the question whether Germany still existed as a subject of international law. The first conferences of experts on international law, under the direction of Rudolf Laun (1882–1975), a jurist of international law from Hamburg, revolved around this existential question. The great majority opted for the thesis of the "continuation of the Reich" in the western partial state, in order to preserve the law of international treaties and generally remain able to function internationally, to assume the assets and liabilities of the Reich, and not to forfeit the right to reunification. Moreover, in dealing with the occupying powers one wanted to be able to invoke a person of public law that was "incapacitated" but still in existence, for example when it came to interpreting the Allied Occupation Statute, which restricted the sovereignty of the Federal Republic until 1955.

[6] Helmut Quaritsch, *Souveränität: Entstehung und Entwicklung des Begriffs in Frankreich und Deutschland vom 13. Jahrhundert bis 1806* (Berlin, 1986); Helmut Quaritsch, "Souveränität," in *Historisches Wörterbuch der Philosophie*, vol. 9 (Basel and Stuttgart, 1996), pp. 1104–9; Helmut Quaritsch, "Souveränität," in *Handwörterbuch zur Deutschen Rechtsgeschichte*, vol. 4 (Berlin, 1990), pp. 1714–25.

Whatever stood against this—the destruction of the power of the state, a central element in the general theory of the state, the division of the territory, or the assumption of "supreme authority" by the victors—mattered little in the face of the desire to preserve a legal point of connection. Even less accepted were the arguments of East German jurists that the partial West German state was arrogating to itself a "claim to sole representation" by virtually occupying the "Reich."

Initially, then, the "Germany question" absorbed all attention. The most important institutions (the Institute of International Law in Kiel and the Kaiser Wilhelm Institute in Berlin, now the Max Planck Institute in Heidelberg) resumed their work, the first outlines for the classroom were printed, and all experts on international law found jobs again, some at universities, some as advisers to the Foreign Office or in the ministry itself.

By around 1960, however, the situation had changed. Although the Germany question remained unresolved, the Federal Republic was acting as a universally recognized sovereign state, which meant that one could shift one's attention back to the entirety of international law. The European international and economic law of the post-war period now transformed itself into a "unique kind of European law" and was given accounts of its own. As a result, new comprehensive textbooks of international law,[7] and a three-volume lexicon of international law,[8] were published almost simultaneously around 1960. It was especially in the latter that the international connectedness of the discipline was re-established. Thereafter it became the standard in legal training that every faculty had one or two chairs devoted to European and international law. The number of textbooks increased accordingly, especially during the phase when new universities were established beginning in 1970, which also led to an expansion of the field in terms of absolute numbers.

Yet this seemingly smooth path of "normalization" continued to be dominated by the Germany question also when it came to the doctrine of international law. The GDR closed its borders in 1961 to stop the steady exodus of its population. That began the slow farewell

[7] Georg Dahm, *Völkerrecht*, 3 vols. (Stuttgart 1958–61); F. A. Frhr. v. d. Heydte, *Lehrbuch des Völkerrechts*, 2 vols. (Cologne 1958–60); Friedrich J. Berber, *Lehrbuch des Völkerrechts*, 3 vols. (Munich 1960–4); Wilhelm Wengler, *Völkerrecht*, 2 vols. (Berlin, 1964); Eberhard Menzel, *Völkerrecht: Ein Studienbuch* (Munich, 1962).

[8] Karl Strupp and Hans-Jürgen Schlochauer, eds., *Wörterbuch des Völkerrechts* (Berlin 1960–2).

to the Hallstein Doctrine, which had aimed at isolating the GDR internationally, until the GDR finally achieved wide recognition as a separate state and severed the pan-German ties. The new *Ostpolitik* of the Federal Republic after 1969, the Basic Treaty, and the treaties with Poland, Russia, and Czechoslovakia created a new nodal point of scholarly activity. It was joined by another one, this one arising from membership in the United Nations and its sub-organizations. This, in turn, led to a great many legal questions about participation in UN peacekeeping missions and NATO actions, especially after reunification in 1989–90.

Looking back, it is evident that international law always reacted to the circumstances of the day in two ways. Since the sixteenth and seventeenth centuries, it had been a place of theoretical reflection in close association with natural law, state theory, and political science; at the same time, it was always an eminently praxis-focused adviser to foreign policy. This situation continued also in the following centuries. From the late nineteenth century on, the German doctrine of international law, since the fading away of natural law was often connected to "philosophical" criminal law, assigned its discipline increasingly to public law; in fact, it sometimes went so far as to think of it as "external state law." After World War I, the majority of its representatives saw its task as protecting Germany against the impositions and restrictions of the Versailles Treaty and to resolve the border problems. During National Socialism and in the GDR, it was seen as a self-evident obligatory task to support one's own government when it came to issues of international law. In the Federal Republic, scholarship was certainly free in every respect to follow such wishes or not. However, because of increasing specialization and expansion of the material, there has been a certain uncoupling of legal theory, of the history of international law, and of political science from the theory of the prevailing international law.

18

Reunification

1. THE COURSE OF EVENTS

State law and international law had been following developments in the divided Germany from different perspectives. In the east there was the obligatory party line, which permitted at most minor deviations. In the west, the debate evolved in its full breadth, uncensored but without a doubt also in the wake of the prevailing political majority opinion. At first, the two camps in the Cold War confronted each other with irreconcilable hostility. Then, from around the middle of the 1960s, more conciliatory tones were heard, which eventually led to the Basic Treaty. After that, the west gradually made its peace with the two-state theory and pursued change through rapprochement. The political elites on both sides, as estranged as they were from each other, prepared themselves inwardly for the territorial and ideological division to remain in place for quite some time, though exactly how long was impossible to tell.

Even most of the scholars in the east and the west did not expect that the collapse of the GDR in 1989–90 would come as swiftly as it did. But a few careful observers had known for some time that the SED regime would not be able to sustain itself once the Soviet empire as a whole was dissolved. Internally, the socialist planned economy could not compete with the capitalist West; the state's deficit could be concealed only with great difficulty. At the same time, the long-active dissident scene in church circles, among peace activists, among environmentalists, and among artists and writers was growing, especially after Wolf Biermann was stripped of his citizenship (1976). The Final Act of the CSCE Conference in Helsinki (1975) approved by the GDR offered arguments against the denial of basic rights. The endless claim that West Germany was becoming impoverished and that class conflict was intensifying was no longer believed. "Western television" provided different images every day. Finally, the inner-German borders had also become somewhat more permeable in the wake of the policy of "change through rapprochement." The already weak legitimation of the regime was used up. The impatience of the citizens was on the rise.

2. TASKS OF STATE LAW AND INTERNATIONAL LAW

The stages in the rapid fall of the SED and of West Germany's reactions to it, which had to be continuously coordinated with international politics, need only the briefest of summation here.[1] After the Wall opened up surprisingly on November 9, 1989, and millions of GDR citizens poured into the west, the SED collapsed tumultuously in December. On March 18, 1990, the *Volkskammer* of the GDR was freely elected for the first time. To avoid a plebiscite about accession (Article 146 GG, old version), the existence of the East German *Länder* (which had been abolished in 1952) was fabricated, and they were allowed to join the Federal Republic through Article 23 of the Basic Law (old version). With this, the long-desired reunification had been accomplished. Article 146 of the Basic Law, which should have been the final seal on a unification happily attained, was not used and was now given a new and unclear formulation for the future, the product of compromise.

This was an exceedingly stressful time also for the disciplines of state law and international law, which were responsible for overseeing all of these events. Politics and jurisprudence cooperated and competed on several levels. At the international level, the extension of international treaties and memberships to the united Germany had to be regulated, from the UN to NATO and all the way to other

[1] All the details are in Klaus Stern, *Staatsrecht*, vol. 5 (Munich, 2000), pp. 1845 ff.; equally comprehensive, the contributions in Josef Isensee and Paul Kirchhof, eds., *Handbuch des Staatsrechts*, vol. 8 (Heidelberg, 1995); and Michael Kilian in *Handbuch*, vol. 1, 3rd edn. (2003), pp. 597 ff. Summary in Willoweit, *Deutsche Verfassungsgeschichte*, pp. 403 ff.

international treaties, which also settled the debt servicing of the GDR, for example. This concerned, above all, also the refashioning of the relationship with the four victorious powers of World War II, which was in fact achieved in the "Two-Plus-Four Treaty" on September 12, 1990. Internally, this had already been preceded on May 18, 1990, by the "Treaty Establishing a Monetary, Economic, and Social Union." Countless details had to be settled, such as the unwinding of the GDR's industrial assets by the "Trust Agency," the acquisition of the files of the "State Security," and not least the restitution of property expropriated by the GDR. That the expropriations carried out between 1945 and 1949 under the authority of the Soviet Military Administration were not reversed, and that the Federal Constitutional Court and the European Court of Human Rights did not object,[2] remained a lasting source of outrage among those affected.

3. THE MODALITY OF REUNIFICATION

While these dramatic events of reunification were under way, the German teachers of state law gathered for a special meeting on April 27, 1990, in Berlin. Talks by Jochen A. Frowein, Josef Isensee, Christian Tomuschat, and Albrecht Randelzhofer dealt with aspects internal to the state and related to international law. All were agreed that speed was of the essence. A day later, the European political leaders approved reunification. In the weeks that followed, all questions of foreign policy, especially the consent of the Soviet Union, then still in existence,[3] were settled. The treaty on unification was concluded after three rounds of negotiation and ratified by both sides, and the *Länder* of Brandenburg, Mecklenburg-Vorpommern, Saxony, Saxony-Anhalt, and Thuringia joined the Federal Republic in accordance with Article 23 of the Basic Law (old version).

[2] See Art. 143 (3) GG in combination with Art. 41 of the Treaty of Unification, BVerfGE 84, 90; 94, 12; 112, 1 (23, 39); 126, 331 (358 f.). Final decision by the European Court of Human Rights (ECtHR) of June 30, 2005, *NJW* (2005), 2907 ff. Additional references in Joachim Wieland, "Art. 143 GG," in Horst Dreier, ed., *Grundgesetz Kommentar*, vol. 3 (Tübingen, 2008), margin notes 25 ff.

[3] The Moscow Treaty on the Final Settlement with Respect to Germany of September 12, 1990.

It cannot be said that state-law theory and the theory of international law played a leading role in all of these events. As in previous decades, they were the external companion to politics. For reasons of academic self-respect and for the sake of its market value, they did champion the ideal of objective scholarship; consciously or unconsciously, however, they followed the political zeitgeist and provided commentary and analysis after the fact. One of the politically charged questions concerned the above-mentioned decision to opt for the path of unification via Article 23 of the Basic Law (old version), another the modality by which the *Länder* abolished in the territory of the GDR in 1952 were revived, and yet another the problem—which exercised the entire nation—of the restitution or recovery of real estate or agricultural property, of industrial or trade enterprises. And so, as early as 1991, in the immediate aftermath of reunification, a conference of teachers of state law took place in Giessen, which dealt with the follow-up problem connected with the GDR in the areas of criminal law, basic rights, and human rights, as well as with issues pertaining to questions of property and restitution.[4] In the process, the old arguments that had been used after 1945 suddenly reappeared in a new guise: the recourse to natural law; the critique of the law of the GDR with criteria that were derived from West German law, which was endowed, however, with the character of universal law; the debate over the continued employment of soldiers and members of the public sector in a different "value system"; and the antagonism between establishing the truth about the past and protecting the rights of privacy of victims and perpetrators. Which files should remain secret? Which should be made public? And concretely: should experts in state, administrative, and international law in the GDR, nearly all of whom had been members of the SED and many also unofficial collaborators with the "state security," be allowed to continue teaching in their fields at the universities? Had one been guided by the West German model between 1945 to about 1950, nearly all professors would have been transitioned into the new state. However, the model that was followed was that of the GDR, which during the same time had rid itself of its "bourgeois" professors. The members of the law faculties of the GDR, as well as

[4] Christian Starck, Wilfried Berg, and Bodo Pieroth, "Der Rechtsstaat und die Aufarbeitung der vor-rechtsstaatlichen Vergangenheit," *VVDStRL* 51 (1992), 9 ff.

the staff of the Academy for State and Law, were almost completely "phased out."[5]

The meetings of professors of state law in 1990 and 1991 show state law and international law in both a serving and a critical function. They accompanied politics and helped sustain it. The exhilarating feeling that the Wall and the border installations had fallen called for support from the majority. Critical reservations were expressed about the fact that all other conceivable options were blocked out, no matter how unrealistic they may have been (a federal solution, semi-autonomy for the GDR with a currency union, preservation of East German elements in the constitutions of the new *Länder*, and so on). The west, as helpful as it was on the whole, also displayed elements of self-righteousness, and at least the political majority was willing to eliminate the ideological remnants of the GDR. The east, meanwhile, fell silent or responded angrily. Many of its protagonists subsequently became active in the new left-wing party or became lawyers; others still were retired and wrote their memoirs. This much, at least, was beyond question for public law: the positive state and administrative law of the GDR, which was closely tied to the vanished forms of SED politics and the planned economy, could not be practiced or taught any longer. The situation was a little different in international law and legal history.

4. RESTRUCTURING AND THE FOUNDING OF NEW UNIVERSITIES

All of this had consequences for teaching and scholarship on public law in the former GDR. The Germany Academy for Political and Legal Science was closed, along with all of its institutes for public law and international law. On its grounds arose the second university of the state of Brandenburg in Potsdam with new personnel. The first university to be created in Brandenburg was the Viadrina in

[5] Inga Markovits, *Die Abwicklung: Ein Tagebuch zum Ende der DDR-Justiz* (Munich, 1993); Renate Mayntz, ed., *Aufbruch und Reform von oben* (Frankfurt am Main, 1994); Jürgen Kocka and Renate Mayntz, eds., *Wissenschaft und Wiedervereinigung: Disziplinen und Umbruch* (Berlin, 1998).

Frankfurt and der Oder (1506–1811), which was newly established after 1991 in close cooperation with Poland. The law faculty of the old University of Rostock, which had been closed in 1950, was also re-established in 1991, but it had to end the classic judicial education again from 2008 to 2012–13. The training of jurists set up at the same time in Greifswald in 1990 was able to hold its ground. The tradition of legal training—and with that also of public law—was likewise carried on in Halle-Wittenberg, Jena, and Leipzig. The law faculty newly established in Dresden in 1991 survived in the classic form only for a decade, though it continued training with masters' programs. A faculty of state sciences was set up in Erfurt in 1999, which now also offers public law in partnership with the Max Weber Center for Advanced Cultural and Social Studies. What was probably the most important restructuring took place at the Frederick William or Humboldt University of Berlin. It is now among the leading universities in the Federal Republic.

19

Globalization and the Future of the State

Over the last few decades, globalization has become one of the most widely used—and overused—words. It can refer to the geographical compression of the world, to political and economic interdependencies, to the world's population and the entire ecosystem, or to humanity as a species. The pronouncements related to it are accordingly varied—so much so, that the collective term "globalization" is considered an empty formula.[1] And yet there is one core area in its usage. Globalization describes the fact that the world has been nearly completely explored and described; that information, financial currents, and streams of goods course around the world today; that humans have a growing awareness that they inhabit the Earth together, share in its resources (e.g., biological diversity, forests and seas, food and raw materials), and are jointly responsible for its climate. The possibilities of human identification reach from the village community to the region, the nation, and the continent, all the way to the global community. Every person lives in multiple roles, and each of these roles comes with a corresponding legal system.

1. THE FIRST WAVE OF GLOBALIZATION

However, neither the phenomenon itself nor the consequences that flow from it for the law are entirely new. One can speak of a first

[1] Wolfgang Streeck, "Globalisierung: Mythos und Wirklichkeit," in Hans-Jürgen Aretz and Christian Lahusen, eds., *Die Ordnung der Gesellschaft: Festschrift zum 60. Geburtstag von Richard Münch* (Frankfurt am Main, 2005), pp. 355–72; Jürgen Schwarze, ed., *Globalisierung und Entstaatlichung des Rechts*, Teilband I (Tübingen, 2008).

phase of globalization at the end of the fifteenth century. The circumnavigation of the world and the discovery of America by the Portuguese and Spaniards in the late fifteenth and sixteenth centuries led to a spectacular expansion in the experience of the world, and it was probably the necessary precursor to the "Copernican" revolution in astronomy in 1543.[2] The world was now definitively understood as a spherical planet that revolved around the Sun, which could be circumnavigated and taken possession of. The latter happened in the centuries of European expansion from the sixteenth century to the nineteenth.[3]

This was the crucial driver behind the development of a universal natural law. For once the Earth had become a single geographic entity; the step toward a universal legal unity also seemed possible. The flowering of the theological and legal-philosophical school of Salamanca in the sixteenth century—such as the *Relecciones De Indis* and *De iure belli* by Francisco de Vitoria; the writings of the Dutchman Hugo Grotius, *Mare liberum* (1609) and his masterpiece *De iure belli ac pacis* (1625); the work of the Englishman John Selden, *Mare clausum seu de dominio maris* (1635)—were palpably shaped by the atmosphere of change in the great colonial nations. Now that the monarchies of Western Europe encountered one another as rivals during their raids on the high sea and at strategically important trading posts, they needed a basis in international law. Even if the emerging international law could be separated out from natural law quite early as a specialized subject matter, both kinds of law were set up to be universally valid. They were supposed to apply to Christians and heathens, and if not to all heathens, then certainly to those who were living in high cultures and with whom one could negotiate—from a European perspective—as between "equals." In this sense the traditional *ius gentium* changed into a law *inter gentes*. Rivals fought each other economically and militarily and also captured enemy ships, but they jointly set themselves apart from self-serving pirates, who

[2] Nicolaus Copernicus, *De revolutionibus orbium coelestium* (Nuremberg, 1543). On this, see Hans Blumenberg, *Die Genesis der kopernikanischen Welt* (Frankfurt am Main, 1975; paperback edition in three volumes, 1981).

[3] Wolfgang Reinhard, *Geschichte der europäischen Expansion*, 4 vols. (Stuttgart, 1983, 1985, 1988, 1990); Jörg Fisch, *Die europäische Expansion und das Völkerrecht: Die Auseinandersetzungen um den Status der überseeischen Gebiete vom 15. Jahrhundert bis zur Gegenwart* (Stuttgart, 1984).

were placed outside the international legal system as "enemies of the human race."[4]

2. THE SECOND WAVE OF GLOBALIZATION

If one of the essential causes behind the rise of natural law and international law during the early modern period was the first globalization, where do things stand today with the second globalization? If our understanding is correct, it is an accelerated continuation of the industrial revolution since the end of the eighteenth century. What Goethe called the "machine being" has since taken hold of all means of communication and transportation, and with the transition from the twentieth to the twenty-first century it expanded, thanks to the electronic possibilities of communication and storage, de facto into a global society. Within modern international law there is intense discussion over whether—and if so, how—the new world order will be constitutionalized,[5] whether human rights should be valid universally or in a culturally modified form, and whether an overarching international criminal law already exists for political and war crimes or whether it should be further elaborated. It is still open how a new, binding world law can emerge out of all these reflections in the social sciences and legal theory. This would require a shared foundation of unwritten cultural beliefs.

Be that as it may, the de facto changes today are breathtaking. Everywhere there are "erosions of boundaries," indeed a trend toward placelessness.[6] Everything can be observed, photographed, and stored. News, stock prices, financial instruments, and services of

[4] Michael Kempe, *Fluch der Weltmeere: Piraterie, Völkerrecht und international Beziehungen 1500–1900* (Frankfurt am Main and New York, 2010).

[5] Jürgen Habermas, *Die postnationale Konstellation* (Frankfurt am Main, 1998); Ulrich Beck, *Was ist Globalisierung?* (Frankfurt am Main, 2007; English translation *What Is Globalization?* (Cambridge, 1999)); Ulrich Beck, *Weltrisikogesellschaft* (Frankfurt am Main, 2008; English translation *World Risk Society* (Cambridge, 1998)); Otfried Höffe, *Demokratie im Zeitalter der Globalisierung* (Munich, 1999); Andrew Hurrel, "Die globale internationale Gesellschaft als normative Ordnung," in Rainer Forst and Klaus Günther, eds., *Die Herausbildung normativer Ordnungen: Interdisziplinäre Perspektiven* (Frankfurt am Main and New York, 2011), pp. 103–32.

[6] Helmut Willke, *Atopia: Studien zur atopischen Gesellschaft* (Frankfurt am Main, 2001).

every kind are exchanged globally in seconds. The distances that need to be bridged seem ever smaller or have ceased to matter any longer. The consequences for the normative orders of the historically evolved sub-societies are still unforeseeable. The territorial basis of the state invariably loses importance if the geographic bonds loosen or disappear altogether. Warring parties are also operating increasingly in a "placeless" manner, concealed or through unmanned weapons or surveillance systems. World trade, the communication in electronic networks, monetary transactions, the media-transmitted mass spectacles of sports, and much else are taking place across state borders. The regulatory systems that are followed are non-governmental, but they consist of "law."[7] They are set up by globally operating organizations that are removed from any kind of traditional control. "Jurisdiction" is often exercised by self-elected mediators, since very complex, large cases cannot be decided quickly enough, and perhaps also not with the requisite expertise, by state jurisdictions.[8] Overhead costs can be lowered through the use of non-state legal pathways. In this way, regulatory systems and the settling of disputes escape the state's monopoly of force, which was established between the seventeenth century and the nineteenth against much opposition.

In terms of traditional categories, this means, on the one hand, gains in freedom and, legally speaking, an expansion of private autonomy. On the other hand, the individual is subordinating himself to worldwide networks of agreements, within which he can achieve legal protection only with the greatest of difficulties, especially since the legal venue is usually located in a foreign country that is far away and uses a different language. The individual appears as a consumer, not as a citizen with a claim to political participation. In dictatorships in which such participation does not exist, there is the added threat of the arbitrary shut-down of the networks of communication, provided the regime in question has access to them.

The contrast is especially dramatic between clearly necessary global solutions and national need or self-interest in protecting natural resources. The living space of the growing world population is

[7] Schwarze (Note 1).

[8] Gunther Teubner, "Globale Bukowina: Zur Emergenz eines transnationalen Rechtspluralismus," *Rechtshistorisches Journal* 15 (1996), 255 f.; Paul Schiff Berman, "Globalization of Jurisdiction," *University of Pennsylvania Law Review* 151 (2002), 311 ff.

becoming more crowded, the consumption of common resources is rising, much of the damage caused by humans to the habitats of animals and plants and to the climate has long since become irreversible. The commendable efforts to contain the threats through international agreements are constantly impeded by economic and political interests. A drastic change is not yet in sight. It would presuppose a kind of collective consensus among humankind to abandon the traditional path of exploiting resources and passing the ecological costs on to the anonymous world community. There are signs that this consensus is slowing growing. However, it is unclear whether there is still enough time to take effective steps against the impending dangers.

3. THE FUTURE OF THE NATION STATE

The areas of tasks of the traditional nation state will shift under this scenario. Already its very oldest mandate, to guarantee protection against external enemies and prevent internal feuds and civil wars, appears in an entirely new light given today's possibilities of electronic warfare and decentralized guerilla tactics. Even local conflicts are being globally registered, if by no means resolved. A future international law that can respond to this is only beginning to emerge. It will have to take on anew the task of civilizing and constraining the new forms of warfare. Presumably it will also elaborate further the individualization of international criminal law, a process that has been evident since the Nuremberg trials. Sacrosanct, "untouchable" monarchs no longer exist. Warring politicians who are enforcing the interests of their state by force of arms are subject to international criminal law and are considered potential criminals.

But it is not only wars as extreme cases that have altered the international scenario. Politics is no longer communicating primarily through embassies or missions, but through direct contacts. The global leaders "know one another." By no means all those involved are legitimized by a state. Professional diplomats have been joined by officials of transnational organizations, such as the organs of the European Union, the many institutions created by international law, but also NGOs, world-spanning corporations, and the electronic networks—in short, all those who are interested in global regulation and deregulation. One can hardly still speak of the absolute final decision-making authority of the state over a circumscribed territory.

Parallel to this, the role of states has shifted internally. States give back some of their functions to society via privatization when they run up against the limits of growth or of the financial capacity of the population. Examples of this are the mail, railways, telecommunication, the control of finance, private schools, and the university system, or segments of old-age provision. This is mostly done with arguments about improved competitiveness and greater efficiency, while the high indebtedness of public budgets is often the real reason.[9] As soon as profits loom, there are also countertendencies, such as re-communalization. But if the public sector shifts the task to society, forms of protection by public law must be transferred into private law, or those in the private sector need to be policed by the state. Today observers speak in this regard about "regulated self-regulation."[10] In many areas the state no longer issues direct prescriptions, but controls what is organizing itself. Perhaps the place of the traditional doctrine of legislating will be taken in the future by a new "regulatory science."[11]

Of course, the new legal forms arising here are still supposed to fulfill the old tasks: guaranteeing security and order; regulating traffic; providing energy and water and disposing of waste water; protecting against noise, dust, radiation, and poisons—in short, protecting daily life against dangers. Indispensable in addition are the guarantee of the basic services of the power supply, the central institutions of care and education, health care, and the provision of information for daily life in the broadest sense. And citizens are willing to pay taxes for all of this. In the final analysis, they hold the municipal or regional state

[9] Norbert Frei and Dietmar Süß, eds., *Privatisierung: Idee und Praxis seit den 1970er Jahren* (Göttingen, 2012).

[10] Overview in Martin Eifert, "Regulierungsstrategien," in Wolfgang Hoffmann-Riem, Eberhard Schmidt-Aßmann, and Andreas Voßkuhle, eds., *Grundlagen des Verwaltungsrechts*, vol. 1, 2nd edn. (Munich, 2012), §19; Gunnar Folke Schuppert, *Der Rechtsstaat unter den Bedingungen informaler Staatlichkeit: Beobachtungen und Überlegungen zum Verhältnis formeller und informeller Institutionen* (Baden-Baden, 2011); Peter Collin, Gerd Bender, Stefan Ruppertr, Margrit Seckelmann, and Michael Stolleis, eds., *Selbstregulierung im 19. Jahrhundert: Zwischen Autonomie und staatlichen Steuerungsansprüchen* (Frankfurt am Main, 2011).

[11] Gunnar Folke Schuppert, *Governance und Rechtsetzung: Grundfragen einer modernen Regelungswissenschaft* (Baden-Baden, 2011).

responsible for services and shortcomings. Regardless of whether or not one calls these elementary guarantees and protections "state" (municipality, region, federal state, the state overall), a complex of commanding, constraining, permitting, or prohibiting public law and criminal law will presumably have to be preserved as a hard core, even if non-state and transnational law expands and society itself at the same time regulates certain functions (again) via private law.

4. THE FUTURE OF THE CONSTITUTIONAL STATE

If it is true that the classic state functions are shifting or being handed over to other actors, this raises the question about the future of the constitutional state in the world society.[12] Constitutional law—indeed, all of public law—is confronting "the challenge of globalization."[13] For more than two decades, the changes it has entailed have been registered,[14] and it has become commonplace to speak—in a conciliatory and hopeful manner—of "open statehood." Different from the "end of statehood"[15] proclaimed by Carl Schmitt with an apocalyptic tone, the emphasis on openness intends to assert that in spite of manifold cooperations, interconnections, and dependencies, the state still remains—and should remain—the real frame of reference and the protective umbrella of the individual. Assuming that this is in fact the case, the crucial issue will be the balance between local, regional,

[12] Udo Di Fabio, *Der Verfassungsstaat in der Weltgesellschaft* (Tübingen, 2001); Gunnar Folke Schuppert, *Staatswissenschaft* (Baden-Baden, 2003), 835 ff.; Mathias Albert and Rudolf Stichweh, eds., *Weltstaat—Weltstaatlichkeit: Beobachtungen globaler politischer Strukturbildung* (Wiesbaden, 2007).

[13] Christian Walter, "Die Folgen der Globalisierung für die europäische Verfassungsdiskussion," *DVBl* 115 (2000), 1–13; Matthias Ruffert, *Die Globalisierung als Herausforderung an das Öffentliche Recht* (Stuttgart, 2004); Georg Nolte and Ralf Poscher, "Das Verfassungsrecht vor den Herausforderungen der Globalisierung," *VVDStRL* 67 (2008), 129 ff., 160 ff.

[14] Gunnar Folke Schuppert, "Was ist und wie misst man Wandel von Staatlichkeit?," *Der Staat* 47 (2008), pp. 325–58, with a response by Philipp Genschel and Stephan Leibfried, "Schupperts Staat: Wie beobachtet man den Wandel einer Formidee?", ibid., pp. 359–80.

[15] Thomas Vesting, "Die permanente Revolution: Carl Schmitt und das Ende der Epoche der Staatlichkeit," in Andreas Göbel, Dirk van Laak, and Ingeborg Villinger, eds., *Metamorphosen des Politischen* (Berlin, 1995), pp. 191–202.

national, and transnational tasks, as well as between the relevant competencies and institutions. This balance, which is likely to remain constantly precarious given the diversity of elements, is a task that concerns all legal disciplines. The spectrum ranges from the theory of private law, to a newly conceived administrative law, to the doctrine of constitutional law, all the way to international law. What will always be at stake are the free spaces and constraints of societal self-realization, but also the de facto security and legal protection. It is not only the legitimacy of the modern state that depends on whether it respects and protects human rights; the same holds for the credibility of those institutions that are to take its place in the future within the context of globalization. For if they do not fulfill the protective tasks for which the modern state was created in the early modern period, they do not deserve to be financed communally by those they serve. Above all, however, they fail to obtain what is indispensable for their functioning: legitimacy through "acceptance." Inseparably linked to the protection of human and civic rights is therefore the major project of transposing democratic decision-making processes from the state to "suprastate realms."[16] In this way, the mechanisms that have stood the test of time should be given a larger radius and incorporate a growing number of actors.

Others think in the opposite direction by interpreting the networks that already exist today as "global governance" and proclaim the international society to be the future normative order. Of course, this order still seems incomplete and needs to be gradually improved in such a way that it becomes "more democratic" and protects human rights. Since a Eurocentric world order no longer exists and a new "Pax Americana," even if desirable, evidently cannot be established, hopes are invested in cooperative, discursive, or deliberative solutions that incorporate all other cultures or at least their more powerful representatives.[17] These solutions should promote "just" and

[16] Uwe Volkmann, "Die zwei Begriffe der Demokratie: Von der Übertragbarkeit staatsbezogener Demokratievorstellungen in überstaatliche Räume," in Klaus Hofmann and Kolja Naumann, eds., *Europäische Demokratie in guter Verfassung?* (Baden-Baden, 2010), pp. 14–32.

[17] Andrew Hurrell, "Die globale internationale Gesellschaft als normative Ordnung," in Forst and Günther (Note 5), pp. 103–32, and Armin von Bogdandy, Philipp Dann, and Matthias Goldmann, "Völkerrecht als öffentliches Recht: Konturen eines rechtlichen Rahmens für Global Governance," in ibid., pp. 227–63, with further references.

"fair" outcomes and derive their legitimacy from the greatest possible participation of the peoples (*demoi*) involved. The questions dealt with are expansive and touch on nearly all disciplines of the social sciences, but especially sociology, philosophy,[18] political science, and jurisprudence.[19] The debate is carried on globally, as is appropriate to the subject. Because this debate is rethinking the state, the latter could change its form or even disappear entirely as a traditional, historically evolved entity. Of course, the latter scenario is not very likely, as least as far as we can discern the outlines of the future.

Historical experience teaches that such a rebuilding of structures requires the exertions of many generations. Institutions, ways of thinking, and expectations change fairly slowly. There will be many mixed forms and transitions, and surely also failed experiments. From a skeptical perspective from within the discipline, one can therefore predict that some of the suggestions and hopeful scenarios that are currently being discussed will not be very long-lived: I am thinking here of a "virtual state in the Internet," an "electronic democracy," a "global civil society," or a "cosmopolitan democracy." Still, these processes of intellectual fermentation are of great interest as the phenomena accompanying a rapid change of the world in which we live. They form the raw material for the dominant interpretive patterns of the future. Along the way they draw upon the stock of ideas from the history of human thought. Either the classic texts are read and reread with new eyes and applied in new ways in order to use them to interpret a present that has still not been conceptualized, or the authors seek to think in new ways on new empirical foundations, though of course without being able to escape the tradition which thoroughly pervades them as a result of cultural osmosis. It is obvious that the strongest impulses for the intellectual creativity of political, sociological, and legal theory emanate today from "globalization," whatever it means. World society is in the same boat, willing or not.

[18] See above, note 5.

[19] Andreas Fischer-Lescano, "Globalverfassung: Verfassung der Weltgesellschaft," *ARSP* 88 (2002), 349–79; Andreas Fischer-Lescano, "Die Emergenz der Globalverfassung," *ZaöRV* 63 (2003), 717–60; Martin Schulte, *Eine soziologische Theorie des Rechts* (Berlin, 2011), pp. 184 ff.

20

Conclusion

The perspective in this introductory text is directed at the history of the discipline of public law. If the historically evolved early modern state, and the sovereign nation state that was built upon it in the nineteenth and twentieth centuries, change so much that entirely new outlines emerge in terms of state law and international law, while the state (under whatever name) must simultaneously satisfy the daily needs of people and ward off everyday dangers, the "public" law that constitutes the state will also change its character. As described, it will be once again more strongly interwoven with private law and criminal law, in both European and non-European legal systems.

If the clearly definable role of public law were to come to an end in this way, it would lead to the reintegration of what are today the largely separate legal histories of private law, criminal law, and public law. Such a development would be appropriate to the subject, since the circumstances of life to be studied never adhered to the boundaries of academic disciplines. A transition to a research perspective that is breaking away from older forms of the curriculum and that undertook to study the function of law and of legal changes within the context of the entire lived legal system would, therefore, be most welcome. If that happened, state and constitution, administration and administrative law, would once again be self-evident subjects of a general history of law. Such a history should already devote itself as much as possible to the interaction of authority and freedom, state and society. The ordering achievement of the "state" is only one of the determinants shaping human life (in terms of its normative side). The better part is accomplished by individual decisions, groups of every kind, or non-governmental institutions, mostly in the forms of private law.

In this situation, the history of law could focus on determining how normative thinking and human actions relate to each other interactively. Historical processes that we believe we can discern through reduction and the interpretation of information arise from countless deeds and spoken words. The latter, in turn, are part of the history of mentalities or ideas. And unless that history is closely interrelated with the historical (social and economic) preconditions of these ideas, it would be as incomplete as a description of real history without the parallel mental labor of its actors or of those who provide them with the keywords. Though ideas may run ahead of practical implementation, just as often the explanation of seemingly chaotic facts was achieved only with hindsight.

What is now being contemplated concerning the change in the tasks of the state, transnationality, and supranationality is part of the process of change itself. From a greater distance we will be able to see more clearly how theory prepared actual development, how the majority perceived and interpreted the change, how some denied the change and withdrew with their thoughts into some corner or another. That will not change: the discipline of history, whatever its doubts about its own interpretations or the reliability of its sources, is quite certain, in any case, that there is no "end of history." Since societal forms of life, the economy, and the general power structures are constantly changing, all of our artful constructs of the law, built with texts, language rules, and conventions, are also subject to permanent processes of adjustment and reshaping. Future generations will govern themselves differently than we do today. For that purpose, they, too, will wisely use regulatory law and legal norms of various levels of abstraction. Future societies will not be free of conflict—that much is certain. Normativity and the breach of norms are interdependent. What will arise from this in the future is not something we can know. But we can hope that future legal norms will also unfold the civilizing power that we ascribe to them based on historical experience.

Further Reading

Friedrich, M. *Geschichte der deutschen Staatswissenschaft*. Berlin, 1997.

Gosewinkel, D. and J. Masing, eds. *Die Verfassungen in Europa 1789–1949*. Munich, 2006.

Huber, E. R. *Deutsche Verfassungsgeschichte seit 1789*. Vol. 1, 2nd edn. Stuttgart, 1995. Vol. 2, 3rd edn. Stuttgart, 1988. Vol. 3, 3rd edn. Stuttgart, 1988. Vol. 4, 2nd edn. Stuttgart, 1994. Vol. 5. Stuttgart, 1978. Vol. 6. Stuttgart, 1993. Vol. 7. Stuttgart, 1984. Vol. 8 (Index). Stuttgart, 1991.

Jeserich, K. G. A., H. Pohl, and G.-Chr. von Unruh, eds. *Deutsche Verwaltungsgeschichte*. Vols. 1–5. Stuttgart, 1983–7. Index. Stuttgart, 1988.

Kley, A. *Geschichte des öffentlichen Rechts der Schweiz*. Zurich and St. Gallen, 2011.

Maier, H. *Die ältere deutsche Staats- und Verwaltungslehre*. 4th edn. Munich, 2009.

Ottmann, H. *Geschichte des politischen Denkens*. Vols. 1–4. Stuttgart, 2001–12.

Reinhard, W. *Geschichte der Staatsgewalt: Eine vergleichende Verfassungsgeschichte Europas von den Anfängen bis zur Gegenwart*. Munich, 1999.

Stern, K. *Das Staatsrecht der Bundesrepublik Deutschland*. Vol. 5: *Die geschichtlichen Grundlagen des deutschen Staatsrechts*. Munich, 1999.

Stintzing, R. von and E. Landsberg. *Geschichte der deutschen Rechtswissenschaft*. Abt. I.II.III.I von Stintzing. Leipzig, 1880–98. Abt. III.2 von Landsberg. Munich and Leipzig, 1910. Reprint Aalen, 1957.

Stollberg-Rilinger, B. *Das Heilige Römische Reich Deutscher Nation: Vom Ende des Mittelalters bis 1806*. 4th edn. Munich, 2009.

Stolleis, M. *Geschichte des öffentlichen Rechts in Deutschland*. 4 vols. Munich, 1988 (2nd edn. 2012). English translations of Vol. 2: *Public Law in Germany 1800–1914*. New York and Oxford, 2001. Vol. 3: *History of Public Law in Germany 1914–1945*. Oxford, 2004.

Stolleis, M. *The Law under the Swastika: Studies on Legal History in Nazi Germany*. Chicago, 1998.

Stolleis, M. *History of Social Law in Germany*. Berlin and Heidelberg, 2014.

Wieacker, F. *A History of Private Law in Europe*. Oxford, 1996

Willoweit, D. *Deutsche Verfassungsgeschichte: Vom Frankenreich bis zur Wiedervereinigung Deutschlands*. 7th edn. Munich, 2013.

Willoweit, D. *Reich und Staat: Eine kleine deutsche Verfassungsgeschichte*. Munich, 2013.

Index

Name Index